Return to

Jacques Lacan's dislocation of psychoanalysis

❖❖❖

SAMUEL WEBER

translated by

MICHAEL LEVINE

CAMBRIDGE
UNIVERSITY PRESS

Published by the Press Syndicate of the University of Cambridge
The Pitt Building, Trumpington Street, Cambridge CB2 1RP
40 West 20th Street, New York, NY 10011-4211 USA
10 Stamford Road, Oakleigh, Victoria 3166, Australia

Parts of this work were published in an earlier form as *Rükkehr zu Freud:
Jacques Lacans Entstellung du Psychoanalyse* (Verlag Ullstein GmbH, Berlin,
1978). An expanded second edition of the German work has appeared
under the same title (Passagen Verlag, Vienna, 1990)

All German editions © Samuel Weber

First published in English by Cambridge University Press 1991 as *Return to
Freud: Jacques Lacan's dislocation of psychoanalysis*
Reprinted 1992

English translation © Cambridge University Press, 1991

Printed in Great Britain by Hartnolls Limited, Bodmin, Cornwall

British Library cataloguing in publication data
Weber, Samuel
Return to Freud: Jacques Lacan's dislocation of
psychoanalysis.
1. Psychoanalysis, Lacan, Jacques, 1901–1981
I. Title II. (Rückkehr zu Freud) English
150.195092

Library of Congress cataloguing in publication data
Weber, Samuel M.
[Rückkehr zu Freud. English]
Return to Freud: Jacques Lacan's dislocation of psychoanalysis /
Samuel Weber; translated by Michael Levine.
p. cm. – (Literature, Culture, Theory: 1)
Translation of: Rückkehr zu Freud.
Includes bibliographical references and index.
ISBN 0-521-37410-3 (hard). – ISBN 0-521-37770-6 (pbk.)
1. Lacan, Jacques, 1901–1. 2. Psychoanalysis. I. Title.
II. Series.
BF 173.W41213 1991
150.19'5'092–dc20 90-44979 CIP

ISBN 0 521 37410 3 hardback
ISBN 0 521 37770 6 paperback

Return to Freud

Literature, Culture, Theory

❖❖❖

General editors

RICHARD MACKSEY, *The Johns Hopkins University*
and MICHAEL SPRINKER, *State University of New York*
at Stony Brook

Samuel Weber's *Return to Freud* is the opening title in a new Cambridge series. *Literature, Culture, Theory* is dedicated to theoretical studies in the human sciences that have literature and culture as their object of enquiry. Acknowledging the contemporary expansion of cultural studies and the redefinitions of literature that this has entailed, the series includes not only original works of literary theory but also monographs and essay collections on topics and seminal figures from the long history of theoretical speculation on the arts and human communication generally. The concept of theory embraced in the series is broad, including not only the classical disciplines of poetics and rhetoric, but also those of aesthetics, linguistics, psychoanalysis, semiotics, and other cognate sciences that have inflected the systematic study of literature during the past half century.

Titles published

Return to Freud: Jacques Lacan's dislocation of psychoanalysis
SAMUEL WEBER
(translated from the German by Michael Levine)

Wordsworth, dialogics and the practice of criticism
DON H. BIALOSTOSKY

The subject of modernity
ANTHONY J. CASCARDI

Onomatopoetics: theory of language and literature
JOSEPH GRAHAM

Other titles in preparation

Paratexts
GERARD GENETTE
(translated from the French by Jane Lewin)

The object of literature
PIERRE MACHEREY
(translated from the French by David Macey)

Parody: ancient, modern, and post-modern
MARGARET ROSE

Kenneth Burke: a rhetoric of the subject
ROBERT WESS

Narratives of narrative: the reflexive tradition in the
English novel
JEFFREY WILLIAMS

This book provides an introduction to the thought of Jacques Lacan. Samuel Weber approaches his subject from a dual perspective: he reads Lacan in the light of Freud (whose work Lacan is concerned to interpret); and from the perspective of structuralism, above all that of Saussure, from whom Lacan borrows and develops a distinctive conception of language as "signifier." Through his use of the category of the signifier, Lacan dislocates the traditional understanding of the "Unconscious," thereby revealing it to be *linguistic*, and not psychological, in essence. Lacan is thus shown to contribute crucially to the rethinking of *subjectivity* that marks much of contemporary literary theory.

What Samuel Weber calls Lacan's "return to Freud" – the complex relationship between his work and its Freudian antecedents – is explored extensively in the context of Saussure, Jakobson, and structural linguistics generally.

In memory of
Eugenio Donato

Contents

Preface

This book has had a rather curious history. It was initially conceived not as a book at all, but as notes for lectures held at the Free University of West Berlin in the early seventies. At that time, there was very little material of or on Lacan available in German, and consequently the lectures I held were designed to serve as a general introduction to the *Ecrits*, which had been published in French some years earlier. The most salient characteristic of these scripts was, and doubtless remains, their pedagogical aspect: they constitute an attempt to delineate the contours of what at the time, at least, was – and for many, still is – a tantalizingly enigmatic rereading of Freudian psychoanalysis. As is often the case when a work emerging from one intellectual field – in this instance, that marked by French Structuralism – is transposed to a different linguistic and cultural area, the contextual underpinnings tend to disappear. This explains why so much of the book is devoted to reconstituting the Saussurean conception of language, which at the time was little known in German, outside of specialized linguistic circles.

In this respect, the situation has changed since then, in Germany no less than in the English-speaking world. And yet, such changes are not as simple or as straightforward as one might suppose. Freud's remarks about repression hold for these changes as well: they do not take place once and for all, but rather must be renewed constantly in order to remain effective. What often happens, by contrast, is that what we call "proper" names begin to circulate widely, suggesting a sort of permanence or at least durability. But these names, far from rendering what they name accessible, function as *screens*, isolating rather than simply repressing, by seemingly arresting the movement of signification. This can be a powerful means of justifying the familiar. Indeed, if culture, as Emerson remarks, consists in the number of things that can be taken for granted, the currency of such proper names is both an index of and a factor in the formation and stabilization of culture. In this sense, "Lacan" has become an integral part of our culture.

The notion of language that underlies the writings attached to that name, however, moves in a very different way, and this difference may well explain both the fascination and the resistance it has elicited. To open the questions of naming and predication as problematic processes of signification is to call attention to the irreducible alterity that inhabits language and that renders it so uncanny: all too familiar in its very strangeness. This sort of move can only undercut the desire for clear-cut relations and decisions that is a particularly conspicuous feature of North American society.

In the face of insistent efforts to foreclose such questions, it may still be useful, even today, to retain the notion of "Poststructuralism." If Structuralism can be described as the rediscovery of language as a semiotic system of binary relations, Poststructuralism marks the delimitation of that semiotics in the wake of the system. What emerges is a movement of marks and traits, of differences and deferrals, that can no longer be contained or comprehended in the oppositional categories that constitute the system, as such and in general.

The writings of Lacan, together with those of Derrida, remain, today perhaps more than ever, two of the most powerful forces working to keep the alterity of language from being isolated and foreclosed. The efficacy of these texts, however, is never indifferent to the singular idiom – and not just to the particular language – in which they are articulated. Whence the risk, but also the challenge of a book like this one. The difficulty in whose shadow it is inscribed is not just that of translating a difficult text from one language to another, but even more, of *rendering a sense of signifying movement* that is irreducible to conceptual discourse. And yet, reduced it must be by a style informed, *grosso modo*, by the conventional rules and norms of academic discourse. The ineluctability of this reduction undoubtedly constitutes the most serious internal limitation of this kind of undertaking.

It is not, to be sure, its only limitation. To avoid confusion, however, it should be kept in mind that the subject-matter of this book, to which the name "Lacan" refers, consists primarily of the writings published in 1966 and entitled, simply, *Ecrits*. In short, the name "Lacan" in this book could be described as a synecdoche, were there a "whole" of which the *Ecrits* could be considered a part. Although it is a matter of record that much significant material was written and published under the name "Lacan" since this text was written, the question of whether it can be considered to form a whole remains entirely open. For my part, I doubt that it can be assembled into anything like a system without the most incisive and pathbreaking aspects of Lacan's "return to Freud" being lost in the process.

Although the texts discussed in the following pages comprise a relatively small portion of Lacan's published work, their discussion can perhaps still help readers to *make their ways* in(to) the *Ecrits*, which remain the most densely charged laboratory of the Lacanian experiment. Contrary to the laboratories of experimental science, however, the walls of Lacan's laboratory are as unstable as the margins of a text: not entirely inchoate, to be sure, but also never completely under control. It is this instability that distinguishes what Lacan calls "l'expérience psychanalytique" – a phrase which *also* means psychoanalytical *experiment* – from its scientific homonym. To make one's way under conditions that can never be entirely controlled is part of what constitutes psychoanalytic truth. To learn how to read Lacan involves making one's way in this sense. The pace of such *reading* is laborious, if also often exhilarating; it has little in common with the rush to judgment that often goes by the same name.

If this book itself is now able to contribute to such reading, it is as a result of the efforts and dedication of Michael Levine, who initiated and undertook the arduous and thankless task of translation. Bruce Fink provided invaluable assistance in revising the manuscript, as did Don Eric Levine. In going over the English text, I have made certain modifications, not so much to the translation, as to the initial German version. Since the two final chapters were written after the book's German publication, they are placed in an Appendix. Both appear here for the first time in English. The result is a considerably revised and expanded English text. A new German edition, published by

Passagen Verlag (Vienna, 1990), contains certain essays that have not been translated into English.

Finally, I would like to dedicate this book to the memory of the person who introduced me, as he did many others, to the work of Lacan, with an unforgettable vivacity and enthusiasm: to Eugenio Donato. His absence is keenly felt by those fortunate enough to have studied and worked with him.

Translator's introduction

Accentuating *Ent-stellung*

Samuel Weber's *Return to Freud*, which appears here in English translation for the first time, has for some time had the status in German intellectual circles of what they call a *Geheimtip*, a hot piece of information circulating semi-privately through unofficial channels. Between its short-lived distribution by Ullstein (1978) and its re-publication by Passagen Verlag (1990) copies of this insider's guide to Lacan have passed from hand to hand and have been much xeroxed throughout the Federal Republic's university towns and "alternative scenes." No less popular than the book itself in these circles is the story often accompanying it about its author, a young American writing with ease and rigor in German about a notoriously impenetrable Frenchman. While it is certainly no exaggeration to say that Samuel Weber is someone who is very much at home in these languages, a more accurate description might compare him to the convalescent of Nietzsche's *Zarathustra* – that is, to someone perpetually *on his way* home.[1] Indeed, in many ways the text which follows traces the itinerary of this "return."

As the reader will have noticed, Weber's *Return* is itself already a quotation, already a repetition of another "return," and of another's "return to Freud." Moreover, if one reads the subtitle of the text as a gloss on this quotation, it becomes clear that this itinerary is not simply a return home, a return to a proper name, or a return to the authenticity of an original, but is instead a movement of dislocation. In order to follow this movement we should recall how Freud instructed his followers

---

[1] See Martin Heidegger, "Who is Nietzsche's Zarathustra?" in *The New Nietzsche*, Cambridge: The MIT Press, 1985, pp. 64–79.

to listen a little differently, to displace accents, and to hear as though with the ears of a foreigner, while Lacan's advice to future analysts was to "do crossword puzzles." If Weber's text may be said to heed the call of a "return to Freud," it also seems to transfer that call in its own peculiar manner, for it is itself a practical lesson in the cultivation of foreign accents and unusual ways of listening. In short, his repetition of Lacan's return to Freud is an act of transference and translation that only familiarizes foreign audiences with the language of psychoanalysis in general and with Lacan's French in particular to the extent that it alienates the reader from his or her "own" language.[2]

While the signs of this kind of defamiliarization are present throughout Weber's text, they are most immediately and paradigmatically evident in the subtitle of the German edition, which describes what has been translated here as "Jacques Lacan's *dislocation* of psychoanalysis" as a process of *Entstellung*. On the simplest level Weber's strategic hyphenation of this term has the effect of drawing attention to the signifying matter, which, instead of making itself transparent as it conveys a particular meaning, becomes somewhat opaque like a piece of stained or faceted glass. Thus, in the most basic way the reader is invited to look *at* rather than *through* the linguistic surface.

It is also significant that this invitation to attend to the signifying surface is only *silently* extended; that is, a shift in focus is effected exclusively via the strategic deployment of a written punctuation mark. A mere change in spacing draws attention to the spatial, graphic, and literal dimension of the text, a gesture which also prefigures Weber's approach to the vexed question of the relationship of speech and writing, spirit and letter in Lacan.[3] The hyphenation of *Ent-stellung* prompts the reader not only to view this signifier in terms of its concrete, visual, and graphic aspects – what might be called the materiality of the letter – but also to take it literally, *à la lettre*, (or in German *buchstäblich*).

While such hyphenations have in recent years become an all too familiar tic of critical writing, this particular "literalization"

---

[2] See Walter Benjamin, "The task of the translator," in *Illuminations*, New York: Schocken, 1969, pp. 69–82.
[3] See chapter 4 on "The rise and fall of the signifier."

of a term seems to reflect the spirit of Freud's own very literal understanding of *Entstellung*. Whereas this term is usually translated as "distortion," Freud comments in *Moses and Monotheism* how

> one could wish to give the word . . . the double meaning to which it has a right, although it is no longer used in this sense. It should mean not only "to change the appearance of," but also "to wrench apart," "to put in another place." That is why in so many textual distortions we may count on finding the suppressed and abnegated material hidden away somewhere, though in an altered shape and torn out of its original connection. Only it is not always easy to recognize it.[4]

It should come as no surprise then that such a potentially ambiguous term should be linked to questions of repressed conflict in Freud's writing. As Weber points out in chapter one, *Entstellung* is used in *The Interpretation of Dreams* to designate the general distortion of dreams. These distortions, which also involve the distorted articulation of repressed wishes, are brought about through the interaction of the mechanisms of the dreamwork – condensation, displacement, considerations of representability, and secondary revision – with the dream censorship. While much remains to be said about the precise nature of this interaction, it is sufficient at this point to notice how from the outset the Freudian notion of *Entstellung* is involved in the power struggles of (self)censorship in particular and in psycho-linguistic conflict in general.[5]

What distinguishes this particular form of conflict is that it is never simply waged by opposing forces meeting on a common field of battle. The implications of this are twofold: first, that the seemingly opposed forces of censorship and the mechanisms of the dreamwork are more intimately connected (or are more intensely at odds with themselves) than it at first appears; secondly, that the *site* of such conflict is difficult to locate.

This brings us to the other more "outmoded" sense of *Ent-stellung* as dis-placement or dis-location referred to by Freud which Weber's hyphenation of the term helps to sound out. By

---

[4] Sigmund Freud, *Moses and Monotheism*, trans. Katherine Jones, New York: Vintage Books, 1939, p. 52.
[5] These interactions are discussed at length in my essay "Censorship's self-administration" in *Psychoanalysis and Contemporary Thought*, 9, no. 4 (1986), pp. 605–640.

re-introducing the issue of displacement through the disarticulation of a key Freudian term, Weber also seems to suggest that in order to understand psycho-linguistic conflict and its dislocations, immunity cannot be granted to the terms used to describe it. Thus, rather than privileging the level of the signified of Freud and Lacan's texts, which would involve reading them "qualitatively" as positive descriptions of an objective reality, Weber pays particular attention to the "quantitatively" defined level of the signifier; that is to say, he treats the language of psychoanalysis as a network of negative, differential terms (or chains of signifiers), whose specific value can only be established in relation to their "surroundings" and in the context of other relevant texts.

There is a certain affinity between Weber's approach to Lacanian terminology and Freud's way of dealing with images in dreams, which, he says, should not be read according to their "pictorial value" [*Bilderwert*: their value as images of something else], but instead according to their "semiotic relationship" [*Zeichenbeziehung*] – that is, like a rebus according to the relations obtaining among the signifying elements themselves. Thus, rather than dealing straightforwardly with Lacanian "concepts" in terms of their positive content, Weber reads Lacan through Saussure for whom concepts are purely differential and not defined positively by their content but negatively by their relations with other terms of the system. Their most precise characteristic is in being what the others are not.

Yet in contrast to Saussure, Weber's "differential" approach to Lacan's texts involves reading his conceptual apparatus not only negatively, but moreover as particular *avoidances, displacements,* and *perversions* of a received tradition. As he says, Lacan's "aim is to disorient and if possible to transform the psychoanalytic orthodoxy."[6] Thus, it is never simply a question of Lacan's adoption or application of a particular model (even – and especially – that of Saussure's linguistic theory), but instead of a specific displacement, "critical appropriation," and "strategic deployment" of such models.

As Weber suggests, Lacanian discourse can only be situated with regard to what and whom it is polemically setting itself off

---

[6] See chapter 7 on "The subject as 'fader': the imaginary and the symbolic".

from at a particular point in time. Thus, the *place* of that discourse, which is differentially and *conflictually* determined, is always only a negative *dis-place*, an *"Ent-stellung."*

In order to delimit these "dis-placements" of Lacanian psychoanalysis Weber is compelled by the logic of his own argument to stage a series of encounters – which are often not so much "face-offs" as *aversions* and strategically *skewed* encounters – with Freud, Hegel, Saussure, Jakobson, Benveniste, Husserl, Laplanche, and others.

Yet while the particular "dis-placements," which are (or rather *will have been*) Lacanian discourse, may perhaps only be differentially located in terms of what they are not – that is, through a process of determinate negation – these negative determinations are rarely as fixed and defined as they at first seem.[7] In order to stress the necessary and inevitable *indeterminacy* of these "dis-placements" and in order to set them off however provisionally from the related Hegelian notion of determinate negation [*bestimmte Negation*], Weber introduces the term "differential articulation" in his reading of Saussure and uses it throughout the text as a means of avoiding the traditional language of representation [*Darstellung*]. His plays on *Ent-stellung* not only serve to accentuate this tricky veering away from more traditional notions of *Dar-stellung*, but also to link the process of "differential articulation" to other psychoanalytic notions such as dream distortion, displacement, and condensation. Indeed, the signifier *Ent-stellung* functions as a veritable nodal point in Weber's text, the specific value of which can only be appreciated by examining the various signifying chains in which it is enmeshed. Some of the more crucial links in the chain run as follows: *Ent-stellung* – as distortion – as displacement in the sense of differential articulation – displacement as a particular mechanism of the dreamwork – displaceability in the sense of *Übertragbarkeit*: the volatility of psychical energy in the primary process – displace as a dis-location or negative site – in German literally an *Ab-ort*, a term whose more conventional sense of toilet is linked to the

---

[7] See Weber's discussion of the importance of the future perfect tense for Lacan, its difference from the present perfect of Hegelian discourse, and its connection to issues of belatedness in Freud in chapter 2 on "Mistaken identity: Lacan's theory of the "mirror stage."

closed restroom doors examined in Weber's reading of Lacan's "Instance of the Letter in the Unconscious."

While Weber's text thus acknowledges and accedes to the particular indeterminacy of "Lacan's *dis-location* of psychoanalysis" through its pointed distortions of standard Freudian terminology and its strategic exploitation of linguistic ambiguities, this indeterminacy also seems to manifest itself as an oscillating movement of the argument itself. A decisive first step of this movement, which is often accompanied by a rhetoric of "radicalization," traces a movement "beyond" or "outside" a particular tradition (be it metaphysics or the *"idées recues* of psychoanalytic orthodoxy"), while a more tentative second step examines how what has presumably been supplanted, displaced, or "precipitated out of the signifying chain" still functions as a determinate absence, as a spectral signifier that continues to haunt what supplants it.

While one might indeed link this rhythm of dis-placement to the Freudian mechanism of repression, a term coined by Lacan to describe the way that "Saussure *genuit* Jakobson" is worth examining in this context since it adds a twilight cast to the crisis of succession (beyond-not beyond) repeatedly enacted by Weber's text. As though no one term could quite describe this hesitant movement, which is neither progessive nor regressive, neither generative nor degenerative, Lacan forms the oxymoronic verb *genuire* by extracting the "genes" from terms like *genèse* and *génération* and combining them with the noxiousness of the verb *nuire* thereby begetting not so much a monstrous product as a disturbing [*gênant*] mode of "production."

Rather than simply describing this crisis of succession involving the linguists Saussure and Jakobson, Lacan's language awkwardly "deproduces" it by enacting its own generational crisis; that is, without introducing a new, competing, alternative mode of (linguistic) production Lacan displaces the anthropomorphic terms in which we usually discuss "generational" issues (in the largest sense of the term). The excessive word play and coinage of an oxymoronic neologism are at the very least an indication of the disruptive energy which seems to be required to shake up traditional thinking about such matters. What erupts in this word play is not so much an ersatz linguistic or "genetically engineered" mode of production, but rather the conflicts which are necessarily repressed and misconstrued in the production of an identity, in the fetishistic identity of a production process.[8]

To understand how these deproductive or generational crises manifest themselves (or rather silently "insist" since this movement is precisely not one of pro-duction) as a rhythm or cadence of Weber's text, let us briefly turn to his introduction of the notion of differential articulation in his chapter on "The unconscious chess player: the linguistic theory of Ferdinand de Saussure." According to Weber,

> The radical difference between Saussure's theory and this [metaphysical] tradition is to be sought . . . in the radicalization of the idea of *difference* as the principle of the linguistic sign [. . .] What Saussure describes as the "two amorphous masses" of acoustical and ideational material can only crystallize and precipitate out as signifier and signified by virtue of their differentiation; a sound can only operate as a signifier insofar as it is distinguishable from other sounds; a thought can only be signified insofar as it is distinguishable from other thoughts. Thought of in this way, signification is no longer conceived as a process of representation, but as one of *articulation*. (p. 27)

This first movement thus has all the markings of a "radical" break, a decisive step beyond, and a supplanting ("signification is *no longer* conceived as a process of representation, but as one of articulation"). Yet in a second step Weber goes on to describe "this radicalization of differentiality" as that which "defines Saussure's *ambivalent* position with respect to traditional metaphysical approaches to language." (p. 28) This second more hesitant *pas* seems to suggest that it is less a question of supplanting or deposing a powerful tradition than of bringing out certain contradictions and ambivalences within it.

The point is *not merely* that Saussure does not go far enough in breaking decisively with tradition (although this is *also* the case particularly in light of the long chapter of the *Cours* devoted to the traditional subordination of writing to speech); rather, what is most important for Weber is that the radicalization of difference as "articulation" will never become a *new principle* or a *position* decisively beyond a superceded tradition of metaphysical linguistic theory precisely because it will have always already

---

[8] That is, "misconstrued" in the Lacanian sense of *méconnaissance* which is discussed in chapter 2 on "Mistaken identity."

been linked – as it is here – to sources of contradiction and "ambivalent positions." As Weber states at the opening of chapter four

To properly understand the significance of structural linguistics for Lacan, one cannot overlook its internal contradictions. Saussure's writings are of interest to him less as the site where a certain strain of modern linguistics sought to pose its foundations, than as the theater in which the structure of language and its relation to the subject are staged as questions. (p. 38)

That Weber has recourse to dramatic language here (and indeed throughout the text) is no accident, for as he says in an important footnote, "the theatrical aspect of articulation tends to emerge whenever phonocentric conceptions of language are no longer taken for granted." (p. 73 note) Obviously, the theatricality of Weber's own writing goes beyond his use of certain metaphors to include the cadences and hesitations which scan the text. These rhythms subtly displace accents in a way that effectively re-introduces repressed conflicts, logical aporia, and linguistic ambiguities. They open an equivocal space – perhaps only as wide as a hyphen (or a missing letter) in the term *Ent-stellung* – in which foreign accents may resonate and other unfamiliar ways of listening may be cultivated. Or to put it a little differently, the graphic dis-articulation of *Ent-stellung* silently re-enacts the uncertain shift in signification from a notion of re-presentation to a process of differential articulation. For the reader this means that instead of being able to narcissistically view the word as a discrete *body* and unit of meaning, one is compelled to focus on the letter – that is, on the dislocated joints, hinges, and differential spacing of articulation.[9] In short, accentuating *Ent-stellung* is but a way of displacing and dislocating an accent, a way to begin to beat out the complex rhythms of a "return to Freud."

I would like to thank Bruce Fink for his careful revisions of the translation, the Mellon Foundation and the Center for Advanced Study at the University of Virginia for their generous support of this project, and my grandfather, Harry Levine, for the endless delights of his immigrant's accent.

[9] See chapter 2 on "Mistaken identity" and chapter 6 on "Spades and hearts: the subject as stylus."

1

Introduction

The attempt to translate Lacan's French and to discuss his work in another language might well be met with a certain amount of skepticism. We usually expect from a theoretical discourse a transparency of language and a clarity of concept that in principle seems to guarantee the possibility of translation. Particularly in the realm of theory, the verbal representation is supposed to efface itself before that which it represents. We assume that an articulation in one language can be translated into another so long as the "represented" may be said to be truthful, since truth is supposed to be the same in all languages. Even if, as in recent times, we conceive of truth as being inseparable from its verbal expression, we have little doubt that its self-identity makes possible the kind of repetition in different languages that we commonly call "translation."

Why then should the attempt to translate Lacan arouse skepticism? His discourse is undoubtedly theoretical and claims not only to speak about truth but indeed to enact it. Nevertheless, what his texts give voice to and in a certain sense "stage" is not simply something represented, an object that would be self-identical, but is itself representation, translation, staging. The "object" of Lacan's entire theoretical discourse, its "sense," entails a mode of articulation which might best be described as a "slip-up" or derailing of sense: the language of the unconscious, the unconscious as language.

What distinguishes this particular linguistic form is that it never simply speaks directly (in the first or any other person) but rather misspeaks itself, concealing, denying, disavowing. Its repetition always involves distortion and dislocation. In this way the unconscious forms a language of representation that is not constituted by what it designates, but that instead always deconstructs the "represented," a translation without an original or, as Freud would say, another scene.

In order to demonstrate that this understanding of the unconscious as a translation without an original or as a representation without a "represented" is not simply an invention of Lacan's, but is already prescribed in the texts of Freud, it suffices to recall the description of the primary process and dreamwork in *The Interpretation of Dreams*. The "other scene" of the unconscious is governed by the primary process, which is characterized by an instability of energy cathexes (under the sway of the pleasure principle); this instability manifests itself by interacting with the censorship in dream distortions, making use of the mechanisms of displacement, condensation, and considerations of representability. Freud, though using linguistic concepts such as translation, transmission, and coding in order to describe the unconscious' necessarily distorted forms of articulation, can still be read as having never called into question the existence of an original text. For instance, his famous distinction between "latent" and "manifest content" seems to presuppose just such an original:

The dream-content seems like a transcript of the dream-thoughts into another mode of expression, whose characters and syntactic laws it is our business to discover by comparing the original and the translation.[1]

A closer reading of *The Interpretation of Dreams*, however, shows that the so-called original constituted by the latent dream thoughts always takes the form of grammatically correct sentences that as such owe their structure to the secondary process of preconscious-consciousness. The primary process of the unconscious appears only in the distorting mechanisms of displacement, condensation and considerations of representability. In a long note added in 1925 to *The Interpretation of Dreams*, Freud stresses the importance of the dreamwork – in the sense of a distorting translation:

I used at one time to find it extraordinarily difficult to accustom readers to the distinction between the manifest content of dreams and the

---

[1] S. Freud, *The Interpretation of Dreams*, ch. 6, *The Standard Edition of the Works of Sigmund Freud*, translated and edited by James Strachey, [henceforth: *SE*], London: Hogarth, 1953–74, vol. IV, p. 277. Here and throughout, I have modified the translation when necessary.

latent dream-thoughts. Again and again arguments and objections would be brought up based upon some uninterpreted dream in the form in which it had been retained in the memory, and the need to interpret it would be ignored. But now that analysts at least have become reconciled to replacing the manifest dream by the meaning revealed by its interpretation, many of them have become guilty of falling into another confusion which they cling to with equal obstinacy. They seek to find the essence of dreams in their latent content and in so doing they overlook the distinction between the latent dream-thoughts and the dream-work. At bottom, dreams are nothing other than a particular *form* of thinking, made possible by the conditions of the state of sleep. It is the *dream-work* which creates that form, and it alone is the essence of dreaming – the explanation of its peculiar nature.[2]

A dream is thus a *form* of thought and this form is constituted by the dreamwork, not by the dream-thoughts, the latent content. For any particular dream there is a manifest and a latent content, and yet this content is not the essence of the dream qua content, but only its material. Furthermore, as a result of the characteristic overdetermination of dreams, the wish realized in it is itself enmeshed in a network of other wishes, among which the infantile ones are the most decisive. This gives the ostensibly original text the character of a palimpsest, superimposed upon other texts that are both referred to and effaced by it. This double and antithetical movement, which Freud calls, significantly, "transference" (*Übertragung*), entails a process of translation which is potentially interminable and which assumes a relatively stable form only when the structures of early childhood sexuality have been stabilized through the "decline" of the Oedipus complex.

Indeed, although at times in *The Interpretation of Dreams*, Freud seems to suggest that representations have their origin in some prior presence, upon closer scrutiny such presence reveals itself to be a representation that in turn refers to other representations. Dream images thus should not be read simply according to their "pictorial value" [*Bilderwert*], but instead according to their "sign-relationship" [*Zeichenbeziehung*]; like a rebus, this relationship treats concrete images as material that serves to signify "a syllable or word."[3]

[2] *SE*, v, pp. 506–507.
[3] *Interpretation of Dreams*, *SE*, iv, p. 278. Significantly, Freud describes the dream here as "a pictographic script," a *Bilderschrift*.

We thus gradually arrive at a notion of the unconscious as a movement of translation without an original, as a process of representation without a "represented," something that, "logically" speaking, is unthinkable – whether as a substratum or as a substance. This logical scandal requires linguistic markers like the curious German prefix, *ver-*, which is found in so many of Freud's decisive terms (*Verdrängung*: repression, *Verschiebung*: displacement, *Verleugnung*: disavowal, *Verneinung*: denial), and which prefigures the way in which those terms *slip* away and out of the grasp of traditional conceptual discourse.[4] The unconscious has no identity, "is" radically other, without being *the* Other as such. Thus, when Lacan writes that "the unconscious *is* what one says,"[5] we should not forget to add: insofar as one says something other than what one *means*, i.e. intends to say. For Lacan, no less than for Freud, it is never a mere accident when language and intention diverge: such divergence derives from the signifying structure of language. As a signifying medium, language *is* the articulation of non-identity and this is

---

[4] The German prefix, *ver-*, stems from the Gothic, where it signifies "out," "before," "past," and "away from." The Latin *per-*, *por-*, *pro-*, as well as the Greek *peri-*, *par-*, *pro-* and *para-* belong to the same word family. In modern usage, the meaning of *ver-* points in two distinct, if interrelated directions: first, a movement *away from*, a dislodging or dislocation (as in *Verschiebung*: displacement); second, the execution or intensification of an operation (as in *Verdichtung*: literally, "thickening," "condensation"). A word such as *Verdrängung* combines both meanings: it signifies a certain dislodging expulsion, and an intense impulsion (*Drang*, *drängen*). This etymological–lexical survey, however summary, turns out to read like an abbreviated description of the Unconscious, a word that Lacan glosses as follows: "Freud didn't find a better one, and there's no going back on it. The disadvantage of the word is that it is negative, which allows one to assume anything at all in the world about it, plus everything else as well. Why not?; To that which goes unnoticed, the word *everywhere* applies just as well as *nowhere*. It is nonetheless a very precise thing." ("Freud n'en a pas trouvé de meilleur, et il n'y a pas à y revenir. Ce mot a l'inconvénient d'être négatif, ce qui permet d'y supposer n'importe quoi au monde, sans compter le reste. Pourquoi pas? À chose inaperçue, le nom de 'partout' convient aussi bien que de 'nulle part'. C'est pourtant chose fort précise.") J. Lacan, *Television*, English translation by Denis Hollier, Rosalind Krauss and Annette Michelson, in: *October*, 40 (Spring, 1987), p. 9. French: *Télévision*, Editions du Seuil: Paris, 1973, p. 15.

[5] Jacques Lacan, *Ecrits*, Editions du Seuil: Paris, 1966, p. 830. To avoid confusion with the French edition of the *Ecrits*, references to the English translation will be to the name of the translator, Alan *Sheridan*. Throughout this book, references to Lacan's writings will be first to the English translation, wherever available, and then to the French edition, in order to facilitate consultation of the original by the reader. As with Freud, published translations will be modified wherever it is deemed necessary.

what allows the unconscious to be described as the discourse of the Other.

In the pages that follow, this relation of the unconscious to language will be elaborated; it is of decisive importance for Lacan's entire doctrine and for the very distinctive character of its "return to Freud." Insofar as this return entails more than a mere paraphrase or translation of an "original," it calls for a reconsideration of the notion of "repetition," and of its particular relation to psychoanalysis. The processes studied by psychoanalysis almost always involve repetition, not however as a return of the same, in any simple sense, but rather as the recurrence of a difference separating that which is repeated from its repetition. An instance of this difference is provided by Freud's description of the genealogy of the wish, in *The Interpretation of Dreams*, as deriving from the hallucinatory memory of an "experience of satisfaction": the hallucination seeks to repeat the remembered experience in the "identity of a perception," while at the same time confirming its absence, qua hallucination. It is this distance, between repeated and repetition, that opens the space of the wish and therefore allows the dream as such to take place.

Lacan's "return to Freud" also follows the ambivalent law of repetition. It draws attention to itself, not so much as a faithful rendering of a self-identical original, but as a turn of phrase or a trope. It is precisely the tropicality of Lacan's use of language that bars the way to any simple presentation. Lacan's "retour" is thus also a detour which describes the Unconscious not as an object, but as a movement whose trajectory it retraces. This is why Lacan's theoretical discourse is at the same time very practical, a "signifying practice" in which the laws of signification, and above all those of the signifier, are not merely objectified or named as much as staged.

Such staging, to be sure, should be identified neither with the language of the unconscious nor with so-called "free association." It remains a theoretical discourse that must be held accountable for the consequences of its conceptuality. Such conceptuality, however, challenges the conventional criteria of accepted academic discourse. In a preface to a dissertation on his work, Lacan asserts that "my Writings (*Ecrits*) are unsuitable for theses, especially academic theses: antithetical in nature,

since one either takes what they formulate or one leaves them."
(*puisqu'à ce qu'ils formulent, il n'y a qu'à se prendre ou bien à les laisser*).⁶ The alternative is drastic, and yet anything but simple. For to "take" to such texts is inevitably to be *taken by* them: to be moved elsewhere by a practice of language in which sense is often overtaken – *surprised* – by sound, just as *se prendre* might easily be taken for *surprendre*. To take to these texts is perhaps above all to follow the lead of such surprises, even if this means taking on more than can be reasonably reckoned with.

For if language is a condition of reason, the games it plays are not always reasonable. We can learn about them, therefore, only by playing along, at least for a while. It is only then that their sense – i.e. their direction – begins to emerge.

⁶ Cf. Anika Lemaire, *Jacques Lacan*, translated by D. Macey, London: Routledge & Kegan Paul, 1977, p. VII; French edition: *Jacques Lacan*, Brussels: Pierre Mardaga, 1970, p. 10.

2

❖❖❖

Mistaken identity: Lacan's theory of the "mirror stage"

❖❖❖

In "Of our antecedents," a short note written for the publication of his *Ecrits*, Lacan comments in retrospect on his early writings:

We thus find ourselves replacing these texts in a future anterior: they will have anticipated our insertion of the unconscious in language.[1]

Lacan uses the future anterior tense to describe not only his own development, but also the historicity of the subject in general, insofar as the unconscious plays a part in its constitution. In his programmatic text, "Function and field of speech and language in psychoanalysis," Lacan writes:

What is realized in my history [i.e. in that of the individual subject] is not the past definite of what was, since it is no more, or even the present perfect of what has been in what I am, but the future anterior of what I shall have been for what I am in the process of becoming.[2]

The peculiarity of this future anterior tense, matrix for the historicity of the subject, can perhaps be explained best by means of a short comparison to Hegel. The (present) perfect tense is undoubtedly the temporal medium of Hegelian discourse, a discourse that presents itself as a self-realization of spirit [*Geist*]. Present in this tense is a spirit or mind that (virtually at least) has always already been perfect. Without this present tense, absolute knowledge and philosophical certainty

---

[1] "Nous nous trouvons donc replacer ces textes dans un futur antérieur: ils auront devancé notre insertion de l'inconscient dans le langage." "De nos antécédents," *Ecrits*, p. 71.

[2] J. Lacan, *The Language of the Self: The Function of Language in Psychoanalysis*, trans. Anthony Wilden, Baltimore: Johns Hopkins University Press, 1968, p. 63. ("Ce qui se réalise dans mon histoire, n'est pas le passé défini de ce qui fût puisqu'il n'est plus, ni même le parfait de ce qui a été dans ce que je suis, mais le futur antérieur de ce que j'aurai été pour ce que je suis en train de devenir." *Ecrits*, p. 300.) Sheridan, p. 86.

7

– i.e. scientific knowledge as such – would never have been representable in Hegel's writings. In his "Introduction" to *The Phenomenology of Spirit*, Hegel criticizes a notion of thought construed as a mere instrument, serving only to recognize something exterior to it. He concludes:

If the Absolute were only to be brought on the whole nearer to us by this agency [*Werkzeug*: instrument] [of knowledge or (re)cognition: *Erkenntnis*], without any change being wrought in it, like a bird caught by a limestick, it would certainly scorn a trick of that sort, if it were not in its very nature, and did not wish to be, beside us from the start.[3]

The Absolute, the mind, must then according to Hegel already be – and want to be – in and for itself with us. Without this prior presence both philosophy as rigorous science and the identity of the subject would be impossible.[4] For how could a subject come to know itself, dialectically realize its identity, if this matrix of presence were not (and did not want to be) at least virtually already there as a form to be filled or as an interiority to be unfolded and explicated over time. The thinking subject (or thought as subject) can only come to know itself to the extent to which the form of this Self has always already been there as a *potential presence*. The course of the Hegelian dialectic may be infinite, but this infinity, according to the claims of the dialectic itself, must not be a "bad" one. Rather, it should be the self-realization of an identity that has always already been virtually present to itself. For the self-conscious mind as it is expressed and represented in Hegel's *Logic*, this in-and-for-itself-having-been-with-us [*An-und-für-sich-bei-uns-gewesen-Sein*] of the Absolute is articulated in the (present) perfect tense. The process of negation and determination, the movement of the dialectic, is defined in the *Logic* from the very start, not simply as the transitional movement of "passing by," but as the perfected past presence of a *passage*, of an *Übergegangensein*, that will have always already taken place as the determinate negation of being and nothing:

---

[3] G.W.F. Hegel, *Phenomenology of Mind*, trans. Baillie, New York: Macmillan Co., 1961, p. 132.

[4] See: M. Heidegger, *Hegel's Concept of Experience*, trans. K.R. Dove, New York: Harper & Row, 1979.

The truth is neither being nor nothing, nor that being passes over into nothing, nor nothing into being, but rather that *each has passed over into the other*.[5]

The history of the subject of metaphysics attaining its most powerful and complete articulation in Hegel, is conceived according to the most self-contained form of presence, that of the present (made) perfect. The temporal structure of the subject that Lacan's reading of Freud strives to articulate, stands in marked contrast to this perfected present. The perfect tense is supplanted by the future anterior, thus calling into question the very foundations of subjective identity conceived in terms of an interiorizing memory. In invoking the future anterior tense, Lacan troubles the perfected closure of the always-already-having-been [*des Immer-schon-gewesen-Seins*] by inscribing it in the inconclusive futurity of what will-always-already-have-been [*Immer-schon-gewesen-sein-wird*], a "time" which can never be entirely remembered, since it will never have fully taken place. It is an irreducible remainder or remnant that will continually prevent the subject from ever becoming entirely self-identical. In the psychoanalytical perspective, then, memory becomes something very different from what it was for metaphysics – not because of a future that the subject will never be able to catch up with fully, but because every attempt by the subject of the unconscious to grasp its history inevitably divides that history into a past that, far from having taken place once and for all, is always yet to come. Consequently, the living present [*lebendige Gegenwart*] (Husserl) of the subject emerges as a focal point whose actuality can reside in an *anticipated belatedness*.

The consequences of such belatedness can be developed through the examination of a second aspect of the future anterior, in which it is considered less as a tense, designating a future past, than as a mode, entailing a conjecture. "You will have understood Freud" (*Vous aurez compris Freud . . .*). Used this way, modally, the "future anterior" designates a surmise, a conditional prediction and hence, a proposition bearing upon an uncertain state of affairs. This uncertainty, which cannot be

[5] *Hegel's Science of Logic*, trans. A.V. Miller, New York: Humanities Press, 1969, p. 83 [translation altered; my emphasis].

identified simply with a future or a past, typifies the language of a subject whose self-consciousness is structured in terms of anticipated belatedness. In accordance with the split temporality of the future anterior, this will have been subject to and of the unconscious.

This split, quasi-temporality affects not only the unconscious as an *object* of theoretical discourse, but also, and perhaps more significantly, the discourse itself. Thus, whereas Lacan stresses the conceptual character of the unconscious – "The unconscious *is* a concept" – the structure of this concept distinguishes it fundamentally from that of the philosophical tradition culminating in Hegel. For Lacan, the concept is construed not as the presentation of a representation in thought through the determinate negation of its properties, but rather as the vehicle of a *search*. As a concept, the unconscious is thus "forged on the trace of what works to constitute the subject."[6]

The tendency of Lacan's earlier texts to use the conjectural quasi-time of the future anterior, thereby deferring the closure of comprehension indefinitely, suggests that the singular movement of the unconscious requires a theoretical discourse capable not merely of *describing* its trajectory, but rather of *staging* its movement. Lacan's use of the future anterior does not imply an absolute knowledge that has, is and will always have been present to itself. Rather, it returns to the *theatricality* that is so powerfully at work in Freud's writings and through which they are clearly distinguished from those of his followers. Lacan renews this Freudian tradition through which psychoanalytic writing gestures towards a stage whose borders are only provisionally determined by what is called the "reader" (or "auditor": the difference in this case is not decisive). This "reader" or "audience," as the provisional "representative of the other," as Freud called Flieβ, serves to delimit the borders of a stage that will always have been at a remove from the place we occupy as self-conscious subjects. Hence, the frequent apostrophes that give Lacan's writings a tone that is even more theatrical than it is pedagogical. For if discourse can be said to set the stage, the unconscious marks the eccentricity of its

---

[6] "L'inconscient *est* un concept forgé sur la trace de ce qui opère pour constituer le sujet." "Position de l'inconscient," *Ecrits*, p. 830.

enabling limits. *There – is* the unconscious, not as an object of perception or of intuition, not as a clinical object, but as a theatrical scene that in turn is inscribed in an ongoing scenario. The future anterior announces the disjunctive immediacy of this *other scenario*, to which we shall have occasion to return.

One may draw a further conclusion from the above: if the conjectural quasi-temporality of the future anterior characterizes not only the historicity of the subject, but also its theoretical articulation in Lacan's texts,[7] this in turn determines Lacan's choice of a *synchronic* perspective and his rejection of the diachronic, developmental point of view that has dominated orthodox psychoanalysis ever since Freud, and even more, ever since Karl Abraham schematized and codified the theory of libidinal stages.[8] Thus if Lacan's entire theoretical project is concerned primarily with replacing the predominant genetic point of view with a synchronic one – his "technique of reading," Lacan writes, "is concerned simply with replacing each of [Freud's] terms in their synchrony"[9] – then what counts for him, as in the case of the future anterior tense, is to replace the temporality of the conscious subject, whose basis is the (present) perfect tense, with that of another, split, disjointed time that would be more adequate to the movement of the unconscious. Against a conception of development based upon identity and presence, Lacan advocates a synchronic perspective that, however, has little to do with mere simultaneity. However apodictic and systematic Lacan's language sometimes sounds, it is accessible only to a reading that does not stop at the seeming stability of individual propositions, but instead seeks out the process of enunciation, and the contradictions that fuel it. Like Freud's unconscious, Lacan's language seems "to know no contradiction," which means, of course, not that there *are* no contradictions but that the "law of non-contradiction" does not hinder them from proliferating and determining thought in its "truth."

[7] Lacan characterizes psychoanalysis as a "conjectural science": cf. *Ecrits*, pp. 472, 863.
[8] Cf. Karl Abraham, *On Character and Libido Development*, trans. Douglas Bryan and Alix Strachey, New York: Norton, 1966.
[9] "Il s'agit simplement de remplacer chacun de ses termes dans leur synchronie" *Ecrits*, p. 856.

With these preliminary remarks in mind, let us now turn to the essay where Lacan's discourse finds its initial articulation: his essay on "the mirror stage." At this point it is important to bear in mind that any interpretation of a discourse whose temporal medium is the future anterior must itself be caught up in processes of repetition difficult to master or to situate temporally. In short, such interpretations will themselves have been inscribed precisely in the temporal *non-identity of the text read*. They are inscribed literally as *inter-pretation* – as attempts to ascertain the price (*pretium*) of textual gaps – of the *inter*. At the same time, interpretation itself strives to reach that future anterior, when it will have done its work, repeating and displacing the gaps, replacing them with other, supplementary gaps that will in turn elicit yet other retrospective anticipations . . .

Let us then begin with Lacan's first psychoanalytic text, "The mirror stage as former of the function of the I." The mirror stage described by Lacan can be briefly summarized as follows: between the ages of six and eighteen months a child displays a reaction to its mirror-image that strikingly distinguishes it from other creatures such as chimpanzees. A chimpanzee loses interest in its mirror-image as soon as it recognizes it to be an image; a child, on the contrary, displays a jubilant reaction when it recognizes its own reflection. From this jubilant acknowledgment of one's mirror-image, Lacan does nothing less than to derive the constitution – and above all: the destiny – of the ego. At this point in time, the child is not yet in control of its body and finds itself in a state of total helplessness and dependency. This situation is an effect of the "premature" birth peculiar to human beings, a consequence of which is that visual perception is much more highly developed than the motor function. A human being is thus able at a much earlier stage to *perceive* the unity of an image than it is to produce this unity in its own body. The sight of another human being, be it the mother, caretaker, or even one's own mirror-image, becomes the *matrix* of a sense of unity, identity and continuity which the child's bodily existence is incapable of providing. Furthermore, the identification of a similar *Gestalt* constitutes the exact opposite of the turbulence and inadequate coordination that the child experiences most immediately. The jubilant reaction of a child who has recognized its mirror-image is a sign not of the recognition of the subject's identity but of its constitution. Later, Lacan will formulate the role of the other as image in the following way: "The mediation of the Other," he asserts, "cannot be considered as deriving from a second instance or as being of secondary importance, if the first or the one does not yet exist."[10] The ego is thus initially constituted through the child's identification with an image whose otherness is precisely overlooked in the observation of similarity. Despite the effort to ignore it, however, such alterity can never be entirely effaced, since it is what permits the identification to take place. Thus, it is only the *anticipated* motor and mental unity, visually represented in the perception of the image and still wholly lacking in the child, which allows the mirror-image, so crucial for the constitution of the ego, to have its effect. The perceived image offers a semblance of wholeness that contrasts sharply with what the child has experienced of its own body: lack of motoric control, deficiency, and dependency. In order to present this semblance of unity and exercise its power, the image need not be a mirror-image; but the recognized relation of the reflecting image to the body reflected, heightens its fascinatory power, while the body's symmetrical inversion in the mirror-image endows the latter with a supplementary moment of alterity, thus heightening its ambivalent attraction.

According to Lacan, the mirror stage hereby locates the constitution of the ego in a dimension of *fictionality* and of self-deception, which will have an alienating effect on the subsequent existence and development of the subject. Or rather, the "self" – insofar as it is determined by the ego – is, as such, a result of alienation and deception (which also makes it problematic to retain the notion of "alienation" . . .). The sense of self-identity – of unaltered and enduring homogeneity and unity – derives from the internalization of a *relationship* that is effective *only* by virtue of its heterogeneity: i.e. by virtue of the difference between the semblance of unity of the image and the disunity of the subject's motoric, bodily functions. The sense of identity and even of reality that the subject obtains from its ego

---

[10] "Discours de Jacques Lacan" (September 26, 1953), *Actes du Congrès de Rome*, in: *La Psychanalyse I* (1956), p. 203.

13

thus harbors in it the irreality, deception, and non-identity that will take on a variety of (familiar) guises, among which Lacan mentions: phantasies of dismembered bodies (studied by Melanie Klein), hallucinations of doubles, Hieronymus Bosch's paintings, and Hans Bellmer's puppets. The *stade du miroir* is thereby defined not primarily as a genetic moment, but rather as a *phase* and as a turning-point or trope, destined to be repeated incessantly, in accordance with a schema whose moments are inadequacy, anticipation, and defensive armoring, and whose result is an identity that is not so much *alienated* as *alienating*, caught up in the "inexhaustible squaring of its own vicious circle of ego-confirmations" ("la quadrature inépuisable des récolements du *moi*").[11] This vicious circle produces an aggressivity that in Lacan's view is initially the effect neither of social conditions nor of subjective interaction; rather, its roots are *intrasubjective*, deriving from a relationship of mis-recognition, through which the ego comes to be by taking the place of the imaginary other.

The subject is thus caught up in a future anterior – it will have been the image whose place it takes. But in order to take place, it must also repudiate or foreclose the alterity of that futural past. In order to say, I am, it must deny the irreducible alterity of the image upon which the ego depends, and instead interiorize that relationship. A hetero-reflective relationship is thus turned into an auto-reflective one marked by the transparency of self-consciousness. The ego forgets, in the words of Rimbaud, whom Lacan quotes in his essay on "Aggressivity in psychoanalysis," that "I is another" (*Je est un autre*).[12]

The ego is thus determined "by a primary identification that structures the subject as competing with itself,"[13] long before the Oedipus complex manifests itself. There are therefore good reasons to suspect that, in view of this kind of imaginary origin, the ego will be perenially alienated, and above all, from itself. For that Self consists essentially in an alienation: not from itself, but from the other.

Already this very early essay, apparently dealing with a developmental problem – the formation of the ego – bears the

[11] *Ecrits*, p. 97; Sheridan, p. 4. [12] *Ecrits*, p. 118; Sheridan, p. 23.
[13] *Ecrits*, p. 117; Sheridan, p. 22.

imprint of a structuralist approach that only much later will be called by that name. The narcissistic structure of the ego and the aggressive tensions that derive from it – which Lacan will later relate to the Freudian notions of primary masochism and the death drive – are as difficult to overcome as the ego itself. Insofar as the subject conceives of its history as that of its ego – insofar that is, as it identifies itself with the ego – there can be no exit from the aforementioned vicious circle of self-affirmations. For Lacan this vicious circle attains its fullest expression in Sartre's existential philosophy. Given his postulate of subjective autonomy, Sartre's philosophy is for Lacan not only a "jeu de l'esprit" but a "je de l'esprit", a spiritual ego that traditional philosophy has never seriously called into question insofar as it has tended to equate subjectivity with self-consciousness. Considered in this way, this ego, Lacan argues, is identified precisely with that part of the subject that renders a true historicity of the individual impossible. This point should be borne in mind when considering not only Lacan's theory, but also what has often – all too indiscriminately – been called the "structuralist attack on history." It is not history as such that is criticized by structuralism, or by Lacan, but the metaphysical conception that construes history in terms of a self-identical subject of self-consciousness.

In these early writings, then, Lacan thus challenges the conception of history as the self-production and self-realization of the subject. Instead, he points to the ego's inertia, which arises from a constitutive identification that leaves it unable to break out of the orbit and spell of its aggressive, narcissistic origins. Not yet able to define structurally an alternative trajectory for the ego's inherent alterity, Lacan can only insist on the non-coincidence of ego and subject. And yet, even at this point in time, it is already clear that this non-coincidence originates in a splitting of the ego that is primary, and not merely external or accidental. In apparent opposition to Freud, who identifies the ego at first with the system perception-consciousness, and later with reality testing within the psyche, Lacan emphasizes the ego's defensive functions, such as misapprehension [*Verkennung*] and denial. As a response to a fundamental predicament of the human being, what is most characteristic of the ego is the function not of reality testing, but

rather of what Lacan calls "derealization," in accordance with
the fictive nature of the ego. Lacan elucidates this fictive
dimension by reference to a work of fiction: the myth of
Narcissus.

In his essay on the "mirror-phase," Lacan calls attention to
the perspicuity of psychoanalytic theory for having been
sensitive to the "semantic latencies" that resonate in the term
"primary narcissism." The recourse to the myth of Narcissus
entails two moments which, Lacan argues, are all too often
forgotten in psychoanalysis. First, the fact that Narcissus, in the
myth, is not merely in love with himself, but rather with an
image of himself. And second, the fact that Narcissus' fascination with this image leads him to take his own life. Lacan links
the suicidal aspect of the Narcissus myth to the process of
identification and to its aggressive consequences, as already
mentioned. More important, however, is the function of the
image, which defines the imaginary realm as such. In philosophy, as well as in everyday usage, an image is generally
construed as a representation that reproduces, with diminished
intensity, a predetermined, structurally and temporally prior
sensation, impression or idea: a subject places an object before
its mind's eye, it imagines something; a picture depicts. Lacan
slightly but decisively displaces this notion of the image: it
de-picts not so much by reproducing or representing an object,
as by taking it apart, dismantling it. Nothing can be said to stand
before the image – its model, for instance – that does not in effect
come *after* it, just as the ego comes after the mirror-image and
depends upon it. This *belated* arrival of the "model" inscribes it
in a chain of doubles, as the "splitting" image of its ostensible
original.

Something similar to this is already intimated in Freud's
discussion of narcissistic identification, insofar as the latter does
not merely *express* a subject, but also re-acts upon it and
transforms it. For Lacan, however, the effect of the image
becomes, as we have seen, constitutive of the ego itself. To be
consistent with this reinterpretation of the image's constitutive
power, its origins can no longer be located in a reality held to be
temporally and structurally prior to it, since this reality, at least
insofar as the ego is concerned, is itself only an after-effect of the
image. That this shift in the conception of the image and of

its powers should raise a number of logical difficulties should come as no surprise, considering the fact that it is the task of traditional logic to determine an order in which first things come first: the model before the copy, the repeated before the repetition, identity before difference. This order of precedence is challenged by Lacan's notion of the *semblable*, meaning the like or the similar. When Lacan claims that the condition of narcissistic identification is the *reconnaissance du semblable*: recognition, reacknowledgement of the *like*, one might ask how the imago can be *re*-acknowledged as being similar, without identity – like Hegel's Absolute – being necessarily presupposed. Distinct from this Hegelian position, which places identity first, ego-identity for Lacan is produced first by the imago, by the representation.

We thereby find ourselves before the very problem already encountered in connection with the future anterior: "is" (the presence of the present tense) should be understood only as an "anticipated past," which has yet to arrive. The paradox can hardly be resolved according to the familiar rules of logic, and this is perhaps due to the fact that the subject implied by the Freudian unconscious cannot be conceived according to the traditional logic of metaphysics. Whether this must lead to a renunciation or revision of Freudian doctrine, or instead to a rethinking of the scope of traditional logic, must be regarded as an open question. Nevertheless, by virtue of what is illogical in this view we can understand why ego-recognition – whether as an objective or subjective genitive, or as both – must for Lacan always and of necessity remain a mis-recognition, a misconstruing implied in the reiterative structure of (re)cognition as such, a misconstruction and ultimately: a case of mistaken identity. For Lacan, the "coming into its own" of the thinking spirit, of the subject as ego and as self-consciousness, always entails "coming to *another*": *an* other, and never *its* other, in the dialectical sense of Hegelian determinate negation. In the strange light of Lacan's mirror-stage, *there* is the mirror, and then image; first the image, and then that which it depicts. And if we seek to be rigorous, we cannot even assert that the mirror *is*: that is, is present, as an entity, a being, but rather only that that *there is* the mirror, and that *there*, on that *other stage*, the ego *superimposes* itself upon its mirror-image, forever to be haunted by that reflection, beyond the wildest stretch of the imagination.[14]

The imaginary can be defined as that fictive, illusory realm of the mirror-image, of the optical illusion, of the image which can no longer hope to be an accurate and faithful representation of its model, since the latter is fashioned in its image: I am the image of that image, a mirror without end.

Beyond the looking glass, there is nothing. Does that mean that there is nothing *else*? The mirror-stage, Lacan remarks, is "the moment that decisively tilts all of human knowledge into mediatisation through desire of the other."[15] With this remark, desire enters the (narcissistic) picture. Before, the discussion of the mirror stage dealt only with the physiological prematuration of the human organism and with the formatory effects of images in the maturation of pigeons and migratory locust. Although in this essay desire is only mentioned in passing, as it were, it indicates the way that Lacan's future thought will take, a way that will lead away from physiology and which will allow the mirror stage to appear in a very different light: no longer as the expression of an organic deficiency, but as the response to the linguistic, "symbolic" nature of human being. Looking back years later on the mirror stage, in "Of Our Antecedents," (1966), Lacan remarks that it defines the rule by which the imaginary differs from the symbolic "at this moment of capture by an historical inertia . . ."[16] To be sure, the rules of this differentiation, in which the symbolic dimension of desire is articulated, will only begin to be worked out from 1953 on, some fifteen years after the first formulation of "The Mirror Stage," which was initially presented in 1936 and then published for the first time in 1949. In the intervening years, much has happened, but for Lacan nothing will have been of greater importance than his encounter with the linguistic

---

[14] On the problem of the "there is," cf. Martin Heidegger, "On time and being," trans. Joan Stambaugh, New York: Harper & Row, 1972, pp. 5ff. The relation of Lacan to Heidegger should be explored less in the manifest adoption of philosophemes, than in the ways the linguistic and rhetorical practices of both authors tend to jar established theoretical discourse into motion.

[15] *Ecrits*, p. 98; Sheridan, p. 5.

[16] "Le stade du miroir donne la règle de partage entre l'imaginaire et le symbolique à ce moment de capture par une inertie historique . . ." *Ecrits*, p. 69.

theories of Ferdinand de Saussure, the founder of structural linguistics. It is this encounter that turns the *stade de miroir* from a *stadium* (to which Lacan compares it), to a *staging area* where forces and figures of a very different kind are preparing to make their appearance.

3

✧✧✧✧✧✧✧✧✧✧✧✧✧✧✧✧✧✧✧✧✧✧✧✧✧✧✧✧✧✧✧✧✧✧✧

The unconscious chess player

✧✧✧✧✧✧✧✧✧✧✧✧✧✧✧✧✧✧✧✧✧✧✧✧✧✧✧✧✧✧✧✧✧✧✧

The name, Ferdinand de Saussure, is generally associated with two insights: first, a semiotics based on the principle of the "arbitrary" or "unmotivated" nature of the sign, and a division of language into language-system, *langue*, and speech, *parole*. Were this all that Saussure had to say, however, it would be little enough. The conception of the arbitrary character of the sign is at least as old as Plato's *Cratylus*, and the separation of language into system and speech is hardly any less ancient. If Saussure was able to exercise a certain influence upon French Structuralism, and through it, upon its "post-structuralist" transformations, it was only insofar as his rethinking of language diverged, in decisive ways, from the more familiar conceptions that his terminology, it is true, often suggests. Let us therefore, as a first step in defining this divergence, briefly recapitulate certain main traits of what might be called the dominant metaphysical theory of language, as explicated by the thinker who first laid the groundwork of that theory: Aristotle.

According to Pierre Aubenque, Aristotle's entire philosophical project, far from being simply a critique of Platonism, should be seen as an effort to repair a fatal flaw in Plato's thought, one which rendered the truth-claims of philosophy vulnerable to the skeptical challenge of the Sophists.[1] At the end of the *Cratylus*, Socrates reminds his interlocutor that "knowledge of things cannot be derived from their names, but only from the things themselves which must be studied and examined independently." (439d) Yet, Plato never explains how a thought process that is only accessible through the medium of language, would be able to examine things "independently" of their "names," nor what the role of language would thereby be.

---

[1] Pierre Aubenque, *Le problème de l'être chez Aristote*, Paris, 1964; see especially the chapter entitled "Etre et langage" (Being and language), pp. 94–205.

The Sophists, by contrast, had made language the focus of their thinking and had elaborated two seemingly contradictory accounts of its relation to reality, both of which worked effectively to undermine philosophy's claim to truth. The first, formulated by Gorgias, held that it is impossible for language to correspond adequately to extra-linguistic things, since language itself is a thing among things – namely a phonetic entity that, in its specificity, is unable to render entities different from itself. Language, in short, is one thing among others, which, by virtue of their otherness, cannot be rendered by it. While language, according to this view, can serve as a means to intersubjective ends, its peculiarity excludes it from being a medium of objective knowledge.

The second, contrasting position, associated with Antisthenes, a disciple of Gorgias, has the following formulation:

All discourse has an element of truth, for whosoever speaks, says something, and to say something means to say some entity, and whosoever says an entity, says something true.[2]

These two apparently contradictory views of language share a common basis: both conceive of language as something self-identical, be it as one natural thing among others, be it as an entity that partakes of Being. Most importantly, both radically question the idea of objective truth, since according to Gorgias, language is separated from other things by virtue of its difference from them, whereas for Antisthenes, language, by always referring to something beyond its own immediate being, always possesses an element of truth (but only an element). The upshot of these arguments is that truth itself becomes increasingly difficult to distinguish from non-truth.

Aristotle's linguistic theory seeks to counter such Sophistic challenges by arguing that language is inherently neither true nor false, but rather a process of signification. In his treatise "On interpretation," Aristotle states that

spoken sounds are symbols of affections in the soul, and written marks symbols of spoken sounds. And just as written marks are not the same for all men, neither are spoken sounds. But what these are in the first place signs of – affections of the soul – are the same for all; and what

---

[2] Cited by Aubenque, p. 100.

these are likenesses of – actual things – are also the same. (*De Interpretatione*, 16a)

Aristotle thus sets up two relationships: that of resemblance, a natural correspondence of things and mental experiences, and that of signification or symbolization, which is not related in any natural way to what is signified; this relation is first produced by convention. One can already see here the division into referent (the things themselves), the ideational content or the "designated" (the mental experiences), and the designating function (language). Linguistic symbols are arbitrary, since they bear no natural resemblance to that which they designate; they necessarily indicate an ideational content, which in turn is a faithful reproduction of a state of Being of an entity. Error is then possible insofar as the designated things – here the mental experiences – are infinite, whereas the number of available linguistic media – the linguistic signs – is limited. A situation thus arises which we would call ambiguity and which Aristotle calls "homonymy."

It is not possible here to follow Aubenque in his fascinating account of Aristotle's struggle to construct a theory of language and of argumentation which effectively answers the Sophists' challenge to the truth-claims of philosophy. The interested reader can consult the study of Pierre Aubenque. Instead, I want to cite a passage in which Aristotle polemicizes against the Sophists, since it relates to our topic in a number of important ways. Towards the end of the fourth book of the *Metaphysics*, Aristotle attempts to demonstrate the untenable nature of the Sophistic position by means of the following *reductio ad absurdum*:

But if all are alike both right and wrong, one who believes this can neither speak nor say anything intelligible; for he says at the same time both "yes" and "no". And if he makes no judgment but thinks and does not think, indifferently, what difference will there be between him and the plants? – Thus, then, it is in the highest degree evident that neither any one of those who maintain this view nor any one else is really in this position. For why does a man walk to Megara and not stay at home, thinking he ought to walk? Why does he not walk early some

[3] *The Complete Works of Aristotle*, edited by Jonathan Barnes, Princeton University Press: Princeton, NJ, 1984, vol. 1, p. 25.

morning into a well or over a precipice, if one happens to be in his way? Why do we observe him guarding against this, evidently because not thinking that falling in is alike good and not good? Evidently, he judges one thing to be better and another worse. And if this is so, he must judge one thing to be man and another to be not-man, one thing to be sweet and another to be not-sweet. For he does not aim at and judge all things alike, when, thinking it desirable to drink water or to see a man, he proceeds to aim at these things; yet he ought, if the same thing were alike man and not-man. But, as was said, there is no one who does not obviously avoid some things and not others. Therefore, as it seems, all men make unqualified judgments, if not about all things, still about what is better and worse. And if this is not knowledge but opinion, they should be all the more anxious about the truth, as a sick man should be more anxious about his health than one who is healthy; for he who has opinions is, in comparison with the man who knows, not in a healthy state as far as the truth is concerned. (1008b)[4]

To begin with, it should be noted that, in order to demonstrate the legitimacy of truth-claims in language, the philosopher finds himself forced to resort to an *ad hominem* argument, a pragmatical move that might rather be expected of a Sophist. One is reminded of the kind, and above all of the *tone*, of the arguments employed by Callicles, in Plato's *Gorgias*, in which Socrates' coming death is made the occasion to deprecate those philosophers who are unable or unwilling to avert approaching danger. Aristotle's pragmatics in this polemic nevertheless appear here to be a necessary result of his theory of language, for it is precisely the priority of the *pragmata* – of the things themselves – over the language which symbolizes them, that Aristotle seeks to defend at all costs against the Sophists. According to Aristotle, the referents of language (the things themselves) and their signifieds (the mental experiences) are both present; they exist prior to all language, although human beings can only have cognitive access to them through language. Aristotle can only demonstrate the priority of the *pragmata* by referring to factual, pragmatic human behavior. Human beings thus differ from plants insofar as they choose to do one thing rather than another; for example, if someone chooses first thing in the morning not to throw himself or herself right into a well or a ravine, this shows that things are

---

[4] *Metaphysics*, Book IV, chapter 4, *Complete Works of Aristotle*, vol. 2, p. 1592.

not indifferent and of equal importance and that such differences are also commonly presupposed as known, and as such form the basis of decisions, preferences and of action: one drinks water when one is thirsty and above all protects oneself from certain things rather than from others. Even anxiety, insofar as it determines human behavior, indicates, according to this argument, that a human being is not indifferent to everything, and perhaps above all, that one cannot be at once human and non-human. The reality principle and the necessity of self-preservation thus become arguments in favor of the real and knowable existence of objective essences.

It is precisely the existence of such beings that determines language in its function as symbol – that is, as a substitute for things, or rather, for their Being. Language is conceived of by Aristotle – and by much of the metaphysical tradition that will follow – as representation, and more precisely, representation in the sense of a substitute, proxy, deputy, or stand-in. Its immediate *reality* resides in the *absence* of the thing it signifies, which in turn is construed as already self-identical, prior to all symbolization. Such self-identical things can thus be called to mind as such, without mediation, whereas in language they can be present only in mediate form, qua representation. Language accordingly has no identity of its own, if it is not that of a medium of representation: it is not a full-fledged entity, in the Gorgian sense, for it only *is* as signification, as the absence of that which it signifies or represents. Language construed as representation becomes a place of irreducible difference, defined in terms of the identity and presence of the things it signifies. Language exists only in view of its meaning or sense, and this sense is in turn conceived as being prelinguistic: it proceeds from the speaker's intention and abides in the mind. Thus Aristotle's rebuttal of Sophistic argumentation must ultimately have recourse to the speaker's intention, for though one can expose contradictions and paralogisms in an argument, and one can trace their necessity to the poverty and dependence of the linguistic medium, precisely because of this poverty one cannot convincingly demonstrate the principle of contradiction in purely intralinguistic terms. The presence of the things themselves can at best only be inferred from the day to day behavior of men, as we have just seen.

Language, determined as representation, is thus considered by Aristotle from the vantage-point of its meaning and referents. What thereby remains to be seen is just how something is *capable* of functioning as a symbol: how language *is able to* signify. It is precisely this question which defines the point of departure of Saussure's reflections upon language. Like Aristotle, he is concerned with the conditions of possibility of scientific knowledge, but unlike most of his predecessors, his ultimate goal is to lay the groundwork for a rigorous *science* of language. Metaphysically speaking, this project is not without its contradictions: on the one hand it is informed by a notion of *episteme*, of scientific knowledge; on the other hand, the object of this knowledge is not a domain constituted by meaningful objects or processes, but a medium characterized by non-identity and absence. It is this contradiction, and the manner that Saussure confronts it, that constitute the originality of his conception of language, and it is to this contradiction that I now turn.

The first requirement of an autonomous science of language is the construction or delineation of a self-contained and homogeneous object of study. Guided by this principle, Saussure divides the field of language into three spheres: *langage, langue,* and *parole. Le langage,* language in the largest sense, designates the ability to constitute and to exercise language in general. Yet precisely because of this generality, language in this widest sense can never serve as the object of study of a single science: "Straddling various domains . . . it belongs to none of them; it cannot be classified within any particular category of human relations for one does not know how to determine its unity."[5] At the other end of the spectrum is speech (*parole*), which, like *langage,* does not possess a self-contained structure, but entails rather the empirical realization and actualization of language by individual speakers. Thus, in order to investigate speech, it is necessary to study the conditions of individual

---

[5] F. de Saussure, *Cours de linguistique générale,* Paris: 1964, p. 25. *Course in General Linguistics,* trans. by Wade Baskin, London: Fontana/Collins, 1974, p. 9. Future references to this work will be given in the body of the text, first to the French edition and then to the Baskin translation. References to this translation are given for purposes of comparison: the English translations used here are largely my own. The reader may also wish to consult the recent English translation of Saussure by Roy Harris, Lasalle: Open Court Press, 1986.

existence from different points of view, including those of psychology, physiology and physics. An independent science of speech is therefore no less difficult to conceive than a science of language as *langage*. Only language considered as a self-contained system of signs, which Saussure designates as *la langue* – can provide the basis upon which an autonomous science of linguistics can be constructed. Although language considered as a sign-system forms part of *langage*, it is only by virtue of the closure of that semiotic system that linguistic phenomena can be said to have any degree of consistency. For Saussure, it is only "the language-system (*la langue*) that constitutes the unity of language (*du langage*)." (27/11) Thus, although *la langue* is actualized in speech and has no existence independently of it, it still retains a structural priority, relating to speech as does the collective to the individual. As a sign-system, Saussure argues, language forms part of a field that is destined to become the privileged domain of a future science of semiology; although linguistic signs form only a relatively small part of this domain, they provide a privileged access to understanding the nature of the semiological problem.

Considered as a closed system, language is determined by the structure and function of the sign. And it is precisely in his theory of the sign that Saussure's paradoxical and original position in relation to metaphysics emerges most forcefully. His discussion of the "Nature of the linguistic sign" begins by rejecting the notion of *naming* as a relevant category in analyzing the operation of language. Compared to many of his predecessors, this move of Saussure's does not at first seem to be very radical: "The linguistic sign does not unite a thing and a name, but rather a concept and an acoustic image." (98/66) Aristotle, we recall, had in a similar way already differentiated between referent, signified (i.e. psychic state) and verbal sign (spoken or written). Moreover, as has frequently been observed, Saussure's introduction of the terminological distinction between signifier and signified – "We propose to retain the word sign to designate the whole, and to replace concept and acoustical image respectively by 'signified' and 'signifier'" (99/67) – continues a venerable tradition going back to the Stoical distinction between *signans* and *signatum*. The fact that Saussure thus distinguishes sign from name, that he construes the former as constituted by the opposition of signifier and signified, and finally, that he conceives this constitutive relationship to be "arbitrary" – all of this can be inscribed easily in the metaphysical concept of the sign. The radical difference between Saussure's theory and this tradition is to be sought elsewhere.

It resides not in the theory of the arbitrary structure of the sign, but rather, as Derrida has argued in *Of Grammatology*, in the radicalization of the idea of *difference* as the principle of the linguistic sign. For, as we have seen in Aristotle, the notion of semiotic arbitrariness is entirely compatible with a conception of language as the representation of entities existing independently of and prior to all such representation. In Saussure, however, the primary distinction is neither that of representation and referent, nor that of signifier and signified. Rather, it is that of *difference* as the principle upon which the function of the signifier as well as that of the signified is "founded." What Saussure describes as the "two amorphous masses" of acoustical and ideational material, can only crystallize and precipitate out as signifier and signified by virtue of their differentiation: a sound can only operate as a signifier insofar as it is distinguishable from other sounds; a thought can only be signified insofar as it is distinguishable from other thoughts. Thought of in this way, signification is no longer conceived of as a process of representation, but as one of *articulation*. Instead of language being considered from the vantage-point of a hierarchically and temporally prior presence as its point of departure, it is construed as an *articulation*, determined and defined by a difference that produces identities only belatedly and retroactively: as concrete and individual signifiers and signifieds. Thus, for Saussure, the "concrete entities" of the language-system are not the perceptible, substantial unities of traditional grammar; rather, they are "values," whose structure is relational or syntactical, not grammatical:

In all these cases [i.e. in the analyses of grammatical and lexical categories] we are thus surprised that instead of pre-given *ideas* [the grammatical categories] we encounter *values* emanating from the system. When they are said to correspond to concepts, it is implicitly understood that the concepts are purely differential, defined not positively, by their content, but negatively, by their relations with other terms of the system. Their most precise characteristic resides in being what the others are not. (162/117)

This radicalization of differentiality as the structuring principle of linguistic signs defines Saussure's ambivalent position with respect to traditional metaphysical approaches to language. The ambivalence is perhaps most evident in the manner that Saussure conceives the relationship of the signifier to the signified. The relationship can be described as "arbitrary" or "unmotivated" only insofar as there is no necessary, "natural" or perceptible connection determining the link between signifier and signified *in any particular sign*. Yet Saussure also emphasizes that the sign as such forms a unity, and that *in general*, a signifier without a signified is unthinkable. Indeed, the function of the language-system, he states, is "to maintain the parallelism between the two orders of differences." (167/121) This amounts to asserting that the function of language consists precisely in stabilizing those differences. Such stability is required if linguistics is to constitute itself as a rigorous science, at least as science has traditionally been understood. This leads Saussure to modify and moderate the principle that "in the language system there are only differences" so that it becomes compatible with the stability required of language qua scientific object:

But the statement that everything in language is negative is true only if the signified and the signifier are considered separately: as soon as we consider the sign in its totality, we are confronted by something positive in the realm of language [*dans son ordre*]. A linguistic system is a series of differences of sounds combined with a series of differences of ideas; but the pairing [*mise en regard*] of a certain number of acoustical signs with as many segments [*découpures*] made in the mass of thought engenders a system of values; and it is this system that constitutes the effective link between the phonic and psychic elements within each sign. Although both the signified and signifier are purely differential and negative when considered separately, their combination is a positive fact; it is even the sole type of fact that obtains in language, since the property peculiar [*le propre*] to the linguistic institution is to maintain the parallelism between the two orders of differences. (166–167/20–121)

Language is, as it were, called to *order*, invested with positivity, its unruly differential principle subordinated to the category of binary opposition, which, as it were, contains and stabilizes the arbitrary but necessary connection between signifier and signified. Language is thereby rendered an appropriate object of linguistic science: well-defined and self-contained. Since the determining linguistic relationship is now the binary opposition, the significance of syntax is rejected: according to Saussure syntactic structures play no role in language apart from "the concrete material unities" constituted through the a priori principle of binary opposition.

It would be a mistake to believe that there is an incorporeal syntax outside of these material unities distributed in space [. . .] in reality, the material unities, arranged in a certain order, alone create [syntactic] value. Outside of a sum of concrete terms, a case of syntax would be incomprehensible. (191/139)

Language is now – and in terms of the metaphysical tradition, once again – considered as an established *institution, maintaining itself*, i.e. its "peculiar properties." These reside in the dual, parallel "order" of signifier and signified, combining in stable oppositions to form total, positive signs. Syntax thus is seen as nothing more than as a function of these parallel, synchronized, linear dimensions, segmented into series of individual signs. The linear arrangement of the linguistic sign is largely taken for granted, and is indeed justified in terms of an ideal of understanding and communication, which Saussure presupposes to be a simple but decisive *fact* of language:

Besides, the very fact that we understand a linguistic complex . . . shows that this sequence of terms is the adequate expression of the thought. (191/139)

Thus, insofar as language is held to be essentially a means of communication and of understanding, linguistic difference is ultimately brought under the sway of a theory of representation: the function of the sign is to serve as the adequate expression of a thought.

Nevertheless, this line of reasoning, informed by the necessities of determining language as a stable system of signs, contradicts the thrust of Saussure's insight that it is difference, not binary opposition, that keeps the process of signification moving. That the former is in no way reducible to the latter in the functioning of language is evident throughout Saussure's lectures, as for instance, in the description of linguistic value as determined solely "by what is outside and surrounding it." (161/116) The difference that constitutes value is identified not with a fully determinable relationship of opposition, but instead with an externality or a surrounding. The examples that Saussure provides in order to illustrate the operation of difference, for example, the difference between the letters of the alphabet required in order that handwriting be legible, or the morphological, etymological, acoustical relations between words, clearly indicate that signification depends upon a play of differences that are in no way reducible to binary oppositions.

Perhaps more important still is the fact that difference only *seems* to function symmetrically in the realm of signifieds and signifiers. However, since it is only through difference that these two realms are determined as such, the signifier leaves its imprint, "as signifier," upon the realm of the signified. In order for the "undifferentiated, amorphous mass of thought" (155/ 111) to be articulated in and as particular thoughts – that is, in order for it to become thought at all – its constituent elements must first set themselves apart from each other, demarcate and distinguish themselves; in short, they must relate to one another *as signifiers* in order to be determinable as signifieds. The Saussurian bar, stroke, or slash that is supposed to separate signifier from signified, cuts through the signified, dividing each and every signified from itself, and allowing its identity *qua* signified to appear only as an effect of this separation. Meaning thus emerges as a function of signification. Thus, when Saussure observes that "there are no pre-established ideas and [that] nothing is distinct before the apparition of language"[6] (155/112), he is not merely referring to the connection of two separately constituted, structurally symmetrical spheres, but rather to the indispensable operation of difference working through signifiers, without which identities could not be determined, whether as "signifieds" or as "signifiers."

Two fundamental and contradictory consequences may be drawn from the above: first, the "concrete," "positive" entity of language – the sign as a binary opposition of signifier and signified – appears as the effect of one of its parts: of the

---

[6] See Samuel Weber, "The apparition of language," MLN, vol. 91/no. 5 (1976).

signifier, insofar as it materializes and realizes the operation of difference. Secondly, it is precisely the materiality and realization of the signifier that constantly elude rigorous definition or determination. This is reflected in Saussure's contradictory attitude toward sound as the medium and material of language. On the one hand, Saussure is obliged by the principle of difference as articulation to consider every materialization of language – thus also sound – as a mere vehicle or support of difference. "Thus," Saussure remarks, in attempting to define language as the object of linguistics, "language cannot be reduced to sound" (24/8), and "the essence of language [. . .] is unrelated to the phonic character of the linguistic sign." (21/7) At the same time, however, Saussure writes a long chapter in which the sign-system of writing is subordinated to phonetic language, repeatedly asserting that the signifier is "of a phonetic nature," and that the "natural connection," between signifier and signified, "the only true one, is that of sound." (46/25) Why then this striking contradiction in Saussure?

Derrida has shown in *Of Grammatology*[7] how closely Saussure's privileging of phonetic language and his reduction and subordination of writing as phonetic writing continues the logo- and phono-centric tradition of Western metaphysics. But, what motivates this repetition and the contradictions implied by it? Whence does it derive its force? The response to these questions – which also play a determining role in Lacan's use of structural linguistics – is related first of all to Saussure's attempt to establish linguistics as a rigorous science; and secondly, to the wish that this attempt strives to fulfill.

As we have already seen, in order for language to be considered as an object of scientific study, it must be autonomous, homogenous, concrete, and self-contained. Nevertheless, it is precisely difference that in a curious way is not autonomous: neither a transcendental a priori nor a founding principle, it exists only in and through the play of articulation; still, it is never fully present in this play. It is impossible to reduce or determine, in terms of a binary opposition, since

[7] Jacques Derrida, *Of Grammatology*, trans. Gayatri Chakravorty Spivak, Baltimore: The Johns Hopkins University Press, 1967; see especially the chapter, "Linguistics and grammatology." The following discussion of Saussure is deeply indebted to Derrida's reading.

differential articulation is always both more and less than any given "concrete" pair of opposites. Or to put it another way: though language as difference and articulation produces representation as an effect, this effect is inscribed in a network of differences that only retroactively produces the possibility of presence – of meaning, of an object or of a subject. In Derrida's apt formulation, "the signified must always already have been in the position of the signifier,"[8] always already differing and deferred, always in relation to something else, in order to be itself. To be able to construe language as a closed system, however, Saussure has to disavow just this implication of difference; he must depict it as a means of representation and "concretize" it. Thus Saussure finds himself forced – in his chapter on "The concrete unity of language" – to repeat an Aristotelian gesture and declare *meaning* to be the criterion of language: "A sequence of sounds is linguistic only if it functions as the vehicle of an idea; taken by itself it is only the material of physiological study." (144/103) Here one can see how Saussure's argument restricts difference in language by treating the latter as a medium of expression: since a sound as such cannot be linguistic, it must be determined through meaning; yet meaning taken by itself is just as indeterminate as sound, it only becomes meaning – as signified – through the play of difference. This play, however, produces identities only retroactively and in a certain context that must of necessity resist closure. To serve as a means of communication or of understanding is undoubtedly *one* of the functions of language, but not necessarily its most essential one. In any event, the conception of language as communication entails certain presuppositions concerning the subject of language, or rather the *subject of linguistics*, and these demand attention.

Saussure's contradictory attitude toward the linguistic function of sound reappears in his description of the role of the speaking subject. On the one hand, he claims that the "language-system [*la langue*] is not an entity and [. . .] exists only in the speaking subject" (19/5 note); on the other hand, he also emphasizes that "the language-system is not a function of the speaking subject." (30/14) This contradiction is only

[8] Ibid., p. 73.

apparently resolved by Saussure's distinction between the individual and the social or collective subject, the former being said to belong to the realm of speech, the latter to *la langue*. Speech (*parole*) implies an historical, "diachronic" dimension, *langue* a static, "synchronic" one. Speech, moreover, as a function of the individual speaker, is essentially random and unpredictable, while the language-system is by nature accessible to conscious consideration:

Synchrony knows but one perspective, that of speaking subjects, and its entire method consists in collecting their testimony; in order to know to what extent something is real, it is necessary and sufficient to examine to what degree it exists for the subjects' consciousness. (128/90)

The closure of the synchronic dimension, its self-presence, and its priority over the diachronic dimension of language, are determined by its capacity to be present, that is, conscious for a "collective" subject. This priority of synchrony over diachrony depends primarily on the regulated closure of the language-system, as compared with its actualization and realization in speech:

The synchronic law is general, but it is not imperative. Doubtless it imposes itself on individuals through the constraint of collective usage, but this relates only to speaking subjects. What we mean [by its non-imperative character] is that, *within the language-system*, whatever the force may be that happens to prevail at any given moment, it can never guarantee the maintenance of this regularity. The synchronic law is therefore merely the expression of an existing order at a given moment. [. . .] Diachrony, on the contrary, supposes active forces through which an effect is produced, a thing executed. But this imperative character is not sufficient to warrant applying the term "law" . . . [since] diachronic events always have an accidental and singular character. (131/92–93)

The synchronic system of language does not completely determine the actual behavior of individual speakers, but it does regulate their behavior, subordinate it to a system of laws, and thereby render it comprehensible as a scientific object of study. Diachronic "events," on the other hand, while they can produce facts, can never generate a language, insofar as language must possess the quality of a system.

Saussure attempts to illustrate this difficult relationship between synchrony and diachrony by means of two comparisons. First he compares synchrony to

the projection of a body on a flat surface. Any projection depends directly on the nature of the body projected and yet differs from it – the projection being a thing apart. Otherwise there would be no science of projections; it would suffice to consider the bodies themselves. In linguistics the same relationship obtains between the historical facts and a language-state; the latter is like the projection of the facts at a particular moment. It is not in studying bodies, that is, diachronic events, that one learns about synchronic states, any more than one acquires an idea of geometric projections by a detailed study of different types of bodies. (124–125/87)

The diachronic dimension of language, that of speech, and the individuals that correspond to it, thus appear in this comparison to constitute the body of language, its living presence. This presence, however, cannot as such be formulated in laws or codified; it is essentially unconscious and can at best be described. Only by virtue of a projection of the body on a surface, does it become visible, consciously perceptible, and susceptible of regulation. Saussure here resorts to the same image as does Freud, when he compares the formation of the ego to a projection upon a screen; in both cases, an ostensibly self-contained, identifiable and systematic structure is produced by projection. For Freud, however, the body that is projected is itself already a surface: "The ego is first and foremost a bodily one, it is not merely a surface entity but is itself the projection *of a surface*" [my italics].[9] Thus, for Freud, the body is not defined by depth, in opposition to surface: it functions itself as surface. And if we recall Lacan's theory of the imaginary-fictive constitution of the ego, we can see how his description of this function in terms of *misapprehension* [*verkennen*] is directly derived from Freud's insight into the "superficial" character of the ego. For Saussure, by contrast, the bodily nature of language as speech is regarded from the very beginning as a living

---

[9] Sigmund Freud, *The Ego and the Id*, SE, xix p. 26. In a footnote, added in 1927, Freud explained his remark as follows: "The ego is ultimately derived from bodily sensations, chiefly from those springing from the surface of the body. It may thus be regarded as a mental projection of the surface of the body, besides, as we have seen above, representing the superficies of the mental apparatus."

substance and as self-identical, although according to Saussure's own comparison, it only comes to be and acquires its systematic identity as language-system through a mechanism of projection. As in the case of the signifier and the signified, Saussure is thus impelled to posit an identity prior to all articulation and difference: that of the speaking subject in *la parole*.

And yet, strangely and significantly enough, this subject, as we have seen, lacks what in modern thought, at least since Descartes, has been considered to be the constitutive attribute of all identity: self-consciousness. As it turns out, for Saussure, everything in the dimension of speech is unconscious not merely in the contingent, descriptive sense, but in the Freudian sense of being necessarily inaccessible to consciousness. This becomes clear through the second comparison used by Saussure to clarify the relationship between diachrony and synchrony in language:

> But of all comparisons that might be imagined, the most fruitful is the one that might be drawn between the play of language [*langue*] and chess. In both instances we are confronted with a system of values and with their modifications. A game of chess is like an artificial realization of what language offers us in a natural form. (125/88)

Saussure goes on to elaborate the similarities between language and chess games: the value of particular elements depends upon their given position within the system; the system is only momentary and changes from one moment to the next; the values, however, depend upon an immutable agreement, through which the rules of the game are set; these exist before the game starts and continue to exist after each move. And whereas changing the position of the elements (making a move) changes the state of the system in accordance with the rules of the game, it does so in a way that is never entirely predictable. Finally, the manner in which this change comes about has absolutely no bearing on the course of the game or on the significance of a given state of the system. Saussure nevertheless adds that his comparison is unsatisfactory concerning one essential point:

> While the chess player has the *intention* of operating a shift and affecting the system, the language-system premeditates nothing. The

pieces of language are displaced, or rather modified, spontaneously and fortuitously . . . In order for chess to resemble the play of language in all points we would have to imagine an unconscious or unintelligent player. (127/89)

In order, then, to do justice to the game of language, it does not suffice to trace its system back to a collective consciousness; at most this consciousness can belatedly conceive the system in its static condition, and in so doing, it coincides with the consciousness of the linguist. Yet in contrast to the chess game, Saussure argues, the rules by which language is transformed remain scientifically inconceivable.[10]

In thus acknowledging that his comparison is deficient on an essential point, which has to do with the decisive relationship of the game to the rules of transformation, Saussure comes very close to reopening the entire issue his example is intended to close: the relation of synchrony and diachrony. For the comparison with chess, if pursued, turns out to be incompatible with the opposition between the two perspectives Saussure is at pains to establish. What Saussure does not mention – although he, like Freud's patients, "knew it all the time" – is that there are two kinds of rules in chess. There are those that regulate the formal conditions of the game: the squares on the board, the ways in which the different pieces move, etc. But there are also those which are less fixed, that regulate the different ways games have been played. These are rules of *strategy*, and although they never allow the game to become entirely predictable, they are also far from being merely "individual," "contingent" and "empirical." They structure the transforma-tions, and hence, the *game* of chess. And if they can do this; indeed, if chess is a game at all, it is because the "synchronic structure" that Saussure saw exemplified in the state of the chessboard, at any given moment, is never present as such in any chess game. Rather, the synchronic state of the board is, in principle, and not just in practice, split, divided from itself, by the *move*. It is this that distinguishes the "position" of the board from that of the synchronic state of language: the position of

---

[10] This is one of the reasons why it is perhaps even more apt to speak of the *apparition* of language in English than in French. See the article of that name mentioned above.

the board is, as it were, structurally dislocated, disarticulated, through the fact that the game requires that there be *two* players, and that their relation to each other is intrinsically dissymmetrical, since *one* of them has the *next move*. In this sense, the example of chess suggests that the temporal, diachronic dimension of discontinuous successivity is inscribed in each "present state" of the system; and that the subject of this system, far from being unitary – be it as individual or collective consciousness – is split, agonistically. Through his example, then, Saussure anticipates the notion of language-game, developed years later by Wittgenstein; but he anticipates it with a Freudian flair, for the essence of that game is an unresolvable, constitutive *conflict*. And its rules, therefore, can only be *strategic*. The rules of this strategy and their unconscious calculation will constitute one of the major concerns of Lacan's return to Freud. We begin to see how and why that return should pass by way of Saussure, although it will be a Saussure read in the same manner that Freud reads the unconscious: in terms of what is not said, but what implicitly has been "known all the time." In terms, that is, of a knowledge that eludes consciousness through a certain *inscription*.

4

❖❖❖❖❖❖❖❖❖❖❖❖❖❖❖❖❖❖❖❖❖❖❖❖❖❖❖❖❖❖❖❖❖❖❖❖❖❖❖

The rise and fall of the signifier

❖❖❖❖❖❖❖❖❖❖❖❖❖❖❖❖❖❖❖❖❖❖❖❖❖❖❖❖❖❖❖❖❖❖❖❖❖❖❖

To properly understand the significance of structural linguistics for Lacan, one cannot overlook its internal contradictions. Saussure's writings are of interest to him, less as the site where a certain strain of modern linguistics sought to pose its foundations, than as the theater in which the structure of language and its relation to the subject are staged as questions. As we have seen with the example of the chess game, this staging is only indirect and implicit, rather than thematic and declared. This is due not to individual inadequacy, but to the incapacity of a discipline such as linguistics to address the problem of the subject as such. Though Saussure's determination of the language-system in terms of differential articulation subverts the traditional concepts of object (as referent) and of subject (as self-consciousness), this disturbance is minimized or effaced so as not to disturb the project of establishing linguistics as a rigorous science. As we have seen, the principle of linguistic difference is partially, at least, revoked when Saussure situates the reality of language not in "value," but in the "totality of the sign," itself a result of binary opposition. It is precisely this ambivalence in the thought of Saussure that serves as Lacan's point of departure. "The instance of the letter in the unconscious or reason since Freud" was written in 1955, three years after the Rome discourse in which "The function of speech and language in psychoanalysis" is set forth with the help of Saussurean concepts for the first time. This address, which has the character of a manifesto, resembles in this respect the lecture delivered in Vienna in 1955, on "The Freudian thing" (*La Chose freudienne ou sens du retour à Freud en psychanalyse*), which also displays a certain programmatic character, in demarcating, often polemically, the Lacanian position from the prevalent psychoanalytic tendencies of the period, including, above all, the powerful New York School of Ego Psychology (Hartmann, Kris, Loewenstein), but also with respect to those efforts to assimilate Freudian thought to neurophysiology. It is a demarcation that insists upon the importance of Saussurean linguistic theory for psychoanalysis, without, however, giving a detailed account of just what in Saussure is of decisive significance. Only with the lecture on "The Instance of the Letter," does Lacan begin to put his cards on the table, while at the same time making clear that his brand of "teaching" – "*enseignement*" is a favorite term of self-description – in no way implies putting all one's cards on the table. We will have occasion to examine the structure and certain of the consequences of the argumentation deriving from this strategy. But it is advisable to begin with the essay that is surely most explicit about the linguistic moment in Lacan's thought, and in particular its relation to Saussure, "The instance of the letter," which, as Lacan remarks, is situated halfway between the written and the spoken word. Only after having worked out some of the more general aspects of this relationship, will we return to some of the issues raised in the earlier, more programmatic lectures of Rome and Vienna.

As is well-known, Lacan takes as his point of departure the Saussurean concept of the signifier. The hidden problematic of this concept, as we have attempted to elaborate it, is silently but unmistakably foregrounded by Lacan, in one bold graphic stroke, as it were, through which the Saussurean diagram of the sign is stood squarely on its head. The S of the Signifier is no longer on the bottom, but on the top. The reverse, which is how Saussure represented the sign, is itself a symptom of the ambivalence of his semiotics, torn, as it were, between the notion of radical difference as the principle mechanism in allowing signs to signify, and the fear that this would render a systematic classification of signs ultimately impossible. The consequent reduction of the differential notion of "value" to "the totality of the sign," now determined to be the basic "reality" of language, could only result in the privileging of the signified over the signifier, of meaning over articulation in Saussure's approach to linguistic processes. Considered from the perspective of the totality of the sign, it is hardly fortuitous that Saussure places the signified *above* the signifier in his diagrammatic representation of the sign. And it is no less significant that this representation would ultimately take the form of an image, in which linguistic noun and extralinguistic referent would be properly matched to one another. Saussure's own graphic representation thus winds up contradicting his attempt to conceive of language in a way that would not render it structurally dependent upon extralinguistic reference. And yet, as already indicated, the project of construing language as an object capable of scientific study leaves Saussure little choice. If language is to be conceived as a closed system, it is not difference, but rather opposition, not the signifier but only the signified that is capable of closing it and of containing the centrifugal and exorbitant tendencies of "value," "difference" and of the "signifier." Thus, although Saussure distinguishes between meaning (signification) that re-presents an idea, and value, which is an intralinguistic relation, it is meaning that has the last word. How could it be otherwise insofar as language is conceived from the point of view of the *word*, since what is commonly used to define the word is precisely the meaning it is held to signify.[1]

In contrast, and without wasting words, Lacan inverts the Saussurean sign. The relationship of signifier to signified is, however, not merely inverted; it is also twisted, dislocated, turned around. The Saussurean symmetry, ultimately based on the priority of the signified, is displaced: the line used by Saussure to separate the two dimensions of the sign from each other, did so only in order then to unite them all the more definitively. This line is now turned into a "bar" – an obstacle or barrier – which, while making meaning (*signification*) possible, at the same time resists it.[2] What is brought into relief here is not merely the separation between signifier and signified, but instead what is implicitly at work in Saussure but

[1] Saussure's description of the linguistic function of the *word*, however, betrays once again a certain ambivalence. He begins – in the published notes of his lectures, at least – by declaring the word to be far too abstract and indeterminate, to be considered the "concrete entity" of language, that a scientifically rigorous linguistics requires as its foundation. Elsewhere, in determining the sign as an oppositional but total structure, he refers to the word as though it were precisely the fundamental linguistic phenomenon. On some of the implications of this oscillation, cf. "The apparition of language."

[2] Signifier and signified, Lacan observes, designate "distinct orders initially separated by a barrier resistant to signification." "The instance of the letter in the unconscious," Sheridan, p. 149; *Ecrits*, p. 497.

also explicitly disavowed: a certain structural primacy of the signifier over the signified, the latter considered as dependent upon the former. This primacy of the signifier implies in turn that language is no longer understood as re-presentation, but instead as differential articulation. If Lacan thus writes that "there is no signification that sustains itself other than by referring to another signification," he concludes from this that "the function of the signifier does not have to answer for its existence to any signification whatsoever."[3] On the contrary, it is by referring to other signifieds, that is by means of the signifier, that the signified first becomes self-identical, that is, a signified. Its identity thus must be conceived as an effect of the signifier, insofar as the signifier embodies the process of signification in terms of the play of differential relations. The signifier, conceived as a movement of difference, thereby becomes co-extensive with language itself, insofar as the latter is no longer understood as a function of representation, but instead as articulation. "The structure of the signifier is, as is commonly said of language in general, that it is articulated."[4] What is criticized here is not only the metaphysical view of language as re-presentation, but also the ontological premises upon which this conception of language is based, above all, the priority of the referent, held to be self-identical above and beyond the differential relations of language.

With the status of the referent, that of the *object* is also radically problematized. Lacan indicates this by describing how "the signifier actually enters into the signified; that is, in a form that, not being immaterial, poses the question of its place in reality."[5] To illustrate the process, Lacan adduces an example

---

[3] "Dans cette voie les choses ne peuvent aller plus loin que de démontrer qu'il n'est aucune signification qui se soutienne sinon du renvoi à une autre signification [. . .]" However, Lacan continues, we shall never be in a position to take on the question of language, which *it* imposes upon *us*, "as long as we have not rid ourselves of the illusion that the signifier answers to the function of representing the signified, or, better put: that the signifier has to answer for its existence to any signification whatsoever." Sheridan, p. 150; *Ecrits*, p. 498.

[4] "Or la structure du signifiant est, comme on le dit communément du langage, qu'il soit articulé." Sheridan, p. 152; *Ecrits*, p. 501.

[5] "Ceci [est] pour montrer comment le signifiant entre en fait dans le signifié; à savoir sous une forme qui, pour n'être pas immatérielle, pose la question de sa place dans la réalité." Sheridan, p. 151; *Ecrits*, p. 500.

that takes the place of the tree (*arbre*) used by Saussure to represent the sign, and which at once places the latter in a distinctly different light. Lacan supplements Saussure's diagram:

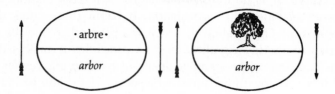

with his own:

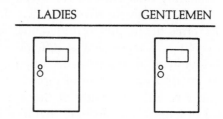

The tree is replaced by two words: *Hommes* and *Dames*, Gentlemen and Ladies. The doubling of the signifier by Lacan – or is it the splitting of the signifier? – into Gentlemen and Ladies seems to do greater justice to the Saussurean difference than the single word "tree," with all of its organic and holistic associations. Yet, it is the signifieds chosen by Lacan which make the difference striking: the two words are inscribed at the top of the figure, as a kind of title, underscored by a line beneath them; below, separate from the legend, as it were, two doors, with rectangles where the words should go. The two doors point to the verbal signifiers above, which however are separated from them. In addition, then, to choosing an example designed to remind one of "the urinary segregation typical both of western culture and of 'primitive' societies,"[6] the separation of signified (the words)

---

[6] On voit que, sans beaucoup étendre la portée du signifiant intéressé dans l'expérience, soit en redoublant seulement l'espèce nominale par la seule juxtaposition de deux termes dont le sens complémentaire paraît devoir s'en consolider, la surprise se produit d'une précipitation du sens inattendue; dans l'image de deux portes jumelles qui symbolisent avec l'isoloir offert à l'homme occidental pour satisfaire à ses besoins naturels hors de sa maison, l'impératif qu'il semble partager avec la grande majorité des communautés primitives et

and signifier (the doors) illustrates the dependency of meaning upon relations of signification, which cannot simply be taken for granted. Without the signifier, no signified, and furthermore no identifiable, definable referent. Yet how do things stand with the subject, with the gentlemen and ladies, who take the lead of the signifier in satisfying their "needs"? To answer this question Lacan tells a short, "true" story:

A train arrives at a station. A little boy and a little girl, brother and sister, are seated in a compartment face to face next to the window through which the buildings along the station platform can be seen passing as the train pulls to a stop. "Look," says the brother, "we're at Ladies!"; "Idiot!" replies his sister, "Can't you see that we're at Gentlemen."[7]

Are we confronted here with a simple example of perspectivism or relativism? Hardly, since the first thing that has to be taken into account is that "the rails" (*les rails*: and the story is also a *raillerie*; a raillery or jest) materialize the bar of the Saussurean algorithm, but "in a form designed to suggest that its resistance might be other than dialectical."[8] The subject here is literally *borne* by the bar separating the signifier from the signified: its place is on the rails, and yet on rails that simultaneously derail. The quarrel between the little girl, who claims to have arrived in "Gentlemen," and the little boy, for whom the place can only be called "Ladies," is impossible to arbitrate, at least as long as the question at issue – the relationship of the sexes – remains couched in the binary structure of an alternative: *either* "gentlemen," *or* "ladies," each ostensibly in its proper *place*. It is therefore no accident that the place described in Lacan's illustrative figure is a toilet, a place that is never entirely "proper," and to which access is generally more or less regulated. In Lacan's figure, the doors seem to be closed. We can, therefore, never be entirely certain about what stands behind it all, and for Lacan, this is probably the most important aspect of the story:

We should add that only someone who has a cockeyed view of things [literally: "who doesn't have holes in front of his eyes" – *n'avoir pas les*

qui soumet sa vie publique aux lois de la ségrégation urinaire." Sheridan, p. 151; *Ecrits*, p. 500.
[7] Sheridan, p. 152.
[8] Sheridan, p. 152.

yeux en face des trous], (it's the appropriate image here) could possibly confuse the place of the signifier and that of the signified in this story, or not see from what radiating (*rayonnant*) centre the signifier sends forth its light into the shadow of incomplete significations.[9]

The traditional pathos of a metaphorics of light and darkness? What radiates behind the bar of the signifier is the light of a *hole*. Not the light that shines through holes, but that *of* the hole as such. For with what Lacan calls the "precipitation of the signifier," with which it leaves its mark upon the signified, the light of the object goes out, or at best becomes a half-light, a chiaroscuro of difference. We can see "objects" only because we can see holes: that is, the *interstices*, through which they relate to one another and delineate themselves. And such interstices are not just *intervals*, not just spaces *between* objects and words, but also cracks and fractures *within* them. The railing of the rails opens to allow the *raillery* of ridiculous word-plays to interrupt semantic seriousness. Insofar as the object is consti-tuted in and through the play of signifiers, it falls through the rails of its railing rays, as is the case of the word, "thing":

The thing [*la chose*], when taken literally, breaks up into the double, divergent ray of the "cause" (*causa*), where it has found shelter in French, and the nothing [*rien*] to which it has abandoned its Latin garb (*rem*).[10]

This etymological word play – chose/cause, rien/rem – reflects the ambivalence of an object as soon as it is viewed in its dependence upon the signifier: while the object may function as a *cause*, insofar as every signifier as such refers – and by virtue of its form must refer – to a signified, the belated priority of the signifier as difference and articulation marks the signified and inscribes it in a structure of radical heterogeneity that cannot be fully contained or comprehended in terms of identity. Thus,

[9] "Il faudrait, c'est bien l'image qui convient, n'avoir pas les yeux en face des trous pour s'y embrouiller sur la place respective du signifiant et du signifié, et ne pas suivre de quel centre rayonnant le premier vient à refléter sa lumière dans la ténèbre des significations inachevées." Sheridan, p. 152; *Ecrits*, p. 500.
[10] "et que la *chose*, à se réduire bien évidemment au nom, se brise en le double rayon divergent de la cause où elle a pris abri en notre langue et du rien à qui elle a fait abandon de sa robe latine (rem)." Sheridan, p. 150; *Ecrits*, p. 498.

relative to the achieved identity of an object, this heterogeneity of signification can be determined as a hole or blank, a *trou*, since what allows one to see – differential relations – is not itself visible and in terms of visibility can therefore be compared to a "hole." Seeing is only possible "through" difference, or demarcation. It is, however, quite a different question whether one is ready to see this hole – or, to stay with the terms of Lacan's story – whether one feels obliged to open the restroom door. Here we touch on a problem which Freud called that of the "lost object," a problem to which we shall return later, in connection with Lacan's theories of the phallus and of desire. Nevertheless, it is already apparent that this problem cannot be separated from the differential operation of language, or from the influence of the signifier on the signified and through it, upon reality as well.

Lacan's use of structural linguistics is thus no simple application of an otherwise unproblematized model, although this is the impression often left by the polemical pathos that accompanies his recourse to Saussure and which is directed against the state of the psychoanalytic theory that dominated the International Association at the time. Lacan's inversion of the Saussurean formula, the emphasis thereby placed on the signifier, develops the internal contradictions of structural linguistics beyond the limits of linguistics as such. Nevertheless, Lacan's adaptation of the Saussurean theory of the signifier by no means entirely frees itself from the aporia of that theory. And since the latter are destined to play a determining role in Lacanian thought, they merit careful examination.

The problem can be localized as, precisely, one of *localization*. Lacan localizes the signifier in what he calls the *letter*. His point of departure is the *articulated* structure of the signifier: "The structure of the signifier . . . is that it is articulated." In theorizing this articulation, Lacan at first follows the determination of the signifier as *phoneme*, elaborated by the Prague School – identified above all, with the names of Trubeckoj and Jakobson. According to this approach, linguistic articulation entails a double mechanism: signifying units "are subjected to a dual condition: that of being reducible to basic, differential elements, and that of combining in accordance with the laws of a closed system." "These elements," Lacan continues, which constitute one of the decisive discoveries of linguistics, are *phonemes*; we must not expect, however, to find any *phonetic* constancy in the modulatory variability to which this term applies, but rather a synchronic system of differential couplings necessary for the discernment of words in a given language.[11]

At first, then, Lacan follows Trubeckoj and Jakobson in determining the signifier as essentially phonemic, and hence, as binary opposition; he thereby also assumes their view, which was shared by Saussure, that language consists of a closed, synchronic system, in turn composed of a limited number of binary oppositions. The heterological heritage of Saussure is thus assumed, as well as its ambivalent revocation. Jakobson's description of the essence of the phoneme as "mere otherness,"[12] is thus cited, while at the same time this "otherness" is identified with relations of binary opposition. Since the notion of binary opposition presupposes a principle of identification for which it, as relation, cannot account, it inevitably if inconsistently recurs to the privilege of the semiotic medium of sound.

In thus assuming the heritage of the Prague School, Lacan comes close to what Derrida has called "phonologism."[13] This phonologism, which, as we have seen, is already at work in Saussure, regards spoken discourse as the exemplary model of language in general. In so doing, it ignores the implications of its own insights into the differential structure of the linguistic sign, which is as little to be identified with a particular medium, as with determinate referents. The most consistent linguistic critique of this "phonological deviation," is to be found in the work of the Danish linguist, Louis Hjelmslev, founder of the so-called school of "glossematics." To the Saussurean distinc-

---

[11] "Ces éléments, découverte décisive de la linguistique, sont les *phonèmes* où il ne faut chercher aucune constance *phonétique* dans la variabilité modulatoire où s'applique ce terme, mais le système synchronique des couplages différentiels, nécessaires au discernement des vocables dans une langue donnée." Sheridan, p. 153; *Ecrits*, p. 501.

[12] Roman Jakobson & Morris Halle, *Fundamentals of Language*, The Hague, 1956, p. 16.

[13] J. Derrida, *On Grammatology*. In "The purveyor of truth," (*Le facteur de la vérité*), Derrida has analyzed what he calls the "phallogocentrism" of Lacan, with particular reference to the latter's reading of Poe's "Purloined letter." English translation by Alan Bass. In *The Post Card*, Chicago: University of Chicago Press, 1987.

tion between signifier and signified, Hjelmslev adds that of "form" and "substance." According to this view the tonal or acoustic aspect of sound would belong to the substance of language, while its differentiality would belong to its form. Thus instead of equating the "signifier" with sound or even with the word – an error that goes back to Saussure, despite the latter's radical critique of the linguistic pertinence of the concept of "word" – Hjelmslev's distinction serves to emphasize that signification is a function of differential relations as such, and not of a particular, privileged material. In this respect, Hjelmslev is faithful to the most original aspect of Saussurean linguistics, whose decisive insight is that of the differential structure of language and not, as phonologism – and at this stage, Lacan as well – holds, that of binary oppositions, above all in the medium of sound. Indeed, the predominance given by Lacan to the opposition of the "full" and "empty" word: "*parole pleine*" and "*vide*," would seem to place him unequivocally in the tradition of Western Phonocentrism.

On the other hand, insofar as Phonocentrism serves to subordinate language as re-presentation or as expression to an extra-linguistic referent, whether this is construed as things themselves or as the subject of self-consciousness – it is clear that Lacan's endorsement of this tradition, and in particular of its privileging of the *parole*, cannot remain unequivocal. And indeed, after having given the (already cited) classical determination of the signifier as phoneme, Lacan goes on to undermine this determination in his own distinctive fashion:

Through this, one sees that an essential element of the spoken word itself was predestined to flow into the mobile characters which, whether Didots or Garamonds, crowding together in lower-case render validly present what we call the letter, namely, the essentially localized structure of the signifier.[14]

"Through this one sees" – *par quoi l'on voit* – this recurrent figure of speech typifies Lacan's discourse, which – like that of the

---

[14] "Par quoi l'on voit qu'un élément essentiel dans la parole elle-même était prédestiné à se couler dans les caractères mobiles qui, Didots ou Garamonds se pressant dans les bas-de-casse, présentifient valablement ce que nous appelons la lettre, à savoir la structure essentiellement localisée du signifiant." Sheridan, p. 153; *Ecrits*, p. 501.

unconscious – often seems to "know no contradictions," or rather, to allow itself to be bound by the "law" of non-contradiction. In this particular case, it is difficult to see just what, in the determination of the signifier as phoneme, would predestine it to flow into typography, much less into its "lower cases." We need only recall the writings of Jakobson, to recognize just how much this figure of the phoneme disfigures the tenets of linguistic phonologism. For Jakobson, as for Saussure, writing is unequivocally subordinated to speech:

Only after having mastered speech does one graduate to reading and writing. There is a cardinal difference between phonemes and graphic units. Each letter carries a specific denotation – in a phonemic orthography, it usually denotes one of the phonemes or a certain limited series of phonemes, whereas phonemes denote nothing but mere otherness. Graphic signs that serve to interpret phonemes or other linguistic units stand for these units, as the logician would say. This difference has far-reaching consequences for the cardinally dissimilar patterning of letters and phonemes. Letters never or only partially reproduce the different distinctive features on which the phonemic pattern is based and unfailingly disregard the structural relationship of these features. There is no such thing in human society as the supplantation of the speech code by its visual replicas, but only a supplementation of this code by parasitic auxiliaries, while the speech code constantly and unalterably remains in effect.[15]

This gesture – the reduction of writing to its phonetic form in order then to assign it a subordinate position as a "parasitic auxiliary" – is not merely an almost verbatim replay of Saussure's attack on the "usurpation" of writing in linguistics; it also repeats a movement as old as metaphysics itself. It is significant, therefore, that such a movement is nowhere to be found in the writings of Lacan – even in their most "structuralist" phase. On the contrary, already in 1956, when this text was written – and thus seven years before the appearance of Derrida's first writings explicitly problematizing the power of phonocentrism – a very clear anticipation of this problematic is evident in Lacan. In drawing attention to Freud's characterization of the dream as a rebus and as a system of inscription, Lacan emphasizes that the dream's plasticity [*Bildhaftigkeit*] –

<hr />

[15] Jakobson/Halle, *Fundamentals of Language*, pp. 16–17.

called by Freud "considerations of representability" – must be understood as part of a hieroglyphics [*Bilderschrift*] (faithfully rendering Freud) and adds:

> This fact could perhaps shed light on the problems involved in certain modes of pictography which, simply because they have been abandoned in writing as imperfect, are not therefore to be regarded as mere evolutionary stages.[16]

Lacan thus clearly distances himself from the teleological tendencies of phonocentrism, in which the latter reveals its complicity with Western ethnocentrism. And this is most clearly the case when dealing with the relationship between letter and spirit:

> Of course, as it is said, the letter killeth while the spirit giveth life. We can't help but agree . . . , but we should also like to know how the spirit could live without the letter. Even so, the pretensions of the spirit would remain unassailable if the letter had not shown us that it produces all the effects of truth in man without involving the spirit at all. It is none other than Freud who had this revelation, and he called his discovery the unconscious.[17]

---

[16] According to Lacan, "considerations of representability," constitute "a limitation operating within the system of writing, rather than dissolving it into a figurative semiology which would approach the phenomena of natural expression ("une limitation qui s'exerce à l'intérieur du système de l'écriture, loin qu'elle le dissolve en une sémiologie figurative où il rejoindrait les phénomènes de l'expression naturelle. On pourrait probablement éclairer par là les problèmes de certains modes de pictographie, qu'on n'est pas autorisé, du seul fait qu'ils aient été abandonnés comme imparfaits dans l'écriture, à considérer comme des stades évolutifs.") Sheridan, p. 161; *Ecrits*, p. 511. Lacan's prudence illustrates at its best what could be called the "structuralist vigilance" – which is in fact a Nietzschean vigilance – with respect to teleological conceptions of history that legitimate prevailing values as the "intrinsic ends" of all "development." Derrida's deconstruction of "phonocentrism" proceeds from a similar suspicion of the normative hypostasis of phonetic writing at the expense of non-phonetic forms of inscription. The term "post-structuralist" can serve, even today, to designate the continuing vigilance with regard to teleological thinking, at least in its more naive forms. The emphasis placed by Lacan on *parole* and on the *letter* should not be isolated from his no less insistent foregrounding of the scriptural – and above all, non-phonetic – nature of unconscious articulation.

[17] "Certes la lettre tue, dit-on, quand l'esprit vivifie. Nous n'en disconvenons pas [. . .] mais nous demandons aussi comment sans la lettre l'esprit vivrait. Les prétentions de l'esprit pourtant demeureraient irréductibles, si la lettre n'avait fait la preuve qu'elle produit tous ses effets de vérité dans l'homme, sans que l'esprit ait le moins du monde à s'en mêler. Cette révélation, c'est à Freud qu'elle s'est faite, et sa découverte, il l'a appelée l'inconscient." Sheridan, p. 158; *Ecrits*, p. 509.

Lacan's views that differential articulation – the signifier – is not a transcendental principle and that the signifier must be localized – namely in the letter – do not co-exist easily with a tendency to conceive of language as a closed system actualized in speech. If it is no accident that in the train example already discussed, the signifiers are clearly inscribed in reality – the signs on the restroom doors – it is no less fortuitous that Lacan makes no explicit mention of this; for on the one hand, he is concerned with the principle by which the signifier is radically separated from its materialization: the letter is determined from the very beginning as an *effet signifiant* – as a signifying effect or as an effect of the signifier – a distinction to which Lacan subsequently returned in a discussion of the work of Serge Leclaire:

That which I have written about the formations of the unconscious, with the aid of letters that themselves are effects of the signifier, does not warrant making the letter into a signifier, and even less, according the letter priority over the signifier.[18]

The letter is thus an "effect" of the signifier, its "material vehicle" and its necessary localization. Yet, on the other hand, the medium of this vehicle is concrete discourse: "By letter I designate that material support that concrete discourse borrows from language."[19]

How *concrete*, however, is this discourse? What is its relationship to the different forms and functions of language: in Saussurean terms, to language in general, including its non-verbal forms? to the language-system? to spoken discourse? to writing? These questions draw us further into Lacan's text.

First, however, a word may be in order on the notion of "discourse," so prevalent in Lacan's writing as in much of structural linguistics, and yet as elusive and hard to pin down as its etymology would suggest: from *dis-currere*, the word "runs here and there," like a broken-field runner. And indeed, perhaps that is precisely its place: a broken field. In Saussure,

---

[18] J. Lacan, "Lituraterre," in: *Littérature* 3, Paris, 1971, p. 5.
[19] "Nous désignons par lettre ce support matériel que le discours concret emprunte au langage." Sheridan, p. 147; *Ecrits*, p. 495.

the notion is never used systematically, but seems to be presupposed, when Saussure distinguishes the two ways that elements combine to form a linguistic structure: the "syntagmatic" and the "paradigmatic." It is in the former that something like "discourse" has its place:

On the one hand, in discourse words enter into relations with each other through concatenation, based on the linear nature of language, which excludes the possibility of pronouncing two elements at the same time. The elements are arranged one after the other in the chain of speech. These combinations, which have [spatial] extension as their support, may be called *syntagms*. The syntagm is thus always composed of two or more consecutive units (. . .) In the syntagm a term acquires its value only because it stands in opposition to what precedes or follows it, or to both.[20]

In thus construing discourse as syntagmatic, Saussure, without raising any further questions, simply transposes the linearity of speech to the language system itself. Thus, although discourse may be called upon to mediate between language as system (*langue*) and language as speech (*parole*), it itself is structured by speaking. And if the syntagm as such is attributed by Saussure to the language system, not to speaking, this is because the syntagm, according to Saussure, is not a product of the free-will of the speaker. To use a post-Saussurean term, the syntagm is *coded*. The fact remains, however, that the linear structure of the syntagm, in its one-dimensionality, as an irreversible sequence, is conceived on the model of speech.

By contrast, the second, "associative" aspect or axis of linguistic relations cannot be conceived as a mode of discourse:

On the other hand, outside discourse, words having something in common are associated [s'associent] in memory and groups are thus formed among which very diverse relations prevail [. . .] They are not structured linearly; their seat is in the brain; they are part of that inner treasure that constitutes the language of each individual. We will call them *associative relations*.[21]

While associative relations may constitute the "treasure of the language system," and may bear the imprint of the language-

---

[20] Cours, p. 170–171/123.
[21] Ibid., p. 171/123.

system, they still seem to lack one of the essential properties of that system: the closure consisting of a limited number of binary oppositions. In contrast to the determinate and limited sequential order of the syntagm, "terms in an associative family occur neither in fixed numbers nor in a definite order. [. . .] A particular term is like the center of a constellation; it is the point of convergence of an indefinite number of co-ordinated terms."[22] Associative relations thus are located outside of discourse, are virtual, in contrast to the actuality of the syntagm, and yet are as much a part of *la langue* as the syntagm.

This division of the linguistic function was taken up and developed by Roman Jakobson in his essay on the "Two types of language and two types of aphasic disturbances."[23] Using Saussure's distinction as a point of departure, Jakobson distinguishes between two "modes of arrangement" at work in every speech act: (1) combination or contexture, Saussure's syntagms, and (2) selection or substitution, involving the equivalence or similarity of linguistic elements. Based on his investigation of different disturbances displayed in aphasia, Jakobson tries to show how disorders involving the linguistic function can be grouped along two axes: either as the inability to recognize similarity or equivalence and consequently the inability to select or substitute; or disturbances involving relations of contiguity limiting one's ability to combine and contextualize. Though these two different operations are carried out by the individual speaker, listener or reader, their roots should be sought, according to Jakobson, in the structure of the linguistic sign itself, the operation of which is no longer conceived of as being linear, but instead as being multidimensional. Saussure's "associative" relation is thereby de-psychologized and his linear conception of the sign broadened.

Perhaps even more important, however, is that concrete discourse no longer is construed in a one-dimensional manner. Instead, it has to be considered in terms of the multidimensionality of the linguistic sign. Jakobson designates these two functions or operations as the *metaphoric* (based on similarity) and the *metonymic* (based on contiguity) poles of

---

[22] Ibid., p. 174/126.
[23] Reprinted as Part II of *The Fundamentals of Language*.

language. In the realm of literature, Jakobson interprets Romantic and Symbolist poetry in terms of a predominance of the metaphoric function, based on similarity or equivalence, while explaining literary Realism as the use of metonymy, that is, of contiguity and contextuality. In addition, he interprets Freud's displacement and condensation as procedures employing what he considers to be a form of metonymy: synecdoche, while claiming that identification and symbolism are based on metaphoric similarity.

From this brief review, it should be clear that Jakobson's elaboration of Saussurean theory provides Lacan with a decisive *precedent* in relating linguistic operations to Freud's description of unconscious mechanisms in the *Interpretation of Dreams*. Jakobson's precedent, however, by no means serves as a *model*. Lacan does not merely apply it unchanged: it is subjected to extensive interpretation and transformation, and indeed, the latter are not without implications for the theories of Jakobson himself. The distinction between metaphor and metonymy, as Jakobson develops it, tends to relapse into a pre-Saussurean conception of language, insofar as linguistic functions are construed in terms of notions – similarity and contiguity – that are determined semantically, rather than syntactically (that is, in terms of differential relations). It is therefore not without significance that Jakobson introduces his discussion of metaphor and metonymy by distinguishing between the "general meaning" of a sign, governed by the function of substitution, and its "contextual meaning" based on combination. This distinction, however, presupposes that a general meaning can be generated *independently* of context, and that it is only the latter which is differentially constituted through the differential relations of signifiers. In short, the Jakobsonian distinction between metaphor and metonymy subordinates the notion of linguistic difference – once again – to a logic of binary opposition based upon the priority of identity over difference.

It is evident, therefore, that Jakobson can offer a precedent, but in no way a model for the Lacanian approach to language, which, in however complex a manner, is based upon the primacy of the signifier, and hence, of differential, syntactical relations over semantic functions. Lacan's use of Jakobson, as of Saussure, is commanded by the strategical imperative of

distinguishing the authority of a *precedent* from that of a *model*.[24]
Thus, although at first Lacan appears to accept Jakobson's
version of Saussure's linear view of the sign, there is an implicit
critique of the linearization of context in his notion of the
"signifying chain":

> There is, in effect, no signifying chain that does not have, as if attached
> to the punctuation of each of its units, a whole articulation of relevant
> contexts suspended "vertically," as it were, from that point.[25]

The fact that the "vertical" dimension of language is, in this
account, "suspended" to "the punctuation of each of its units,"
indicates that the "paradigmatic" or "metaphorical" axis is
construed in terms of syntax, rather than of semantics. The
"associative" aspect of language can no longer be considered in
terms of the multiplication of meaning; rather, the category of
meaning itself is inscribed in the movement of contextual
relations out of which the signifier emerges. The sturdy
Saussurean image of the tree decomposes into the different
meanings of the signifier "tree" (*arbre*), which may also be read
as an anagram of the Saussurean *barre*; such decomposition
problematizes the unity of the word as the basic building block
of language. The linguistic significance of a word can just as
easily be a function of its graphic, phonic or typographic features as of its different meanings. Thus, it is not only in the
verse of Valéry, which Lacan inscribes in his text, that the "tree
says No!":

> *Non! dit l'Arbre, il dit: Non! dans l'étincellement*
> *De sa tête superbe*
> *Que la tempête traite universellement*
> *Comme elle fait une herbe.*[26]

---

[24] In their astute reading of "The instance of the letter," Philippe Lacoue-
Labarthe and Jean-Luc Nancy analyze Lacan's use of predecessors in terms of
a *détournement*, the more or less violent, more or less *perverse* appropriation of
a movement by giving it a different direction. In current French usage,
the word also designates "hijacking." See: Ph. Lacoue-Labarthe, Jean-Luc
Nancy, *Le titre de la lettre*, Paris: Galilée, 1973. Second edition: Paris 1990.

[25] "Nulle chaîne signifiante en effet qui ne soutienne comme appendu à la
ponctuation de chacune de ses unités tout ce qui s'articule de contextes
attestés, à la verticale, si l'on peut dire, de ce point." Sheridan, p. 154; *Ecrits*,
p. 503.

[26] Sheridan, p. 155; *Ecrits*, p. 504.

The tree says "no!" to the storm that in this text and context becomes the signification, which only negatively, through its no and its difference lets the tree have its say, in a verse that is organized not by the signified, but, as Lacan remarks, by the "law of the parallelism of the signifier." This parallelism, Lacan notes, is marked by a "comme" – "as" – which operates independently of the meaning of what it "equates": the tree is treated like a blade of grass by the tempest, which "reduces" its "majestic head" by "treating [it] universally." This movement of "contrast" and "contradiction," Lacan continues, culminates in the "condensation" of *tête* and *tempête*, effectuated through assonance. To this, we might also add that of *traite*. What Lacan calls "the law of the parallelism of the signifier," thereby consists in a repetition of sound, which may produce meaning, but which is not dependent upon it.

Summing up his argument, Lacan writes: "What this structure of the signifying chain discloses," is the subject's possibility "to signify something entirely different from what it says."[27] Insofar as this movement of signification is constitutionally anchored in language itself, and does not depend upon the conscious intention of the subject, the function of discourse is no longer that of disguising – or, one might add: of expressing – thought. Rather, it is to "indicate the place of this subject in the search for truth."[28]

"Truth," is therefore no longer determined as the adequation of a thought to its object, or that of an expression to its thought, but rather has to do with a relation between signifiers, which here is in turn associated with "metonymy." In the "Instance of the Letter . . . ", metonymy is redefined as "the properly signifying function,"[29] which supplements its traditional definition as a relation of "word to word" (*mot à mot*). The traditional example that Lacan cites: "thirty sails," used to designate a flotilla of thirty ships, can serve to introduce this redefinition. The figure of thirty sails, which, in the strict sense, is more of a synecdoche than a metonymy, provides us with little reliable information about the fleet of ships it is said to designate, since a

---

[27] Sheridan, p. 155; *Ecrits*, p. 505.
[28] Ibid., p. 155.
[29] Ibid., p. 156.

ship can as easily possess eight sails as one. Although one might be tempted to reply that a sail remains part of a ship, even if the ship has many of them, Lacan's concern here seems to problematize a notion that is presupposed by all synecdoche, and which itself necessarily depends upon the identity of the signified: that of *totality*. And indeed, the figural movement of this signified – by means of which the ship seems to *split* or *double* itself in the process of conferring its identity upon the sails – is far more pertinent to the effect of metonymy Lacan is discussing than is the familiar relationship of part and whole. The term, metonymy, is designed to call attention to the fact that the chain of signification is constituted of signifiers, linked to one another by their differential function. What, however, does this imply concerning the metaphor? Is it any less concrete?

Before addressing this question, it may be helpful to recall how Lacan defines metaphor in the first place. Lacan adopts Jakobson's notion of substitution, but with an essential difference: insofar as the substitution takes place between signifiers, it cannot be based upon a semantic or substantial equivalence or similarity, as Jakobson often presumes. Lacan's clearest statement on this question is to be found not in the "Instance of the Letter," but instead in a short note entitled "The Metaphor of the Subject."[30] Here Lacan criticizes the theory of metaphor elaborated by Charles Perelman, according to which metaphoric substitution is based upon analogy, and hence upon similarity. In response, Lacan asserts that:

> Metaphor is – radically seen – the effect of substituting one signifier for another in a chain, without anything natural predestining it to this function of *phora* [vehicle], except for the fact that it deals with two signifiers, which as such are reducible to a phonematic opposition.[31]

Metaphor is thus not based either on a substantial similarity or on equivalence – which would once again imply the primacy of the signified – nor is it, as the surrealists (following a long tradition) claimed, the product of the simultaneity of two actualized signifiers; rather:

[30] Published in an appendix to the second French edition of the *Ecrits*, pp. 889–892.
[31] Ibid., p. 890.

It breaks out between two signifiers, one of which has taken the place of the other in the signifying chain, the occulted signifier remaining present through its (metonymic) connexion with the rest of the chain.[32]

A clearly determined relationship of presence and absence of the signifier is thus described here: the replaced, absent signifier is driven under the bar, as it were, into the realm of the signified – one could say it is "repressed" – yet, as an excluded and absent signifier it still remains present through its syntagmatic relationship to the rest of the chain. This suppression, in the most literal sense, is, however, in no way a removal, lifting or surpassing of the bar itself: though it may be crossed over, it still stays in place, for the repressed signifier remains a signifier even in the position of the signified.

Thus, if metonymy marks the proper function of the signifier – that is, the formation of the signifying chain – the function of metaphor is no less indispensable, insofar as no signifying chain can exist without simultaneously depending upon the signified. Metaphor confers its name on that movement of dependence, already noted in Saussure: the self-precipitation of the signifier as signified, which in virtue of the differential structure of signification must have always already been a signifier, in order to become a signified. "One sees," writes Lacan, "that metaphor occurs at the precise point where sense takes place in non-sense."[33] This taking-place, Lacan argues, is described in Freud's theory of jokes, as well as in his account of condensation [*Verdichtung*].

The "precipitation" by which the signifier drops down, as it were, to become a signified, discloses here a further aspect, which we could at most only suppose in Saussure: the process is a deadly one. The verse of Hugo, from "Booz endormi," which Lacan cites to exemplify the function of metaphor, leaves no doubt about this. If the proper name of Booz is replaced, and indeed repressed, in the verse Lacan quotes – and repression, we should remember, always involves the supplanting or

---

[32] "Elle jaillit entre deux signifiants dont l'un s'est substitué à l'autre en prenant sa place dans la chaîne signifiante, le signifiant occulté restant présent de sa connexion (métonymique) au reste de la chaîne." Sheridan, p. 157; *Ecrits*, p. 507.

[33] "On voit que la métaphore se place au point précis où le sens se produit dans le non-sens." Sheridan, p. 158; *Ecrits*, p. 508.

translation of one term by another – this verse: *"Sa gerbe n'etait pas avare ni haineuse"* (His sheaf was neither miserly nor spiteful), still retains the place of Booz by means of the syntagmatic relationship to the predicates denied by the sheaf. The exclusion of Booz becomes definitive, however, when the possessive pronoun "his" (*sa gerbe*) arrives on the scene. Thus – and we are forced to simplify Lacan's commentary here considerably – on the one hand, the surprising fertility, the unexpected paternity of the old man is alluded to, yet at the same time, his ability to produce life is reduced to "less than nothing," when contrasted with the fertility of the sheaf.

One sees here how, by virtue of its significance, Hugo's verse emerges as an exemplary representation of the process of signification itself. For there is no movement of the signifier that would not be dependent upon the signified: the question is only how the signified relates to the signifier, as cause or effect? In this particular case, the structure and meaning of paternity are performed, as it were, through the repression of the name of the father as a proper name. Lacan emphasizes that this repression must be seen in relation to the myth of the parricide, as expounded in *Totem and Taboo*. Without being able to pursue this point further here,[34] we have perhaps caught a glimpse of how the structure of language, like that of the object, comes to be determined by the movement and operations of the signifier.

[34] Cf. "On a question prior to all possible treatment of psychosis," in: Sheridan, p. 179–224, *Ecrits*, pp. 531–583. I have discussed Lacan's reading of the Schreber case in a preface to the American edition of Schreber's *Memoirs of My Nervous Illness*, Cambridge Mass.: Harvard University Press, 1989.

5

Significant fallout: metonymy and metaphor

Before proceeding to the next section of "The instance of the letter in the unconscious," it may be useful to attempt to summarize Lacan's remarks in the first part of that article. He takes as his point of departure the insight that what he calls in French *l'expérience psychanalytique*, and which can be translated as "psychoanalytic experience," but also as "psychoanalytic *experiment*," discovers in Freud's account of the unconscious, not merely speech (*la parole*), but moreover "the entire structure of language."[1] This structure is determined through the distinctive properties of the signifier, which is constituted on the one hand through opposition, on the other, through a capacity to combine with other signifiers to form a chain, "in accordance with the laws of a closed order."[2] This order consists of two radically heterogeneous but interdependent dimensions: that of the signifier and that of the signified, which are separated from each other by a bar – derived from the Saussurean division of the sign, but above all, from its graphic representation. But this bar is not merely a mark of separation: it is also a limit that must necessarily be transgressed, for the signifier is also precipitated into the realm of the signified, leaving its mark upon the latter, and allowing it to be designated as an "effect." Lacan therefore emphasizes a certain "primacy of the signifier over the signified."

The signifier is associated by Lacan with the phoneme, which Jakobson, following Trubetskoj, defines in terms of its "distinctive features," and as "mere otherness." However, from the

---

[1] "Notre titre [*l'instance de la lettre*] fait entendre qu'au-delà de cette parole, c'est toute la structure du langage que l'expérience psychanalytique découvre dans l'inconscient." Sheridan, p. 147; *Ecrits*, p. 495.

[2] Sheridan, p. 153; *Ecrits*, pp. 501–502.

exemplary status of the phoneme, Jakobson still tends to derive the linguistic priority of the spoken word over all forms of inscription, whereas Lacan stresses the *letter* – a graphic sign, albeit a phonetic one – as the necessary materialization and localization of the signifier. As in Freud, Lacan thus attributes to inscription the function of articulation, a fact that considerably relativizes the great emphasis he places on the *parole*.

This foregrounding of the importance of writing and its intimate relation to the signifier leads Lacan to problematize certain other linguistic concepts he adopts from the Saussurean heritage of structural linguistics: above all those of "speech" and of "discourse," although such problems tend to be implied, rather than explicitly stated. These concepts are no longer, as in traditional, metaphysical theories of language, conceived as forms of verbal exchange, as expressions of an identical subject, or as designations of things. It is not the linearity of speaking that is actualized in discourse, but instead the multi-dimensionality of the signifying chain formed by the twin operations of metonymy and metaphor. These two concepts are originally defined by Jakobson as designating the two functions of language: the first, the combination of signs, in the dimension of contiguity or of contextuality; the second, the selection and substitution of signs, based on relations of similarity. Lacan does not, however, merely apply these concepts, he *plies* them, giving them a new twist in the process. By redefining them as a movement of signifiers, the contextuality of metonymy and the similarity of metaphor become a function of differential opposition and cease to depend upon the signified. The only contiguity that metonymy can therefore count on, is that of the signifying chain itself. And the sole "similarity" presupposed by metaphorical substitution is the purely formal similarity among signifiers.

This rapprochement of Saussure and Jakobson in Lacan's text does not so much reconcile the two points of view as mutually dislocate them: Saussure's linear view of the syntagma and the sign gives way to the ambiguity of metaphorical–metonymical operations, while Jakobson's naive realism – according to which metonymy functions "within a predetermined context," instead of producing contextuality as such – is corrected by recourse to Saussure's *implicit* if highly ambivalent privileging of the signifier. Insofar as the signifier remains the primary concept of language, Lacan can state, in a later radio interview, published under the title, *"Radiophonie,"* that metaphor and metonymy are "places where Saussure *genuit* Jakobson:"[3] that is, where Saussure begets Jakobson but also besets (*gêne*) and troubles (*nuit*) him. Literally, then, the statement, "Saussure genuit Jakobson," resounds, radiophonically, as: "Saussure gêne (et) nuit à Jakobson." How, then, do things stand with the trouble-maker himself?

It can equally be said that Saussure *genuit* Lacan. The radicalization of the signifier as the constitutive element of language, throws into question the distinction between metaphor and metonymy – at least in the form in which they have heretofore been considered. Lacan's example taken from traditional rhetoric, thirty sails for the flotilla, is not only a "combination," but a substitution as well: not simply a "word for word," but rather "one word for another" (*un mot pour un autre*), which is the definition Lacan gives of "metaphor." Every operation of the signifier consists of both substitution and concatenation, each depending upon the other, since the signifier is determined only through its relationship to its surroundings, and more precisely, through exchanges that define linguistic "value" as a function of substitution. In his seminar, "The formations of the unconscious," Lacan's remark upon this is rendered by Pontalis as follows:

What characterizes the signifier is not that it can replace an object . . . but rather that it can become its own substitute, which presupposes a concatenation and a law that governs the signifiers.[4]

The search for this law and the attempt to define it in a way that would not make it contingent upon substantial factors (and thereby exclude it from being the law of the signifier), increasingly comes to determine the direction of Lacan's thinking. In "The instance of the letter," Lacan's initial use of an algorithmic model determines the formalization of metaphor

---

[3] "Et pourquoi Saussure se serait-il rendu compte, pour emprunter les termes de votre citation, mieux que Freud lui-même de ce que Freud anticipait, notamment la métaphore et la métonymie lacaniennes, lieux où Saussure *genuit* Jakobson." *Scilicet* 2/3, 1970, p. 58.

[4] "Les formations de l'inconscient", in the *Bulletin de Psychologie* XII/4, 1958–59, p. 251.

and metonymy in the direction of a mathematical topology that plays an ever-increasing role in his later writings.

In order, then, to be able to read Lacan in that future anterior, which he designates as the temporality not only of the discourse of the unconscious, but also of his own discourse, we must strive to read his own texts no less metonymically than they read the unconscious.

To do this, however, the concepts and intellectual habits associated with an Euclidean notion of space, as a homogeneous and empty continuum – in which two bodies cannot occupy the same place at the same time – are only of very limited value. For the laws of the signifier, like those of the unconscious, presuppose a very different kind of space. The Saussurean bar, on the other hand, is Euclidean through and through: it separates two internally coherent spheres and thus allows us to conceive of a movement between and within them, without, however, putting their respective identities into question. In contrast, the Lacanian bar traces the impossible trajectory of the signifier, precipitated into the realm of the signified, which only takes shape as a result.

Lacan's radicalization of the principle of difference thereby deconstructs not only the realm of the signified, but also – at least implicitly – that of the signifier, since every realm as a "closed" order must first of all be articulated as such, and this articulation can be understood only as an "effect of the signifier". That Lacan should retain a spatial notion here, in separating signifier and signified, is not surprising, for his primary concern at this stage in his thinking is to emphasize the radical disparity of the two orders. Nevertheless, the ultimate consequence of this kind of spatial separation would be nothing other than the transformation of the signifier into its own signified and its consequent hypostatizing as a self-identical transcendental principle.

Indeed, just such an interpretation of the signifier was advanced in an article on "The Unconscious" written by two well-known psychoanalysts who studied with Lacan, Jean Laplanche and Serge Leclaire.[5] There, they claim that a signifier can sig-

[5] "L'inconscient, une étude psychanalytique," *Actes du Colloque de Bonneval*, D. de Brouwer, 1966.

nify itself – in order subsequently to ontologize the unconscious as the precondition of language. Lacan sharply criticized this interpretation[6] and we will have an opportunity later, in the context of our discussion of Lacan's concept of the unconscious, to examine the question more closely. What needs to be stressed here, is that only those readings of Lacan's texts guided by the "metonymic movement of signification" – i.e. its contextuality – will do them justice. This means not only taking Lacan "at his word," but moreover taking him *literally*, which is not necessarily the same, any more than a "letter" is the same as a "word." Indeed, the difference between these two kinds of readings may well turn out to be the decisive question of hermeneutics today. To take a text at its word is to assume that signifier and signified are united, as it is precisely this unity that defines the word as such. Thus, to construe the significance of Lacan's writings primarily in terms of the meanings his words convey, however sensitive one may be to their connotations, is to practice reading in a manner that inevitably presupposes the priority of the signified over the signifier, even (and often especially) where one explicitly proclaims the contrary thesis. The form of the "thesis" as such, i.e. as a proposition, assertion or statement, inevitably subordinates the differential relation of signification to its significant "payoff," as the Pragmatists used to call it. It is just this payoff, however, that Saussure, Freud and Lacan seek to problematize.

Concretely, this suggests that the term "signifier" – formally considered, a word – has neither a simple nor a clearly determinate meaning, since what it designates and points toward – a configuration of differences – engenders meaning only retroactively, as the result of the "pointing," as it were. It is for this reason that Lacan insists on the distinction between signifier and letter; the significance of this distinction, however, lies not so much in neatly separating otherwise clear concepts, as in designating the ineluctability of difference, insofar as it coincides with the movement of articulation. The signifier is thus materialized and localized in the letter, which should not be identified with the signifier, since the latter, strictly speaking, has no identity, but instead designates the process through

---

[6] In his Preface to: A. Rifflet-Lemaire, *Jacques Lacan*, Brussels, 1970, p. 18, 404.

which identity is produced in the first place. If this process designated by the signifier forms the condition of possibility of the word, qua meaningful unit, which in turn is an indispensable constituent of the concept, the signifier cannot be grasped in terms of a particular content, but instead can be represented only formally, by what Lacan calls an "algorithm"; this unspeakable formula must be *written*:

$$f(S)\frac{1}{s}$$

If, on the other hand, one attempts to put what is designated here into words, one could say, in French, "l'incidence du signifiant sur le signifié."[7] With regard to its content this formulation is still not much clearer or more complete than the formal algorithm. The decisive word, incidence, decomposes in an ambiguity that again seems to defy any conceptual subsumption or synthesis: taken literally *"incidence"* means "falling in," "on," or occurring unexpectedly. I would, therefore, propose, as a tentative translation, or rendition, of the Lacanian phrase, "the falling *out* of the signifier with the signified." This has at least the virtue of suggesting that the signified is a kind of "fallout" of the signifier, the effect of its decomposition, and at the same time hinting at the conflictual aspect of their relationship. Through its falling out, the signifier bears upon the signified, to be borne in turn by it, in what must be considered to be an intrinsically uncanny "incident."

Lacan's use of algebraic representations as well as his witty and playful discursive language games constitute serious attempts at keeping the "signifying chain" from congealing into the hypostatized meanings of that essentially denominative, conceptual, constative discourse we call the language of theory. By calling attention to the formal processes through which meanings are generated and articulated, the errant and unpredictable "back and forth" of "dis-cursivity" is associated with a surplus of significance that no proposition or concept can fully comprehend. As we have seen, Lacan *calls* this movement a result of "metonymy" and "metaphor." The *actual* function of

---

[7] This formula, as well as the two following, designating metonymy and metaphor, are to be found in Sheridan, p. 164, *Ecrits*, p. 515.

the signifier, we recall, is embodied in metonymy, insofar as the signifier can only be determined as such by being related differentially to other signifiers, that is by means of *the contiguity of a discontinuous concatenation.* The signifier only "is" as an element of a signifying chain, which in turn is part of a network of such chains. The constitution and reproduction of this network, as a concatenation of intrinsically meaningless elements, constitutes the operation of metonymy. Metonymy thus could be said to *actualize* the differential articulation of the signifier. The distinctive *particularity* of such an occurrence – in the sense of the *falling-out* mentioned above – is that its particularization is always at issue, implicitly at least, since the metonymic movement depends upon something else, upon another *missing* signifier: indeed, upon another scene and stage, what Freud, in German called "the other scene" of the unconscious, in order for it to "take place." The place of the signifying change is always *elsewhere*, but that elsewhere is also never simply accessible as such.[8] In German, the *literal* designation for this would be an *Abort*, the restroom of Lacan's famous example. In English, it could be called a *dis-location*. Put another way, one could say that metonymy names the Saussurean "bar," insofar as it dislocates the sign. This formulation provides a fresh look at the dis-located place of the signifier, which, however, remains barred. For its place is none other than that marked by the bar, which divides the sign right down the middle while at the same time turning it inside out, forcing it to point elsewhere. Lacan's formula for metonymy:

$$f(S \ldots S')S \cong S(-)s$$

represents this movement, in which the signifier at hand (S) fulfills its metonymic function only by

$$(S')$$

referring to another latent signifier: which determines the end of one chain, only by pointing toward the beginning of another. And yet at the same time, that further beginning must be

---

[8] All this is an effort to find a suitable English circumlocution for what in the original German text was called an *Abort*: literally, a place that is off-limits, but in everyday language, a toilet.

resisted, excluded, suspended or deferred, if anything is to take place at all. The signified is consequently always excluded or barred by the bar (−).

We can now attempt to trace how Lacan's formalization of metonymy contrasts with that of metaphor. In the latter the signifier that produces an effect of "significance" is not somewhere else, in a dis-location, but instead appears directly in the chain itself, albeit as a substitute that *takes the place of another* signifier, thereby driving it from the chain, repressing and supplanting it. As a result of this substitution, the repressed signifier is banned to the realm of the signified, or more precisely, to a "place" where it functions as a signified while, however, remaining a signifier. Only here does significance, or more precisely, meaning emerge. The bar is cleared (cf. the + in the formula for metaphor):

$$f\left(\frac{S'}{S}\right)S \cong S(+)s$$

Is the dis-location then finally accessible? Hardly, since the signifier that clears (or limbos under) the bar remains a signifier and acts as a signified only in order to operate as a signifier both "in the realm of the signified" and in the signifying chain to which it is still linked as a determinate absence. We see that this "metaphorical" operation, as Lacan calls it, is nothing other than the precipitation of the signifier that produces the signified and at the same time bars it as long it does not cease to be a signifier. Metaphor thus produces an effect of meaning, but in the double meaning of the French *sens: sense and direction.* If metonymy can be said to describe the movement, metaphor provides the *sense of direction.* But to have a sense of direction is not necessarily to arrive at one's destination.

We are thus led to the conclusion that both metonymy and metaphor are "functions of a uniform movement of the signifier," which, on the one hand, can only function in and through its concatenation, and on the other, is always dependent upon what is not part of the chain, the signifier to which it refers. Nevertheless, if the two aspects are necessary and interdependent, they do not have the same status: the signifier only becomes a signifier by means of a concatenation, and this would seem to suggest a priority of metonymy over metaphor.[9] The effect of meaning (that is, of a *determinate* signified), presupposes the functioning of the signifier in a chain. We will be able to examine more closely this priority of metonymy when we discuss Lacan's theory of desire as essentially metonymic and his definition of the symptom as metaphoric. But in order to follow the difficult relationship between metaphor and metonymy, we must first examine how Lacan uses them to reinterpret Freud's analysis of the "dreamwork" in the *Interpretation of Dreams*.

We will leave aside, for the moment, Lacan's discussion of the dream as a system of writing, at the very beginning of this section, in order to proceed to those mechanisms of the dreamwork in which he rediscovers metaphor and metonymy. What concerns us here are those processes that Freud called condensation and displacement. Lacan writes:

Verdichtung, or "condensation," is the structure of the superimposition of the signifiers, which metaphor takes as its field, and whose name, condensing in itself the word *Dichtung*, shows how the mechanism is con-natural with poetry to the point that it envelops the traditional function proper to poetry.

In the case of *Verschiebung*, "displacement," the German term is closer to the idea of that veering off of signification that we see in metonymy, and which from its first appearance in Freud is represented as the most appropriate means used by the unconscious to foil censorship.[10]

If we examine Freud's concept of condensation, we find at first not so much the idea of substitution as that of *accumulation* or "compression,"[11] and it is significant that in his definition Lacan speaks not of substitution but rather of *surimposition*,

[9] It should be noted that Lacoue-Labarthe and Nancy arrive at an opposite conclusion; according to them, Lacan's thought is marked by "the bias of a preference accorded (against difference, in short) to metaphor, including the choice of the paradigmatic (vertical) axis of language against syntagmatic linearity" (*Le titre de la lettre*, p. 145, note). The question around which such an evaluation turns, may be formulated as follows: To what extent does Lacan's writing imply a metalinguistic position for its own propositions? To what extent, in short, should Lacan be read as a *theoretical* discourse? The analyses in this book constitute an attempt to address this question (which, however, remains largely implicit throughout).

[10] Sheridan, p. 160; *Ecrits*, p. 511.   [11] *SE*, IV, p. 279.

superimposition. A single idea or representation serves as the nodal point of different associative chains; considered from an economic perspective, this idea unites in itself the energetic cathexis of the chains with which it is in contact. This process takes place as much in the latent dream-thoughts and repressed wishes as in the manifest dream-content. Not only dreams, but also jokes, symptoms, and slips, are structured by this mechanism of condensation. As one of the forms of unconscious articulation, condensation can be employed in all expressions of the unconscious, insofar as these expressions are necessarily "overdetermined." Nevertheless, although Freud discusses condensation in terms of compression and concentration, it is clear that this process can take place only by virtue of an exchangeability of representations: the condensed representation – be it a nodal point, a composite person, or a montage – replaces other ideas, which it excludes from the manifest chain and yet which it at the same time is bound to allude to. Overdetermination, which is a distinctive aspect of condensation, is conceivable only as a relationship of substitution, even if substitution alone does not seem to describe the compactness of condensation adequately. This difficulty should no longer surprise us, however, since we have already seen that substitution alone does not suffice to distinguish Lacan's conception of metaphor, since it applies equally to metonymy.

One of the questions raised by this problem, therefore, is whether the priority of metonymy that is implicit in Lacan's theory of the signifier, is also to be found in the writings of Freud, in particular with respect to his notion of "displacement." To respond, we must first differentiate various meanings in the Freudian use of the term. In the *Interpretation of Dreams*, displacement primarily has to do with the way elements of the dream-thoughts relate to those of the dream-content. Freud writes:

What is clearly the essential content of the dream-thoughts need not be represented in the dream at all. The dream is, as it were, *differently centered* from the dream-thoughts – its content has different elements as its central point.[12]

[12] *SE*, IV, p. 305.

In thus speaking of the de-centering of the dream-content, Freud seeks to account for the way the demands of censorship are met while still allowing the unconscious wish to be fulfilled. The narrowness of this interpretation makes it possible for Freud to speak of dreams in which no displacement occurs, as in the dream of Irma's injection, where "the different elements are able to retain . . . the approximate place which they occupy in the dream-thoughts." Yet as soon as we turn to Freud's metapsychological discussion of the dream-mechanisms, we see that there is a second, more general concept of displacement at work in his writing, one that is presupposed by the notion of a "primary process" of thought, and hence, of the unconscious. What is decisive here is the displaceability – or as Freud also writes, the *Übertragbarkeit*: the transferability and translatability, infectiousness, and contagiousness – of psychic energy, of ideational cathexes, whose instability constitutes the difference between primary (unconscious) and secondary (preconscious-conscious) processes. The reason for this instability of cathexes is to be sought in the structure of the wish and of the pleasure principle (or as Freud still calls it in *The Interpretation of Dreams*, the "unpleasure principle"). We will have occasion later to return to this structure and to discuss it in greater detail, but here it will be sufficient to indicate the universality of displacement as an essential mechanism of the primary process in order to show that, considered in this sense, displacement is at the basis of all dream-distortion, that is, at the basis of the entire dreamwork. Both condensation and displacement in the narrow sense are only made possible by the displaceability of cathexes.

The structure of this displaceability is nothing other than that of the metonymic movement of the signifier. With this in mind, it is possible to put in perspective a criticism often made of Lacan: namely, that the structuralist interpretation of psychoanalysis neglects or even ignores the economic aspect of the drives. The drive, which according to Freud represents "a concept straddling the psychological and the somatic,"[13] can be determined only in terms of a structure of representation: to proceed otherwise would be to abandon the liminal position of

---

[13] "Drives and their vicissitudes," *SE*, xiv, pp. 121–122.

what Freud calls *Trieb*, situated between the physiological and consciousness, in favor of biologism. However, in determining this structure of representation, Freud himself wavers between two versions, or rather, two emphases: on the one hand, the drive itself is described as being a "psychic representative [*Repräsentant*] of a stimulus emanating from within the organism," albeit one that defines itself precisely by "making its way into the psyche,"[14] and thereby distancing itself from its physiological origins; on the other hand, the drive is described as itself a *Vorstellung*, a "representation," or more precisely, by a *Vorstellungsrepräsentanz*, a term forged by Freud himself, extremely difficult to render in English, and generally translated as: "ideational representative":

A drive can never become an object of consciousness, only the *Vorstellung* that represents it can be consciously perceived. In the unconscious as well, it is only by means of the *Vorstellung* that [the drive] can be represented.[15]

Freud's difficulty in deciding whether the drive is a representative, or that which is represented, is rooted in the ambivalent nature of the concept of drive, which entails both aspects. Our discussion of the process of signification can be helpful in determining their configuration: the drive is determined by Freud as the movement of representation *qua* *signification*; that is, insofar as it is not grounded in a predetermined signified (the traditional notion of representation), but instead in a differential relation of signifiers. That Freud's concept of the drive can best be construed in these terms, may be demonstrated by recalling his approach to the categories of *quality* and *quantity* in this context. Freud's insistence on the quantitative aspect of the drive is often summarily dismissed as evidence of an outmoded scientific bias. Such a view, however, misses the significance of Freud's quantitative notion of psychic economy: far from trying to make the drive into something *quantifiable*, Freud's insistence on the quantitative aspect of psychic energy defines its distinctive articulation as a representation that is not constituted by its qualitative aspect, that is

---

[14] Ibid.
[15] "The Unconscious," *SE*, XIV, p. 177.

by its "ideational content," but rather by its incommensurability to any qualitative *object*. This is what distinguishes what Freud calls the "primary process," from the more familiar "secondary" thought processes. Whereas the latter is "qualitative" in nature, the former is determined by relations that are essentially *differential*: by the so-called "pleasure principle," consisting of "reductions in tension." The latter are only "quantitative" in the sense of being irreducible to qualities, i.e. to identities: they are not quantitative in the sense of being quantifiable. Such differential relations function according to the laws of the signifier, as Lacan describes them. In *Totem and Taboo*, Freud brings these laws together under what he calls, in German, *Berührung*, that is, touch, contact or contiguity:

> It is further to be noticed that the two principles of association – similarity and contiguity – are both included in the more comprehensive unity of "contact." Association by contiguity is contact in the literal sense; association by similarity is contact in the metaphorical sense.[16]

If "association by contiguity" might be understood as corresponding to a limited concept of metonymy, the more comprehensive concept of *contact* suggests a broader interpretation of metonymy, entailing nothing less than "the actual function of the signifier," its discontinuous concatenation. The manner in which *contact* contributes to the formation of ideational contents is described by Freud with the help of what he calls "perceptual identities." This notion is developed as an attempt to account for the distinctive plasticity of the dream. Freud conjectures that perceptions first become identities by means of their essentially fortuitous convergence – that is contact – with an "experience of satisfaction"; the association of a particular perception with such an experience then recurs at the next sign of distress. Insofar as a perception is experienced together with a satisfaction, it will tend to be repeated – that is re-presented – whenever satisfaction is lacking. Through such iterability, the perception acquires a certain degree of identity, which in turn, however, is linked to a series – or chain – of other perceptions, as Freud makes clear:

[16] *Totem and Taboo, SE,* XIII, p. 85.

Our perceptions prove also to be connected with one another in memory, and this is especially so if they originally occurred simultaneously. We call this the fact of association.[17]

Perceptual identity, the condition of all ideational content, shows itself to be in turn an effect of a process of *repetition* based on a fortuitous encounter: on contact and contiguity. The place, however, that makes contact and contiguity possible – the place, where such an encounter takes place – is itself determined not by the "quality" or identity of the elements encountering each other, but rather by the "quantitative" variations in tension, that is by the *differential* relations that constitute the pleasure (or more precisely: unpleasure) principle. What Freud attempts to retrace in his account of the formation of "perceptual identity," is thus nothing other than the determination of the signifier.

We are perhaps better prepared at this point to turn our attention to the third mechanism of the dreamwork, which, Lacan asserts, constitutes the distinctive trait of dream language: its "consideration of representability" [*Rücksicht auf Darstellbarkeit*]. Lacan takes some liberties in translating it as "consideration of the means of staging" (*égards aux moyens de la mise en scène*).[18] The aptness of this translation, however, lies in the emphasis it puts on the *theatrical*: for what Freud describes as the *Darstellbarkeit* of the dream involves less a representation, a *Vorstellung*, in the sense of a mental image, than what in German is condensed into the word, *Entstellung*. This word normally signifies "distortion,"[19] but it literally, and etymologically, also suggests a shift in place, a dis-placement, such as that we have already encountered in the movement of the signifier. Above all, however, the term points us toward the precise difference between a mental representation and Freud's notion of *Darstellbarkeit*: whereas the former seems to imply only a binary relation between an object represented and a representing subject, the latter, replacing the "*Vor-*" of *Vorstellung* by *Dar-*, "there", opens what might be called a more public space,

---

[17] *Interpretation of Dreams*, SE, v, p. 539.
[18] Sheridan, p. 161; *Ecrits*, p. 511.
[19] Chapter 4 of the *Interpretation of Dreams* is entitled, "The distortion of dreams" (*Die Traumentstellung*), and must be understood as designating not simply the *effect* of the dream, but the dream itself. To be sure, the structure of the dream cannot be entirely separated from its effects, a fact that underscores the *pragmatic* aspect of the Freudian unconscious.

involving relations more complex than mere binary opposition. If the dream involves distortion, *Entstellung*, it is because of the intervention of a third party – which Freud calls "censorship" – in the figuration of the dream, a party that plays the role both of spectator and of judge in the dream-representation. And it is precisely this that distinguishes *theatrical* representation from other forms: the explicit reference to a third party, to an addressee, and hence, a structure that is at least triadic. This is why the plasticity of the signifier of the dream, as described by Freud, does not have the re-presentative structure of a simple, mimetic image, but rather that of a *scene* or of a *scenario*; and it is also why that scene also inevitably resorts to forms of *inscription*. In this context Freud employs the term *Bilderschrift*, pictographic or ideogrammatic writing:

The dream-content is, as it were, given in a pictographic script [*Bilderschrift*] whose characters [*Zeichen*] must be transposed individually into the language of the dream-thought. If we attempted to read these characters according to their pictorial value instead of according to their semiotic relations, we should clearly be led into error.[20]

While Lacan's translation of *Darstellbarkeit* as *mise en scène* emphasizes the scenic quality of dream-distortion, his explanation of this translation underscores the necessity of that scene becoming a *scenography*, that is, a writing system. If Lacan refuses to render Freud's term as the French *figuration*, it is because *Darstellbarkeit* "takes place within a writing system" and thus clearly distinguishes itself from figuration in general, be it even that of "a figurative semiology."[21] The written structure of the dream language sets itself off not only from the representative image, but also from the spoken word. Speech and word only provide the dreamwork with "material" with which to articulate its distortions. Freud comments:

A word, as the nodal point of a number of ideas, possesses, as it were, a predestined polyvalence, and the neuroses (obsessions, phobias)

---

[20] *SE*, iv, p. 277. Since the pictography of the dream is also distorted, Freud goes on in the next sentence to compare it with a "picture puzzle," a "rebus."

[21] It should be noted that Lacan's insistence upon the non-phonetic, scriptural quality of the dream converges here with an emphasis upon the latter's *theatricality*. The theatrical aspect of articulation tends to emerge wherever phonocentric conceptions of language are no longer taken for granted, as Derrida has shown in regard to Artaud.

take advantage of the opportunities for condensation and disguise afforded by words quite as eagerly as do dreams.[22]

According to the law of the signifier, all elements of the dream – whether images, words, utterances, or their syntactical arrangement"– only become significant as nodal points or as "determinatives," that is, through their contextual relations:

Perhaps the dreamer will say: "My mother was there too" (Stekel). Such an element of the dream-content is then comparable to a determinative in hieroglyphic script, which is not meant to be expressed, but is intended only to explain another sign.[23]

Although Freud seems to present the "determinative" here as comprising a special case of the dream langauge, it should be considered to be its exemplary element. It does not signify by means of its expressive value, but instead solely through its relation to other signs which it serves to "explain." The constitutive function of a shifting context also rules out the possibility of a dream interpreter ever being able to depend on a symbol or code book that might, as it were, serve as a universal key to deciphering dream symbolism. "These (symbols) often possess many and varied meanings, so that, as in Chinese script, only the context can furnish the correct meaning."[24] This also implies, however, that the shifting context of the dream can never be completely determined or exhaustively interpreted, since it itself is only part of a more comprehensive context that must in principle be impossible to close. If the impossibility of closure suggests – as an image – something like an infinite expansion, the figure that Freud uses to name this aspect of the dream shows that such openness leads not only to the periphery of the dream, but also to its most intimate center:

Even in the best interpreted dreams, there is often a place that must be left in the dark, because in the process of interpreting, one notices a tangle of dream-thoughts arising, which resists unravelling, but has also made no further contributions to the dream-content. This, then, is the navel of the dream, the place where it straddles the unknown.[25]

---

[22] *SE*, v, pp. 340–341. In this context Freud refers to the use of verbal wit in dreams.

[23] *SE*, IV, p. 321.

[24] *SE*, v, p. 353.

[25] *SE*, v, p. 525. I have discussed this passage at greater length in *The Legend of Freud*, University of Minneapolis Press: Minneapolis, 1982, pp. 75ff.

If the meaning of the dream requires a certain interpretation in order to be articulated, it is apparent that the latter cannot be conceived as entirely detached from what it is interpreting; interpretation itself cannot avoid being contaminated by the sense-distorting articulation of the dream. This fact leads Freud to introduce another figure in describing the peculiar imbrication of interpretation and text in the dream, one which may well exemplify the peculiar structure of that relationship: the palimpsest. Commenting on the use of this image by the English psychologist, Sully, to describe dreams, Freud asserts that "no statement found in the literature [on dreams] so closely approaches my own account."[26]

If the dream "itself" already consists of a system of superimposed inscription, its interpretation adds a new layer to the dream-text. The latter, as Freud insists, is not merely the representation of a desire, but its "fulfillment," however distorted. It is, therefore, as "wish" that the palimpsest receives its contours and frame, which is why the discussion of the dream as signifying text leads us to the question of the subject and its desire.

[26] If Freud identifies Sully as his closest predecessor in the exploration of dreams, it is because "he was more firmly convinced, perhaps, than any other psychologist that dreams have a disguised meaning." (*SE*, IV, p. 60). The following passage from Sully's article, "Dreams as a revelation," cited by Freud, emphasizes precisely the refusal to regard dreams as absurd: "It would seem, then, after all, that dreams are not the utter nonsense they have been said to be by such authorities as Chaucer, Shakespeare and Milton. The chaotic aggregations of our nightfancy have a significance and communicate new knowledge. *Like some letter in cipher, the dream-inscription when scrutinized closely loses its first look of balderdash and takes on the aspect of a serious intelligible message. Or, to vary the figure slightly, we may say that, like some palimpsest, the dream discloses beneath its worthless surface-characters traces of an old and precious communication.*" (*SE*, IV, p. 135 note; emphasis Freud's)

6

Spades and hearts: the subject as stylus

Until now we have considered the laws governing the movement of the signifier in terms of a metonymic string that in
principle is never closed, since it produces determinate meaning, and hence closure, as a retroactive effect, thereby rendering
meaning a function of the string. Can one therefore ever hope,
from this point of view, to ascertain regularities by which
metonymic contexts themselves are determined? Or to put it
even more radically: are the "contiguity" or "contact" presupposed by metonymy even thinkable without some recourse to a
grounding signified functioning as a principle of closure?

Both contiguity and contact necessarily require some sort of
site, delimited in some way, in order to be able to "take place."
Yet, in order for such a place to be *taken*, it must first be
delimited, marked out and cordoned off. How is this to be
accomplished, if not by some sort of signified? If, until now, we
have investigated *how* the signified is produced by the signifier
in unconscious articulation, we now must ask *why* the movement of the signifier, so resistant to closure, *nevertheless*
succeeds in delimiting itself or in being delimited. How in short
are *particular* signifiers and *individual* signifying chains formed?
Without such delimitation, no single signifier could ever take
place, could ever encounter another, even to demarcate itself
from it; without such delimitation, there would be no place for
either contact, contiguity or difference. It is imperative, then,
that the site of signification be located, and it was such a
necessity that led Freud himself, once he had described the laws
of the dreamwork, to take a further, and fateful step into
darkness:

For it must be clearly understood that the easy and agreeable portion
of our journey lies behind us. Hitherto, unless I am greatly mistaken,

all the paths along which we have travelled have led us towards the light – towards elucidation and fuller understanding. But as soon as we endeavour to penetrate more deeply into the mental process involved in dreaming, every path will end in darkness.[1]

This path into darkness which, in the steps of Freud and Lacan, we must follow, has nevertheless been on the agenda for quite some time. It was already inscribed in the ostensibly simple notion of the dream as wish-fulfillment. In analyzing the dream not simply as wish-fulfillment, but also as an almost inevitably *distorted* one, which therefore encrypts itself in a hieroglyphics and hides the key, Freud raised, at least implicitly, the question: a wish-fulfillment *for whom*? Who or what is the subject whose wishes are fulfilled by the dream in this way? And, perhaps even more significantly: where is its *place*?

The seventh chapter of *The Interpretation of Dreams* may be read as an attempt to outline this place and in so doing, to track down the subject. In following its trail, Freud stumbles upon the question of the unconscious. He approaches it cautiously, indeed, with a certain trepidation. How is one to conceptualize that which, in its essence, is inaccessible to consciousness? Or, put somewhat differently: does the unconscious lend itself to thought? In seeking to respond to such questions, Freud follows two, not necessarily compatible paths. First, he portrays the unconscious as the most comprehensive of psychic domains, implying, as it were, that its very *comprehensiveness* allows comprehension by consciousness:

The unconscious is the larger sphere, which includes within it the smaller sphere of the conscious. Everything conscious has an unconscious preliminary stage; whereas what is unconscious may remain at that stage and nevertheless claim to be regarded as having the full value of a psychical process. The unconscious is the true psychical reality (. . .)[2]

As "the truly psychical," the unconscious appears, in such formulations, to be essentially *intrasubjective* in nature. At the same time, however, Freud tends to portray the conflicts and differences between the unconscious and preconscious-consciousness as *intersubjective* phenomena, as if they involved

---

[1] *Interpretation of Dreams*, V, p. 511.
[2] *SE*, V, pp. 612–613.

entirely distinct persons, something like a master and a slave. And when he writes of an unconscious "intention," this might seem to imply that the unconscious is a kind of second ego, insofar as "intentionality" is generally closely associated with self-consciousness. His initial division of the psychic "apparatus" into dynamic, conflictual instances or systems, leaves the question of the structure of subjectivity to which both belong unanswered. Nor is this lacuna an accident: before Freud, the subject had been largely identified with self-consciousness, the instance that comprises the "smaller circle" of the psyche; hence, for its "larger circle" no theoretical account was readily forthcoming. The theoretical discourse that would be adequate to the subject of the unconscious had to be invented by Freud, although the task was hardly facilitated by his highly ambivalent relationship to those philosophical predecessors who might have aided him in this task, in particular, Nietzsche.

Thus, when Freud claims that the dream is not only a wish-fulfillment, but also utterly "egoistic,"[3] it cannot be taken for granted that we know just which *ego* he is referring to. Certainly not to the ego that coincides more or less with the system of perception-consciousness – that is, with the secondary process. In this connection, a passage from *The Introductory Lectures on Psychoanalysis*, which Freud later inserted as a footnote into *The Interpretation of Dreams*, is helpful:

A second factor, which is much more important and far-reaching, but which is equally overlooked by laymen is the following. No doubt a wish-fulfillment must bring pleasure; but the question then arises, "To whom?" To the person who has the wish, of course. But, as we know, a dreamer's relation to his wishes is a quite peculiar one. He repudiates them and censors them – in short: he doesn't like them. Their fulfill-ment can therefore give him no pleasure, but just the opposite; and experience shows that this opposite appears in the form of anxiety, something still to be explained. Thus, in his relation to his dream-wishes, a dreamer can only be compared to an amalgamation of two separate people linked by some important common element. Instead of enlarging on this, I will remind you of a familiar fairy tale in which you will find the same solution repeated. A good fairy promises a poor married couple to fulfill their first three wishes. They are delighted, and make up their minds to choose their three wishes carefully. But the

---

[3] *SE*, v, p. 322.

woman lets herself be tempted by the odor of sausages being grilled in the cottage next door and wishes for a pair. In a flash they are there; this is the first wish-fulfillment. But the man is furious, and in his rage wishes that the sausages would hang from his wife's nose. This happens too; and the sausages are not to be dislodged from their new position. This is the second wish-fulfillment; but the wish is the man's, and its fulfillment is most disagreeable for his wife. You know the rest of the story. Since after all they are in fact one – man and wife – the third wish can only be that the sausages should be removed from the woman's nose.[4]

We should not be distracted by the seemingly intersubjective character of the scene Freud recounts, since the two "are in fact one, husband and wife;" and yet this unity is split and conflictual. Nor is it accidental that the story recounts a split between husband and wife, in German, between *Mann* and *Frau*, Man and Woman, since it thereby links the conflictual aspect of difference to sexual difference, where "bisexuality," far from naming the reconciliation of this difference, indicates its ineradicable character. By being "one," "Men" and "Women" do not become a harmonious unity, but on the contrary, are inseparably linked in their differences. It is the fairytale version of the irreconcilable difference touched upon in the quarrel over the two signs, "Gentlemen" and "Ladies." Nor is the example itself chosen at random; the woman wishes she had a pair of "little wieners," the man spitefully complies by having a few hung on her *nose*, and both then finally decide to *wish* them *away*, thereby almost returning to their point of departure – almost, but not quite. Freud's story confronts us with nothing less than the constitutive relationship between desire and the phallus – or more exactly, between desire and castration; we shall have occasion to return to this later. Here, what should be remarked is that wish-fulfillment, governed as it is by the unconscious, comes paradoxically close to converging with "wish-renunciation" [*Wunschversagen*]. Husband and wife, in Freud's story, represent not two separate persons, but a situation that is "one" in its *disunity*. Fulfillment and renunciation of a wish turn out to amount to the same thing because the wish, drawing its energy from unconscious desire, must always be abhorrent to

[4] *SE*, v, pp. 580–581, note.

consciousness. A wish only becomes unconscious, insofar as it must be *repressed*. Such repression thus *constitutes* the subject, insofar as it is a subject of the unconscious. Whence, the "special relationship" of the dreamer "to his wishes": he "repudiates them, censors them, in short, he doesn't like them." For such a subject, pleasure and unpleasure coincide.

Thus if what comprises the subject is not simply the separation of the unconscious from consciousness (preconscious), but rather their active exclusion of one other, the site occupied by the subject is *riven* by divergent drives, since no wish is unconscious without at the same time being fractured and split by a striving incompatible with it. If in the terminology of the early Freud, "pleasure" and "unpleasure" are almost exchangeable terms, it is because they designate not self-identical feelings or states, but a relation of "tension," which is irreducible to any one of its components.

When, therefore, Freud designates all dreams as being "egoistic," the ego to which he refers is not that of an ultimately unifiable self-consciousness, but rather of a certain dispersion and repetition:

It is my experience, and one to which I have found no exception, that every dream deals with the dreamer himself. Dreams are completely egoistic. Whenever my own ego does not appear in the content of the dream, but only some extraneous person, I may safely assume that my own ego lies concealed, by identification, behind this other person; I may fill in my ego [*Ich darf mein Ich ergänzen*]. On other occasions, when my own ego *does* appear in the dream, the situation in which it occurs may teach me that some other person lies concealed, by identification, behind my ego. [. . .] Thus, my ego may be represented in a dream several times over, now directly and now through identification with extraneous persons.[5]

Thus, according to Freud all dreams are egoistic, regardless of whether the ego of the dreamer is directly represented or not. Since, however, according to the law of distortion, the most important elements of the dream-thoughts seldom appear as such, there is every reason to think that the ego that appears in the dream will only rarely signify the ego of the wish-distorting

---

[5] *SE*, IV, pp. 322–323.

dreamer. Behind this manifest ego, "another person is usually concealed by means of identification." When "in the dream-content [. . .] it is not my ego but a strange person who comes forth, I may easily assume that my ego is hidden by means of identification." "I may fill in my ego," [*Ich darf mein Ich ergänzen*] Freud remarks. The German phrase is notably ambiguous: "to fill in my ego" means both to complete my ego, and to complete the scene by adding my ego to it, in the place of the non-ego that appears. But it would be more accurate to say, "I may conceal and distort my ego," for this is precisely what the subject does in the dream. And yet, precisely that is what "filling in one's ego" amounts to: creating the illusion of fullness, of complete-ness, of the ego as a self-identical subjective instance. If this is the inevitable illusion of all dream-content, as such, and independently of its specific signification, then this might explain the rather curious "may" in Freud's phrase, "Ich *darf* mein Ich ergänzen." The dream indeed *allows*, permits, but even more, it almost *obligates* the dreamer to "fill in" the ego: that is the "law" of dream-distortion, of the dream *as* distortion. And yet, is this filled-in ego the same as the *subject* of the dream? In the light, or shadow, of the dream, are we certain that we know what an ego is?

Ever since Descartes, modern philosophy has constituted itself, in part at least, through the attempt to provide an answer to this question. The ego is said to be a thinking being which, even if it knows nothing else, knows itself to be thinking. The ego is supposed to be this being thinking itself: *cogito me cogitare*, self-consciousness, reflexive identity of thought itself. Yet at least since Freud's great philosophical contemporary, Husserl, a new specification has been added: the ego is not only an instance of thought, but an instance of language as well. In his *Logical Investigations*, (which appeared in 1900, the same year as Freud's *Interpretation of Dreams*), Husserl includes the ego, as first person pronoun, in that group of expressions which he describes as "essentially occasional"; while these expressions may have a "conceptually fixed" [*begrifflich-einheitliche*] mean-ing, they are nevertheless oriented "by the occasion, the speaker and the situation." Hence, "only by looking to the actual circumstances of utterance can one definite meaning be constituted out of all this mutually connected class for the hearer."[6]

The meaning of the word "I" thus "can only be drawn from living speech and from the perceptual circumstances relevant to it."[7] Accordingly, "I" is intelligible only as an indication of the discursive context in which it occurs. Yet, as Husserl stresses, this indexing function does not coincide with the concrete meaning of the word, since "otherwise we could simply substitute for it the phrase 'whatever speaker is designating himself,'" which is clearly too general to explain the specific meaning of the word as it is sometimes used. Husserl therefore distinguishes "the universal *semantic function* [*Bedeutungsfunktion*] of the word 'I' to designate whoever is speaking," from its concrete meaning, which is "essentially realized in the immediate idea [*Vorstellung*] of one's own personality" as it is experienced in our own silent thoughts: in the mind's "solitary soliloquy" with itself.[8] Husserl thereby attempts to take the "essentially occasional" indicative function of the word "I," which refers primarily to the context of linguistic enunciation [in the sense of Benveniste's *énonciation*], and raise it to ideality of thought. The context of the enunciation – the linguistic context – is thereby negated and surpassed, *aufgehoben*, in that of thought and of transcendental self-consciousness.

Opposing this effort by Husserl to intellectualize the linguistic context, Roman Jakobson defines the status of the word "I" in purely linguistic terms, in his essay on "Shifters, verbal categories and the Russian verb."[9] Whereas Husserl attempts to separate the concrete meaning of the "I" from the linguistic situation by identifying it with "the immediate representation of one's own personality," and thereby with pure thought, Jakobson emphasizes the word's "general meaning," which, he asserts, remains the same regardless of changes in context, by referring to the process of enunciation – to the "message."[10]

---

[6] E. Husserl, *Logical Investigations*, vol. I, trans. by J.N. Findlay, New York: Humanities Press, 1970, p. 315. Cf. *Logische Untersuchungen*, vol. II, part 1, Tübingen: Niemeyer, 1968, p. 81.
[7] Ibid.
[8] Ibid, pp. 315–316.
[9] "Shifters, verbal categories and the Russian verb," Roman Jakobson, *Selected Writings*, vol. II: *Word and Language*, The Hague: Mouton, 1971, pp. 130–147.
[10] Ibid., p. 179.

Husserl would not have disagreed with this; yet Jakobson then goes on to distinguish the specific forms this indexing function may take. First of all, he divides the linguistic process into statement and enunciation, on the one hand, and into process and protagonist, on the other. Shifters are distinguished by the fact that they refer not only to language as that which is enunciated, but also to the process and the protagonists of language qua enunciation.

The distinction Jakobson draws between the enunciated and enunciation will be important for Lacan, not only in his definition of the subject, but also in his choice of terminology. In order to appreciate fully the importance of this distinction, it will be helpful to consult briefly two short essays by the French linguist, Emile Benveniste, which elaborate upon Jakobson's distinctions. The first essay, "The nature of pronouns," was published in 1956 in the collection, *For Roman Jakobson*.[11] In contrast to Husserl, and in agreement with Jakobson, Benveniste argues that the meaning of the word "I" "can only be identified by the instance of discourse that contains it and by that alone."[12] Yet this discourse is itself comprehensible only with respect to the linguistic form "I," which in turn exists only as part of a speech act. Drawing on Jakobson's distinction between enunciated and enunciation, Benveniste concludes that "there is a combined double instance in this process: the instance of *I* as that which refers, and the instance of discourse containing *I* as that which is referred to."[13] The word "I" thus entails a double reference: on the one hand, it refers to the speaker designating himself as part of the content of a particular statement [*énoncé*]; on the other hand, and at the same time, it refers to the speaker designating himself as the subject of a more general process of enunciation that is irreducible to any determinate statement.

This distinction, although implicit in Benveniste's analyses, is qualified by the fact that the linguistic constitution of the subject

---

[11] In the meantime, this has been republished in: Emile Benveniste, *Problems in General Linguistics*, trans. Mary Elizabeth Meek, Coral Gables: University of Miami Press, 1971, pp. 217–222. Cf. in the same volume, "Subjectivity in Language," pp. 223–230.
[12] Ibid., p. 218.
[13] Ibid; translation modified.

described above, relates to the operations of language in the same way as it does, for instance, in Husserl; that is, language continues to be construed from the teleological point of view of appropriation – that of the subject becoming conscious of itself. A speaker referring to herself as "I," positions herself vis-à-vis another subject, a "you." Language thereby is conceived as a medium of intersubjective communication, whereby "language turns into instances of discourse," thus enabling "the process of appropriation by the speaker" to take place.[14]

Is this "I" – whether determined philosophically by Husserl, or linguistically by Jakobson and Benveniste, the same as the "I" which, as Freud writes, is "represented in a multiple manner" in dreams? Is it really, or merely, an "I" that is "filled in" in dreams? And does Lacan's adoption or adaptation of linguistic terms, such as shifter, enunciated/enunciation, involve an endorsement of the linguistic conception of the "I"?

Let us return to the passage quoted from *The Interpretation of Dreams*. After considering the multiple representation of the ego in the dream, Freud tries to reduce the apparent strangeness of this process by comparing it to phenomena from waking thought:

The fact that the dreamer's own ego appears several times, or in several forms, in a dream is at bottom no more remarkable than the fact that the ego should occur at various times, in different places and in other contexts in a conscious thought, for instance, in the sentence, "When *I* think of what a healthy child *I* was."[15]

The example, however, hardly demonstrates what it is supposed to, since in fact there would be nothing "remarkable" about sentences an ego could consciously *remember* – or more exactly, could pronounce at will. The unconscious "I" of the dreamer, were it ever to stage such a sentence, would certainly have something quite different in mind. The example that would enable us to broach the question of the dreaming "I" cannot be one of a speaker reflexively positing its own identity, since this "I" almost always replaces itself with something else – particularly when it is most immediately concerned. Lacan's formulation of the question takes this into account and thus

[14] Ibid, p. 220.
[15] *Interpretation of Dreams, SE,* IV, p. 323.

comes much closer to what Freud, in *The Interpretation of Dreams*, is trying to articulate:

> It is not a question of knowing whether I speak of myself in a way that conforms to what I am, but rather of knowing whether, when I speak of this, I am the same as the one of whom I am speaking.[16]

Whereas the metaphysical tradition – be it in the philosophy of Husserl, or in the linguistics of Jakobson and Benveniste – has generally considered the "I" to be the sign of a reflexive and self-identical subject, it is precisely this self-identity that Lacan, following Freud, calls into question. Making explicit a question that remains implicit in Freud, Lacan asks:

> Is the place that I occupy as the subject of a signifier concentric or eccentric with respect to the place I occupy as subject of the signified? – that is the question.[17]

The answer for a philosopher such as Husserl is clear: the "I" spoken about acquires its veritable meaning only as an expression of the very same I/ego that is now speaking. Where the continuity of such a relationship can no longer be taken for granted, as is the case in written texts, the meaning of the word "I," is, as Husserl puts it, "alienated": "If we read the word without knowing who wrote it, we have a word that is, if not meaningless, at least alienated from one of its normal meanings."[18] As Derrida demonstrates in his pathbreaking reading of this text,[19] it is no accident that Husserl should choose, as his example of "alienation," a written text, since it is precisely in

---

[16] Il ne s'agit pas de savoir si je parle de moi de façon conforme à ce que je suis, mais si, quand j'en parle, je suis le même que celui dont je parle." Sheridan, p. 165; *Ecrits*, p. 517.

[17] La place que j'occupe comme sujet du signifiant est-elle, par rapport à celle que j'occupe comme sujet du signifié, concentrique ou excentrique? Voilà la question." Sheridan, p. 165.

[18] Husserl, *Logical Investigations*, p. 82.

[19] Jacques Derrida, *Speech and Phenomena* trans. David B. Allison, Evanston: Northwestern University Press, 1973. Derrida demonstrates how Husserl is compelled here to contradict his own position concerning the ideality of meaning. For Husserl's "ideality" demands that a meaning be independent of any actual or possible intuition of an object. The example of a written I, cut off from its authorial referent, would therefore have to be considered not "abnormal," but the normative case of ideality. Derrida's conclusion: "My death is structurally necessary to the utterance, 'I.'" p. 96. (Translation slightly modified.)

writing that the presence of the author is least assured. And yet this is no less the case in dreams: for if the dreamer articulates something, he does so not as a speaker, but instead as a scribe. Speech, we recall, provides the dreamwork only with its raw materials, as it were. And if the term, "dreamer," suggests a certain *activity*, that of *scribe* – as distinct from "writer," much less "author" – denotes an operation that cannot be easily accommodated by the alternative, active/passive. The subject of the dream "receives" the dream the way a scribe receives the text to be inscribed. To "have" a dream is to "open" oneself to impulses which cannot be controlled consciously or voluntarily. It entails an "active passivity," the readiness to receive and to retain, but also to follow.

What Husserl therefore describes as an anomaly in the functioning of the "I" is recognized by Freud as that which constitutes the norm. This "norm," then – a word, to be sure, that Freud rarely employs, – entails a certain relation, not to self, but to the other, an alterity that Lacan will variously describe as that of the signifier, of enunciation, or of the unconscious. The instance that sums up the effects of such alterity is what Lacan calls the "subject": it is defined, quite literally, by being *subject to the other*.

While structural linguistics defines the "I" as a shifter, Lacan demonstrates how this shifting extends far beyond the limits imposed on it by a linguistics still under the sway of metaphysics. If, as Benveniste writes, the "I" has "no reference other . . . than the actuality of discourse,"[20] then such "actuality," we must conclude, extends beyond the present moment of discourse – and thereby also beyond the "I": at the same time, in so extending, it also reaches *back* to what comes "before." Let us attempt to retrace the contours of this divided movement. To do so we will have to make a short detour, by way of Freud's definition of the "ego"; more precisely, we shall reconsider a particular aspect of this definition.

This aspect could be called "the linguistic condition of the ego." For it is nothing but language, or more exactly, a particular function of language, that permits the ego to constitute itself, at least insofar as the ego harbors what Freud

[20] *Problèmes*, p. 262.

describes as preconscious and conscious thought. To be sure, the ego cannot be simply identified with such thought; but it is its psychical "home," as it were. The role of language in the constitution of the ego becomes clear when Freud explains how it is possible for something to be admitted to consciousness, or more specifically, how it enters the preconscious. The problem is dealt with at length in his study of "The Unconscious." In that text, Freud seems to have a sudden insight, which leads him to modify his earlier, topological view of the "double inscription" held to be characteristic of the unconscious:

> It strikes us all at once that we now know what the difference is between a conscious and an unconscious representation. The two are not, as we supposed, different inscriptions of the same content in different psychical localities, nor yet different functional states of cathexis in the same locality; but the conscious representation comprises the thing-representation [*Sachvorstellung*], plus the corresponding word-representation, the unconscious one consists in the thing-representation alone. The system Ucs contains the thing-cathexes of the objects, the first and authentic object-cathexes; the system Pcs originates in a hypercathexis of this thing-representation, linking it to the word-representations that correspond to it. [. . .] We can now also formulate precisely what it is that repression denies to the rejected representation in transference neurosis: translation into words capable of remaining attached to the object. The non-verbalized representation, or the non-cathected act, then remains repressed in the Ucs.[21]

It might seem at first that for Freud, as in the Gospel of St. John, "In the beginning was the Word," and that consequently, language begins with the word and belongs exclusively to the system, preconscious-consciousness, while the unconscious, by contrast, is concerned only with images of objects. And yet, as the discussion of "considerations of representability" already has suggested, what the unconscious involves is not just different from such objects and images, but in fact radically distinguished from them. Perceptual identities, which may be equated with what Freud refers to here as "thing-representations," and which provide the unconscious, primary process with its privileged *material*, become signifiers through the processes of condensation and displacement; word-

---

[21] S. Freud, "The unconscious," *SE*, XIV, pp. 201–202.

representations too are subjected to the same transformation, insofar as they undergo the elaborations of the primary process. An example, not from dreams this time, is furnished by a case of schizophrenia:

> Now it is in this respect that the essential difference between the dreamwork and schizophrenia becomes clear. In the latter, what becomes the subject of modification by the primary process are the words themselves in which the preconscious thought was expressed; in dreams, what are subject to this modification are not the words, but the thing-presentations to which the words have been retraced.[22]

Whether or not the difference singled out by Freud here suffices to distinguish dream and psychosis is dubious, since, as he himself acknowledges in *The Interpretation of Dreams*, it is entirely characteristic of the dream to submit words to distortion and transformation through the primary process: one need only recall the dream in which "the vividly remembered word *Autodidasker*" plays such an important role.[23] More significant, however, in Freud's description is the implication that what determines whether or not a representation is admissible to consciousness or not is its *translatability*. In the sense that Freud gives to the term here, this means the ability to translate a signifier into *the signified that belongs to it*. It is this notion of "belonging," of *Zugehörigkeit* or of *Entsprechung*, that defines admissibility to consciousness, and hence, consciousness itself. And this in turn is tantamount to privileging the "word," at least as it is traditionally understood – namely, as a unity of signified and signifier – as the basic unit of language. The language of consciousness is thus defined as that of verbal discourse, in this sense. In the word, so understood, the movement of signification proceeds from the signified, as its beginning, traverses the signifier, as its middle – and manifestation – and comes full circle, ending again in the signified.

In Lacanian terms, the movement of the signifier through displacement and condensation – through metonymy and metaphor – is thereby brought to a standstill; unstable, unconscious cathexes are *arrested*, psychic energy is *bound up* or

[22] S. Freud, "Metapsychological supplement to the theory of dreams," *SE*, XIV, p. 229.
[23] *Interpretation*, *SE*, IV, p. 299.

"cathected" to a signified; and the principle of identity asserts itself – asserting as well the identity of the ego. That identity is based on the signified, for it is the signified that marks the arresting of signification – the movement of signifiers – and makes possible a repetition or fixation of the same. This repetition of the same authorizes the formation of the apparent identity of the two "I's" in Freud's phrase, "When *I* think of what a healthy child *I* was." The form of this identity is based, as we have seen, on the unity of the "I" as a word, having a fixed, albeit formal, meaning. In the history of Western thought, this form appears most clearly in the Cartesian *cogito ergo sum*.

"The philosophical cogito," Lacan writes, "is at the center of the mirage that renders modern man so sure of being himself even in his uncertainties about himself."[24] Why a mirage? Because the cogito construes the subject in terms of the signified, rather than as an effect of the signifier. In one of his most important essays, "The subversion of the subject and the dialectic of desire," Lacan makes this clear with unusual directness:

The promotion of consciousness, in the historical aftermath of the Cartesian *cogito*, to the essence of the subject, signifies for us [both] the deceptive accentuation of the transparency of the I in action, at the expense of the opacity of the signifier that determines it, and the slippage through which the *Bewußtsein* serves to cover up the confusion of the *Selbst* (. . .)[25]

Insofar as language is defined as a system of articulation governed by the play of signifiers, a subject constituted through this play can never be reduced to the reflexive identity and transparency generally associated with the ego. Instead, it must go the way of the "I" construed as a shifter, or, we could add, as a drifter, whose only "home" is the rails of the signifying train (or the metonymic chain). What deranges in this re-inscription of the subject is that its destiny is no longer simply to follow the

---

[24] "Il n'en reste pas moins que le *cogito* philosophique est au foyer de ce mirage qui rend l'homme moderne si sûr d'être soi dans ses incertitudes sur lui-même . . ." Sheridan, p. 165; *Ecrits*, p. 517.

[25] "La promotion de la conscience comme essentielle au sujet dans la sequelle historique du *cogito* cartésien, est pour nous l'accentuation trompeuse de la transparence du Je en acte aux dépens de l'opacité du signifiant qui le détermine, et le glissement par quoi le *Bewußtsein* sert à couvrir la confusion du *Selbst* [. . .]" Sheridan, p. 307; *Ecrits*, p. 809.

rails of the signifier, but rather to be *derailed*. The differential nature of the signifier thereby affects the metonymic movement itself: it does not merely carry the subject somewhere else, but rather locates the subject in a place where it can never arrive. The signifying structure of the subject assumes value only through its position relative to others, within the chain, but also without. The place of the subject thereby becomes impossible to demarcate fully, since it is always "there where I am not, because I cannot situate myself there," as Lacan puts it.[26] One can even go so far as to say that the subject, in the Lacanian perspective, *determines itself* in and as this impossibility. The latter, translated into an image, is called: *fader*. The subject only appears, insofar as it *fades*. The emergence of the subject *is* its *fading*.[27] Lacan describes this movement in the following way: "I am not, wherever I am the plaything of my thought; I think of what I am, wherever I do not think [that I am] thinking."[28]

Not to think that one is thinking, is to think of what one is. Or rather, of what the "I" is: a mode of thought, that, far from attaining self-reflexivity, is determined precisely by its destiny of not thinking that it thinks. A form of thought that is not self-identical, that only thinks of itself when it is not thinking that it is thinking, this way of thinking is incompatible with self-consciousness. Rather, it is the thought-process of the unconscious, the unconscious *as* a mode of thought, albeit one whose essence consists in "the radical eccentricity of the self to itself." Put in general terms, "the truth discovered by Freud" can be said to be the truth of a "radical heteronomy."[29]

Perhaps it is possible to indicate the location, or – for it amounts to the same – the dislocation of the subject by examining a particularly telling anecdote recounted and ana-

[26] Sheridan, p. 166; *Ecrits*, p. 517.

[27] Lacan's notion of "truth," here, seems close to that of Heidegger, as, for instance, it is discussed in the essay on "The origin of the work of art," namely as "the dispute of clearing and concealing" (*als der Urstreit von Lichtung und Verbergung*). M. Heidegger, *Der Ursprung des Kunstwerks*, Stuttgart: Reclam, 1967, p. 60. The Heideggerian motif of the *rift* (*Riß*), could be compared to the Lacanian notion of *la béance*, the gap, gash or gaping hole that opens and traverses the "symbolic."

[28] "Je ne suis pas, là où je suis le jouet de ma pensée; je pense à ce que je suis, là où je ne pense pas penser." Sheridan, p. 166; *Ecrits*, p. 517–518.

[29] "L'excentricité radicale de soi à lui-même à quoi l'homme est affronté, autrement dit la vérité découverte par Freud [...] l'hétéronomie radicale [...]." Sheridan, pp. 171–172; Ecrits, p. 524.

lyzed by Freud. The example I have in mind involves "the forgetting of proper names," the case of "Signorelli." It was first discussed in print by Freud in 1898, in "On the psychical mechanism of forgetfulness," and was later included, in modified form, in *The Psychopathology of Everyday Life*, published in 1904. Because of the extremely complex nature of the story, I prefer not to try to summarize it, but rather to quote Freud's account of it at length:

During my summer holidays, I once took a carriage-drive from the lovely city of Ragusa to a town nearby in Herzegovina. Conversation with my companion centered, as was natural, upon the condition of the two countries (Bosnia and Herzegovina) and upon the character of their inhabitants. I talked about the various peculiarities of the Turks living there, as I had heard them described years before by a friend and colleague who had lived among them for many years as a doctor. A little later, our conversation turned to the subject of Italy and to painting, and I had occasion to recommend strongly that my companion visit Orvieto some time, in order to see the frescoes of the end of the world and of the Last Judgment, with which a great artist had decorated one of the chapels in the cathedral there. But the artist's name escaped me and was not to be recalled. I exerted my powers of recollection, let all the details of the day I had spent in Orvieto pass through my memory, and convinced myself that not the smallest part of it had been obliterated or become indistinct. On the contrary, I was able to conjure up the paintings more vividly than is usual for me. I saw the artist's self-portrait before my eyes, with unusual clarity: a serious face and folded hands – which he has put in a corner of one of the pictures, next to the portrait of his predecessor in the work, Fra Angelico da Fiesole; but the artist's name, ordinarily so familiar to me, remained obstinately in hiding, nor could my travelling companion help me out. My continued efforts met with no success, beyond bringing up the names of two other artists, which I knew could not be the right ones: *Botticelli* and, in the second place, *Boltraffio*.[30]

It is only much later that Freud is able to recall the forgotten name, and only then with the help of a

cultivated Italian who freed me from it by telling me the name: *Signorelli*. I was myself able to add the artist's first name, *Luca*. Soon my extra sharp memory of the master's features, as depicted in his portrait, faded away.[31]

---

[30] "On the psychical mechanism of forgetfulness," *SE*, III, pp. 290–291.
[31] Ibid., p. 291.

Let us review the situation: the name that Freud is trying to recall has been forgotten, repressed; in its place, paintings by the repressed artist appear with a visual intensity that is highly unusual for Freud's memory. Even the self-portrait of the painter appears with extraordinary clarity. And finally, the names of two other painters of the Italian Renaissance, Botticelli, and the lesser-known Boltraffio, appear in place of the forgotten name. Yet as soon as Freud is told the name, Signorelli, "the extra sharp memory of the master's features, as depicted in his portrait, faded away." We discover here both the result of a regression from word-representations to thing-representations, occasioned by the repression of a proper name, "Signorelli," and the effect of the primary process – namely displacement and condensation; these operations increase the intensity of the remembered picture far beyond what might otherwise be expected. As soon as the thing-representation is reunited with the word-representation, the intensity diminishes. And yet perhaps most importantly, the mental image does not function as a mere reproduction of the original picture, but rather as a significant nodal point at which various metonymic chains converge. Its role as a signifier is apparent in Freud's explanation. Viewed as a process of repression, forgetting cannot be explained in terms of any kind of "immanent" meaning that the forgotten information might contain, since it is not the picture that Freud forgets – far from it – but rather the name of the painter. Forgetting, here, can be explained only by considering the particular significance, the contextual value [*Stellenwert*] of the name within the context of the conversation leading up to it:

Shortly before I asked my travelling companion if he had been in Orvieto, we had been discussing the customs of the Turks living in *Bosnia* and *Herzegovina*. I had related what I heard from a colleague who was practicing medicine among them, namely that they show full confidence in the physician and complete submission to fate. When one is compelled to inform them that there is no help for the patient, they answer: "Sir [*Herr*], what is there to say? I know that if he could be saved, you would save him." It is only in these sentences that we find the words and names *Bosnia*, *Herzegovina* and *Herr* which can be inserted in the series of associations between *Signorelli* and *Botticelli* – *Boltraffio*.[32]

[32] S. Freud, *The Psychopathology of Everyday Life*, SE, VI, p. 3.

Freud thereby uncovers the linguistic material that the process of repression works on, but we still do not know the motivation for the repression. Why "Signorelli"?

I recall that I wished to relate a second anecdote which was close to the first in my memory. These Turks value sexual pleasure above all else, and upon encountering sexual disturbances, fall into utter despair, one which contrasts strangely with their resignation when faced with the danger of losing their lives. One of my colleague's patients once told him: "For you know, sir [*Herr*], if *that* doesn't work any more, life is no longer worth living."[33]

Freud suppresses this anecdote not only because he does not dare speak about such delicate matters with a stranger, but also because he himself is particularly preoccupied with the problem of sex and death at this time.

I was at that time under the after-effects of a message I had received a few weeks before, during a brief sojourn in *Trafoi*. A patient on whom I had spent much effort, had ended his life on account of an incurable sexual disturbance. I know positively that this melancholy event, and everything connected with it, did not come to my conscious recollection on that trip in Herzegovina. However, the similarity between Trafoi and Boltraffio forces me to assume that this reminiscence was at that time activated, despite the deliberate distraction of my attention.[34]

Freud thus draws the conclusion that his forgetting was not only motivated, but that the forgotten material itself was significant only in view of its symbolic function:

I wanted to forget something, *I had repressed* something. To be sure, I wished to forget something other than the name of the master of Orvieto; but this other thought produced an associative connection between itself and this name, so that my act of volition missed its goal, and I forgot *the one against my will*, whereas what I *intentionally* wished to do was *to forget the other*. The disinclination to recall directed itself against the one content, the inability to remember appeared in another.[35]

This story contains two moments which are of particular interest here: first, it shows how the mechanism of repression works as a metonymic–metaphoric movement; and second, in

[33] Ibid.
[34] Ibid., pp. 3–4.
[35] Ibid., p. 4.

so doing, it articulates the structure and motivation of repression. In order to explicate these processes further, let us refer to the diagram used by Freud, on which he comments in the following manner:

The name *Signorelli* has undergone a division into two pieces. One of the pairs of syllables (*elli*), recurs without alteration in one of the substitute names, while the other, by means of the translation of *Signor* into *Herr*, has acquired numerous and diverse relations to the names contained in the repressed theme, but for this very reason is lost to [conscious] reproduction. Its substitute has been arrived at in a way that suggests that a displacement along the connected names of "*Herzegovina* and *Bosnia*" had taken place, without considering the sense or acoustic demarcation of the syllables. Thus, the names have been treated in this process like pictograms of a sentence that is to be transformed into a picture-puzzle (or rebus). Of the whole course of events that have in ways like these produced the substitute names instead of the name *Signorelli*, no information has been given to consciousness. Any relation between the theme in which the name *Signorelli* occurred, and the theme, the repression of which must have chronologically preceded it – any such relation, other than that consisting in the mere recurrence of syllables (or rather of sequences of letters), seems at first to be impossible to find.[36]

Freud's diagram of the incident is shown in Figure I:[37]

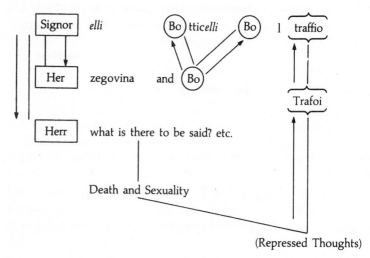

Figure I

[36] Ibid., pp. 4–5.   [37] Ibid., p. 5.

Before turning our attention to the apparent absence of a thematic connection between Signorelli and the motifs of sex and death that led to the repression, let us first consider the movement and structure of signification operating here. As Lacan remarks in his seminar on the "Formations of the unconscious," the properly metaphorical dimension here is the absence of the signifier, "Signorelli," in the manifest and conscious chain, and the substitution of "Botticelli" and "Boltraffio" for it. An effect of sense is produced here; yet the signifier that falls out as a signified, still functions as a signifier, although in relation to the substitute formations that replace it, it has now become a signified. As a signifier, "Signorelli" is over-determined in at least three ways: first, as a translation of "Signor" into "Herr," it refers to Her-zegovina and to "Herr" ("what is there to say," and "Herr, if that doesn't work anymore . . ."); second, as the name of the painter of the "Three Last Things," it refers to the Day of Judgment; third, it signifies the instance to which the statement is addressed, the addressee. Other significant moments, such as the painter's narcissistic relation both to his image and to his predecessors, might also be mentioned. Even though these relationships do not appear in the manifest chain, they may still be considered as being metonymic in nature, since they are less dependent upon a fixed meaning than upon a movement of signification. *Botticelli* and *Bol*traffio refer to *Bos*nia, and Bol*traffio*'s connection to *Trafoi*, like Botti*celli*'s to Signor*elli*, may also be described as metonymic. The names acquire signification as *vehicles of repetition and recurrence*, and this function is effective even if there is no connection between the signifiers and the "proper" meaning of their vehicles.

Let us now turn from the metonymic–metaphoric movement of the signifier to the problem of repression and of its motivation. This in turn again returns us to our former question, namely: what is the place of the subject in this process? When Freud writes, "*I* thus wanted to forget something, something *I* had repressed," who is this "I" and where is it located with respect to the movement of signification? It would be beyond the scope of our investigation to attempt an exhaustive response to this question – if one can be envisaged at all; I will therefore refer the reader to an article by Anthony Wilden, the English translator of Lacan's Rome discourse, that examines the matter in great detail.[38] Nevertheless, what should already be clear is that the strength of the so-called "death and sex" motifs, and the effect of the news Freud receives in Trafoi and his patient's suicide, are intelligible only in a context that is organized "in terms of the structures of infantile sexuality" (this holds not only for the case at hand, but also for dreams and in fact for all expressions of the unconscious). Neither any conscious concern about the issues of "death" and "sexuality," nor even the shock of the patient's suicide, can suffice to account for the strength of the repression; only when these factors are reinforced by the phantasies of infantile sexuality, reported by Freud in the context of his "self-analysis," can they elicit such a vigorous response. The signifier, "Herr," refers both to the role of the father, and to the problem of the Oedipus complex (sexuality and death). If one now asks where the subject Freud is in all of this, the answer, as in the dream, is quite simply, *everywhere*: the *Herr*, both as the physician and as the Creator who depicts himself in his work; the follower, who portrays (ambivalently) his predecessors – i.e. his own "Herren" – in his work; but also in the heart [*Herz*], since Freud is concerned at this time about a heart ailment. *Everywhere*, and yet also: *nowhere*, i.e. in no single place, for everywhere here is an *alibi, since it signifies elsewhere*:

On one occasion (. . .) when I was meaning to describe the same small incident to a colleague of mine, the name of my authority for the stories about Bosnia suddenly escaped me. The reason for this was as follows. Just before, I had been playing cards. My [Bosnian] authority was called Pik. Now "Pik" and "Herz" ["Spades" and "Hearts"] are two of the four suits in the deck. Moreover the two words were connected by an anecdote in which this same person pointed to himself and said: "I'm not called 'Herz,' but 'Pik.' "Herz" appears in the name "Herzegovina," and the heart itself, as a sick bodily organ, played a part in the thoughts I have described as having been repressed.[39]

"I'm not called *Herz*, but *Pik*": what better description could there be of the place of the "I" in the metonymic chain of signifiers; that is, the movement of signification does not come to an end with hearts and spades, but instead is effectively continued by them. At the same time, the relation of the "I" – as

[38] Anthony Wilden, "The repression of the signifier," *American Imago*, 23/IV (1966), pp. 322–366.
[39] "The psychic mechanism of forgetfulness," *SE*, III, p. 296 note.

instance of identity in the subject – to the calling of a proper name is also manifest: the Ego is the signifier that would call itself by its proper name, if such were possible.[40] But such "property" is always caught up in the web of language, in which a name can only signify – that is, name – by demarcating itself from other, improper names. Not *Herz*, but *Pik*; not the innermost organ of body, symbol of the soul, but an instrument that *punctures*: this is a true, and truly improper name, for the ego.

Through this reading of Freud, one can gain a sense of what Lacan calls "the radical eccentricity of the self to itself," of the "radical heteronymy" that betrays its heritage. We also see that if Freud describes the unconscious as the "core of our Being," at its *heart* what we find is a pick and a *pike*, which do not just puncture, but also punctuate. At the heart of the subject is a certain *punctuation*. As such, it can never in and of itself constitute "an object of cognition,"[41] since it consists in the interruption and suspension of beings, rather than in their codification. Such were the aberrations and slips that drew Freud's attention to dreams, symptoms, jokes, and parapraxes, none of which is consciously controlled or intended. Which is why the subject of the unconscious is not the author or proprietor of "its" language, but rather, the bearer of a name that is never entirely proper, never quite a proper fit. A remark of Lacan's about neurosis could be extended to the unconscious in general:

It does not pose (the question) *before* the subject (. . .) but *in place of it* (*à la place du sujet*), i.e. it poses it in this place *with* the subject, as one poses a problem *with* a pen . . .[42]

The question *of* the subject thus becomes a question in (the) stead of the subject, which is neither the author nor the object

---

[40] The game of cards, here, becomes a game of naming, which in Lacanian terms involves, ultimately, the "name of the father." Since the name of the father must be able to function in the radical absence of the named – "death and sexuality," in Freud's words – it is hardly accidental that the only suit suitable to name the "I" is: *spades*.

[41] Sheridan, p. 174; *Ecrits*, p. 526.

[42] "Il ne la pose pas *devant* le sujet puisque le sujet ne peut venir à la place où il la pose, mais il la pose *à la place* du sujet, c'est-à-dire qu'à cette place il pose la question *avec* le sujet, comme on pose un problème *avec* une plume et comme l'homme antique pensait *avec* son âme." Sheridan, p. 168, *Ecrits*, p. 520.

of the question, but its vehicle, or more precisely: its stylus. The apparently generic name, "subject," and the ostensibly "proper" pronoun, "I," thereby emerge as punctuation marks, with all the depth of a pack of cards. Saussure's chess game has shifted to a game of cards. Between hearts and spades, however, the stakes have become slightly clearer.

❖❖

7

The subject as "fader": the imaginary and the symbolic

❖❖

The polemical moment, the attack and parry style of distinguishing one's own position that is so characteristic of Freud, plays an even more decisive role in the evolution of Lacan's thinking. Almost from its inception, Lacan's "return" to Freud is polemically aimed at the psychoanalytic establishment.[1] Many issues are at stake in Lacan's controversy with mainstream psychoanalysis, especially as institutionalized in the International Psychoanalytical Association: the length of the psychoanalytic session and the training of analysts being those explicitly mentioned by the IPA in excluding him from its ranks. But from a theoretical point of view, the decisive difference that separates Lacan from the conceptions predominant in the IPA involves the concept of the subject implied in the Freudian notion of the unconscious. Looking back upon the development of his thought, Lacan demonstrates his awareness of the importance of "strategic" factors, and in particular, as they relate to this question:

I shall not return here to the function of my "mirror stage," that first strategic point that I developed in opposition to the favor accorded in psychoanalytic theory to the supposedly autonomous ego. The academic restoration of this *"autonomous ego"* justified my view that a misunderstanding was involved in any attempt to strengthen the ego in a type of analysis that took as its criterion of "success" a successful adaptation to society – a phenomenon of intellectual abdication that was bound up with the aging of the psychoanalytic group in the

---

[1] On the history of Lacan's relationship to the International Psychoanalytical Association, see the *Dossier on the Institutional debate*, trans. Jeffrey Mehlman, *October* 40 (Spring, 1987), 51–81, and *La scission de 1953*, supplement to *Ornicar?*, no. 7, edited by Jacques-Alain Miller, with a note by Lacan, Paris: 1976. Cf. also Elisabeth Roudinesco, *L'histoire de la psychanalyse en France*, vol. II, Seuil: Paris, 1986.

diaspora of the war, and the reduction of a distinguished practice to a label suitable for exploiting the "American way of life."[2]

Such lines make it clear that polemics are indispensable to Lacan not only as a strategy directed against opponents, but also as a constitutent of his thought. In its incipient stages, that thought is characterized by a series of oppositions, designed to invert prevailing conceptual and axiological hierarchies: subject of the signifier, *and not* of the signified; subject of enunciation *and not* of the *énoncé*; subject of the unconscious *and not* the ego of self-consciousness. Only in this light does Lacan's insistence upon the philosophical category of the *subject* – despite its dismissal in the thought of Heidegger, with which Lacan was well acquainted[3] – become understandable; his aim is to disorient and transform the received ideas of psychoanalytic orthodoxy, and the notion of "subject" provides an alternative to that of the "self" so highly accredited by that orthodoxy, although the word, not accidentally, is rarely to be found in the writings of Freud.

If after the previous chapters we are better prepared to follow the Lacanian conception of the subject through a new conceptual opposition, we should not forget that Lacan's language must itself be understood in the context of the theory it elaborates, that of the signifier. Lacan's discourse is, not surprisingly, itself a signifying practice, which means that the terms inscribed in it function less as traditional concepts, than as ciphers in a dream. We recall how the dream's pictorial writing acquires meaning through the position the dream-elements occupy in relation to one another, and not through the particular content they appear to depict.

Lacan's own language must be read in this light: "Our statements [*énoncés*] are designed primarily for a function that

---

[2] "Nous ne reprendrons pas ici la fonction de notre 'stade du miroir,' point stratégique premier dressé par nous en objection à la faveur accordée dans la théorie au prétendu *moi autonome*, dont la restauration académique justifiait le contresens proposé de son renforcement dans une cure désormais déviée vers un succès adaptatif; phénomène d'abdication mentale, lié au vieillissement du groupe dans la diaspora de la guerre, et réduction d'une pratique éminente à un label propre à l'exploitation de l'*American way of life*." *Ecrits*, pp. 808–809; Sheridan, p. 306–207.

[3] Lacan translated Heidegger's essay, "Logos," in the first number of the journal he edited, *La Psychanalyse*, 1, 1956.

they perform only in their place."[4] Inasmuch as it is subject to the signifier, however, this place can be determined only by means of an *alibi*, since it can only *take place* by taking the place of another, for which it then stands and fills in. Such a place can never be definitively located, which is why the *place* of a signifying element is always the dissimulated place of another and hence its alibi.

In returning to the mirror-stage, then, it should come as no

---

[4] "Nos énoncés sont faits premièrement pour la fonction qu'ils ne *remplissent* qu'à leur place." *Ecrits*, p. 834. Lacan's theory of *enunciation*, which is proposed in his discourse explicitly, that is, as statement, as *énoncé*, can hardly fail to have consequences for its own mode of articulation. Where, one might ask, is the proper place of a "statement"? That Lacan himself is quite aware of this aspect of his thought, is indicated a few lines before the passage just cited: "Psychoanalysts themselves comprise part of the concept of the unconscious, since they constitute its addressee. We cannot therefore avoid including our own discourse on the unconscious in the thesis it enunciates, namely that, insofar as it is situated in the place of the other, the unconscious must be sought in all discourse, in its enunciation." ("les psychanalystes font partie du concept de l'inconscient, puisqu'ils en constituent l'adresse. Nous ne pouvons dès lors ne pas inclure notre discours sur l'inconscient dans la thèse même qu'il énonce, que la présence de l'inconscient, pour se situer au lieu de l'Autre, est à chercher en tout discours, en son énonciation.") For the reading of Lacan's writings – whether in the *Ecrits* or elsewhere – certain consequences result from this, including the following: first, such writings call for a *reading*, in the strong sense of the word. Notwithstanding the calculated play with oral rhetoric in the *Ecrits*, Lacan's utterances are eminently *textual* in character. Not, to be sure, in the sense of an opposition to oral delivery, but rather in distinction from that language of statement and of proposition, of *énoncé* and of the signified, that it is incessantly at work to deflect and derail. Thus, if one can speak of a priority of enunciation over enunciated in Lacan's writing, it is because it does not merely utter statements, but also de-scribes the movement of what it says, i.e. inscribes its statements in its movement. This description determines and localizes itself as writing: in Freud's analysis of the pictography of the dream no less than in Lacan's determination of the letter as localization of the signifier. Whatever divergences separate Lacan's emphasis on *parole*, truth and what Lacoue-Labarthe and Nancy have called his "negative ontology," (*Le titre de la lettre*, p. 131) from Derrida's foregrounding of writing, the motifs of utterance and of the signifier retain considerable deconstructive force. The latter does not stop short of the notion of *text* itself. What in Lacan's writings takes the place of *textuality*, is *theatricality*, and in this respect, it anticipates Derrida's own "pragrammatological turn": each utterance localized in the text, "in its place," is determined, post facto as it were – and in this, very much like the dream – by addressees that it did not necessarily intend. The most explicit model for this is undoubtedly to be found in Freud's analysis of the function of the "third person," upon which the joke depends, and which endows it with its social character. It is perhaps this that Lacan, in the wake of Freud, but also of Heidegger, anticipates most clearly: *a form of address not governed by (conscious) intentionality.* This is the indelible, if inaccessible place of the other in the theater of the unconscious.

shock that we do not go back to the *same place*: to the immutable *topos* of an unaltered text, but rather to another place and to other texts, even if they appear under the same title. "The mirror stage," Lacan observes in retrospect, "situates the line dividing the imaginary and the symbolic at that moment in which [the subject] is seized by an historic inertia (. . .)."[5] As we will see, this claim only holds, if we read the "original" text in terms of what "it will have been": that is to say, in relation to two later essays which supplement the earlier one in important ways. These two texts are, first, an essay written in 1958 in response to a paper by the French analyst, Daniel Lagache, and entitled, "Psychoanalysis and the structure of personality"; and second, a note, giving a brief sketch of Lacan's intellectual genealogy: "On our antecedents," written in 1966. Revisited in this perspective, the text of the mirror-stage provides us – at least implicitly – with a preliminary account of what Lacan will subsequently call the "imaginary."

The elements that make up this account, such as the mirror-image, cannot be considered in isolation, as though they were intrinsically meaningful. Rather, they can be understood only within a process of representation that necessarily misrepresents itself, and in so doing produces a semblance of autonomy. Yet, in what sense can the mirror stage be said to describe a process of representation? The child, between the age of six and eighteen months, as a subject-in-the-making, recognizes itself in the Gestalt of its mirror image. At a time when motoric control of its body is still inadequate, the child's powers of perception are already able to grasp *Gestalten*, coherent images that compose a whole. The child's discovery of its reflection provides it with a model for all future feelings of identity. Such an image exemplifies an instance that strives to stay the same no matter how much it may change; it appears as enduring, substantial and solid. This instance in which the subject seems to be unified, transparent and identical with itself, develops into the ego; that is, it develops into the subject of self-consciousness – a being that strives to be present in, for and to itself. This

---

[5] "Le stade du miroir donne la règle de partage entre l'imaginaire et le symbolique à ce moment de capture par une inertie historique dont tout ce qui s'autorise d'être psychologie porte la charge, fût-ce par des voies à prétendre s'en dégager." *Ecrits*, p. 69.

in-for-and-to-itself, this self-identical, unified and self-present subject, is thus the effect of a particular mode of representation: that of its own (or of a similar) body, perceived and introjected as a Gestalt that will provide the matrix for all future presence and identity.

Yet – and this is what makes all the difference in Lacan's theory – the process of projective identification with an image, that is: with something other, something external, with something that appears to be similar or subtly different (the mirror-image symmetrically inverts whatever it reproduces) – this process remains a constitutive force and factor in the ego that develops from it. Thus, although the ego may claim to be self-identical, although it may strive to subordinate and to appropriate heterogeneity as *its* other, it is in fact in constant rivalry with itself and with everything else; aggressive tension is fundamental to it. The autonomy of the ego, conceived as an instance of consciousness, of reality, of perception, or of all of these at once, is constituted only through a misconstruing [*Verkennung*] and denial [*Verleugnung*] of its structural dependence on others.[6]

The misconstruing we are dealing with here can be neither avoided nor reduced to an instance of false consciousness. The structure of consciousness is not merely misrepresented by the ego, in order then to be all the better comprehended by it, in accordance with a dialectical model of absolute knowledge. This movement would be possible only if the ego actually were what it claims to be: self-identical. Only then could it hope to know and recognize itself. Yet if the ego always has and will have been another, all such attempts to "come into its own," must inevitably entail misconception and disavowal.

Having thus touched on the structural necessity of this misconception, let us now turn to its real basis. Lacan's description of the latter is reminiscent of Aristotle's polemic

[6] "Au principe des véritables résistances à quoi on a à faire dans les dédales de ce qui fleurit de théoretique sur le Moi dans la psychanalyse, il y a le simple refus d'admettre que le Moi y soit en droit ce qu'il s'avère être dans l'expérience: une fonction de méconnaissance." *Ecrits*, p. 668. ("At the origin of the veritable resistances with which one is confronted in the labyrinthian excesses of psychoanalytical ego-theory, stands the simple refusal to acknowledge that the I, considered theoretically, is nothing other than what it turns out to be in experience: a function of misapprehension.")

ridiculing the inconsistency of the Sophists,[7] who, when all is said and done, still prefer not to jump into an abyss first thing in the morning. In his "Remarks on the paper given by Daniel Lagache," in which Lacan discusses at length the significance of the ego in Freud's second topology, Lacan describes the resistances that any critical understanding and theory of the ego – namely as a function of misrepresentation – would inevitably evoke:

> Such resistance is nourished by the fact that it is certainly indispensable to know something of reality in order to survive in it, and that practical evidence shows us that experience accumulated in the ego, and particularly in the preconscious, provides us with the surest bearings for getting around in this reality. Yet one thereby forgets – and it is all the more surprising that it is psychoanalysts who forget – that this argument breaks down when it is a question . . . of the effects of the unconscious. Moreover, the sphere of influence of these effects extends to the ego itself: it was precisely to affirm this that Freud introduced his theory of the relations of the ego to the id. Its purpose was thus to extend the field of our ignorance, not of our knowledge . . . [8]

The pragmatic demands of self-preservation thus require a perceptible reality, that is, one that may be identified with itself, assumed to be present and coherent, in order, in its turn, to permit the self-preserving subject to identify with itself, and to identify that Self as a unified and identical ego. What is most important, however, about this subject of self-preservation is that it can be constituted only on the basis of a particular structure, or more precisely, of a particular representation. Subject and object, ego and reality, self and other, all presuppose a form and a matrix of presence in which representation is conceived as the copy of an original [*Abbild eines Urbildes*], as the sign of referent, the signifier of a signified. It is this very

---

[7] See above, chapter 3.

[8] "Cette résistance s'appuie sur le fait qu'il faut bien que nous connaissions quelque chose à la réalité pour y subsister, et qu'il est d'évidence pratique que l'expérience accumulée dans le Moi, spécialement dans le Préconscient, nous fournit les repères qui s'avèrent les plus sûrs. On y oublie seulement, et ne faut-il pas s'étonner que ce soit des psychanalystes qui l'oublient, que cet argument échoue quand il s'agit . . . des effets de l'Inconscient. Or ces effets étendent leur empire sur le Moi lui-même: c'est même pour l'affirmer expressément que Freud a introduit sa théorie des rapports du Moi au Ça: c'est donc pour étendre le champ de notre ignorance, non de notre savoir [. . .]." *Ecrits*, p. 668.

interpretation of representation and the notion of the subject that results from it that Lacan addresses in his theory of the mirror stage. In so doing, he attempts to point out both the necessity and the limits of such an interpretation.

According to Lacan, the child's ego is formed:

1. through the child's perception of its own mirror-image, or of that of someone similar.[9]
2. through the recognition that this image represents its own or a similar body.
3. through the projective, "heteropathic" identification with this other as other in order thereby to anticipate that corporeal-motoric identity which the child still lacks.

This account has significant implications for a theory of representation. First and foremost, the logical priority of the "represented" over the "representative," a priority that defines traditional conceptions of representation, is called into question. In the mirror-stage, the representative, the reflected image, in a certain way produces the "represented": the body "proper," conceived as a totality and as the matrix of the ego's identity. However, if a certain image of the body thus produces identity, it at the same time also threatens it. For the perception of one's own body as a whole perpetuates what it dissimulates: the disunity of the subject, which "returns," as it were, in the phantasies of physical dismemberment described so vividly by Melanie Klein.

Insofar, then, as it describes the immutable structure of the ego, the theory of the mirror-stage suggests that the meta-physical interpretation of representation entails a conception of the subject that Lacan calls *narcissistic*. The subject of the signi-fied is, ultimately, the narcissistic ego. As such, it is determined by a form of articulation which dissimulates the play of difference – that is, that of the signifier – in order to prioritize the signified. Lacan will later designate this difference-dissimulating form of articulation as the "imaginary." The imaginary is defined as an order of representation which misrepresents difference as the

---

[9] It is therefore in no way indispensable that the child see its own image in the mirror, in order to traverse the mirror stage. All it needs is to perceive, or recognize, an image as being similar, as, for instance, the image of the mother.

image of identity. One might say that it seeks to impose a ground upon the groundless "reality" of differential articulation. It is an effort that can never fully succeed, but that in missing the mark engenders powerful effects.

To be sure, the notion of reality implied in the imaginary should in no way be confused with Lacan's concept of the "real" (*le réel*), which in turn is derived from Freud's notion of "psychic reality." In Lacan, as also in Peirce, the "real" is defined by its resistance, which includes resistance to representation, including cognition. It is, therefore, in a certain sense at the furthest remove from the imaginary. At the same time, one could with equal justification describe it as residing at the innermost core of the imaginary insofar as the latter is constituted by an ambivalence and a conflict that, precisely, resists imaginary representation, and in so doing goads it on. For the imaginary aims not at the "real," but at a *reality*, which would be its self-contained and autonomous legitimation. Its constitutive incapacity to produce, or rather: to reproduce such a state results in a highly unstable struggle for power. Lacan's analysis of the imaginary corresponds – mutatis mutandis – to Heidegger's account of the "will to will": both are seen as the necessary but ominous culmination of the Western tradition of autonomous and constitutive subjectivity. Like Heidegger, Lacan stresses that the self-dissimulation of the imaginary, however "unreal" it may be, can have very powerful and dangerous consequences.

What distinguishes the imaginary, and constitutes its peculiar "reality," is not dissimulation or estrangement as such, since – as the Heideggerian comparison would suggest – they are inevitable effects of the signifier. What distinguishes the imaginary is that it is estranged from this inevitable estrangement. For the identity it seductively and alluringly promises is not simply unattainable, or structurally aporetic: it denies and dissimulates the repetition to which it is indebted. Which is to say, it denies its debt to the other.

The result of this denial is an antinomical relation to the other. Repressed, rejected and subordinated to identity, the debt of difference returns, as it were, in a dangerous spiral of destructive rivalry. If the ego is formed in the image of a mirror, this still presupposes a minimal but decisive difference between image and "imaged." It is precisely this difference, after all, that endows the image with its fascinating power. To regard it as an image of wholeness is to overlook the frame that delimits its contours, that separates the "figure" not simply from the "ground," as Gestalt-theory would have it, but from the *rest*. But can this rest: everything that remains "outside" the Gestalt, be reduced to a mere "background"? Can one ever be certain where the background stops, where the back hits ground. Lacan's theory of the mirror-stage, which is initially articulated with the aid of Gestalt psychology, thus tends to put the latter very much into question.

It is only by means of identifying with another, even if that other is its "own" mirror-image, that the ego is constituted. Yet to seek to appropriate that other is tantamount to denying the difference that makes it a suitable object of identification in the first place. The imaginary thus becomes a "trap," or a double-bind: the ego can only emerge by binding itself to the other; but for it to fulfill its image of wholeness, as a Gestalt, it is bound to deny the bond that constitutes it. No wonder the ego, as Lacan sees it, is the subject tied up in knots. Its efforts at self-affirmation and preservation tend to undermine the relationship upon which it depends. Far from appropriating the other, qua mirror-image, the ego is thus permanently suspended in denials that are ultimately as threatening to itself as to the other denied. The phenomenon of scapegoating suggests itself as an instance of such a dual threat.

Such narcissistic ambivalence can be discerned in psycho-analysis itself. To define the goal of psychoanalysis as the thera-peutic strengthening of the ego is to place both the practice and the theory of psychoanalysis increasingly under the self-destructive sway of the imaginary. This, Lacan concludes, is the price psychoanalysis has paid for acceptance into the American establishment. Official psychoanalysis has thereby lost touch with the symbolic processes that were at the heart of Freud's discoveries.

Although the "imaginary" order evidently derives from the "image," it would be a mistake to conceive it as constituting a separate realm. For this would be to overlook that whatever coherence and structure may be attributed to the imaginary must in turn be seen in relation to the signifier as the condition of all articulation whatsoever. As Lacan notes in his remarks on Lagache, "structure is defined by, and in turn defines, the signifying articulation as such, [. . .] that is, the effects determined by the pure and simple combinatorics of the signifier in the reality where it manifests itself."[10]

This reference to Saussure can help to emphasize just how different the "reality" in which the signifier "manifests itself" is from its imaginary counterpart. The reality of the imagination situates the imaginary as "mere" representation. "Reality" is thereby construed as a domain that both precedes and outlasts imagination, its origin and end. The reality in which the symbolic shows itself, by contrast, is that of the showing itself, not of the show. In its movement of "manifestation," the signifier is never fully identical with its necessary localization and materialization – that is, with its realization – but is always both "more and less," more and less than itself. In coming forth, the signifier, as we have argued, *falls out*. The signifier "is" the falling-out, the fall-out of "being" with "itself." It thus both exceeds the reality of its manifestation, and at the same time falls short of it. The signifier falls out with itself as it falls into the signified. No signifier without a signified. But the signified is ultimately only the signifier dissimulating its signification. It is through such dissimulation that meaning takes place. The place of meaning, or rather: the *taking-place* of meaning, *is* (the) imaginary. The imaginary halts the fall-out of the signifier. But the halt remains imaginary, for it does not put an end to the falling-out. The imaginary arrests the fall-out of the signifier, but only at the cost of falling-out with itself, or rather: with the Self.

If the arresting images of the imaginary order are effectively inscribed in the force-field of the signifier, the latter would have neither field nor force without the dissimulation by the imaginary. Left to its own devices, the symbolic, like the primary process, would tend to dissolve and to displace the very determinations upon which it "itself" depends. In short: without the imaginary, the symbolic would self-destruct. It is therefore no less dependent on the imaginary than the imaginary is on it, although it is this latter aspect that Lacan chooses to emphasize, almost to the exclusion of the former. The reason for

---

[10] "La structure définie par l'articulation signifiante comme telle [. . .] à savoir les effets que la combinatoire pure et simple du signifiant détermine dans la réalité où elle se produit." *Ecrits*, p. 649.

this one-sided emphasis is above all strategic: it is the signifying function of the symbolic that had to be introduced into psychoanalysis at the time Lacan was writing, whereas the dissimulation of the imaginary was simply identified with reality per se. Nevertheless, to misconstrue their reciprocal relationship would be, ultimately, only to supplant one ethical norm, that of the autonomous, if imaginary ego, with another: the ontological, but no less hypostatized priority of the signifier. By contrast, the imaginary and the symbolic constitute neither an ethical opposition nor an ontological hierarchy, but a differential relationship that disorders each of these "orders," as Lacan often calls them; each order sets itself apart *from* the other, but in so doing reveals its dependency upon the other and thereby sets *itself apart*.[11]

Such mutual interdependence and undoing of the symbolic and imaginary recall the relationship between metonymy and metaphor. If the metonymic movement may be said to constitute the symbolic function "proper," its "slippage" must in turn be held in check, given direction and hence, distorted by the metaphorical function if it is not to dissolve into sheer indeterminacy. In short, metonymic displacement must itself be dislocated and disfigured – *entstellt*, to use Freud's term – by metaphoric condensation, in order to function at all.

To be sure, for Lacan the metaphorical movement belongs to the symbolic order, and hence, in it the narcissism of the mirror-stage is subordinated to the movement of the signifier, as the following passage, from Lacan's essay on "The situation of psychoanalysis in 1956," asserts:

Without doubt, the imaginary is not simply the illusory, and it supplies material for the Idea. But what enabled Freud to plumb the depths that were to enrich his followers was the symbolic determination to which the imaginary function is subordinated; we are constantly reminded of this in Freud, whether we are dealing with the mechanism by which words are forgotten, or with the structure of fetishism.[12]

---

[11] I have discussed how such *setting apart* works in the writings of Freud in *The Legend of Freud*, part I.

[12] "Sans doute l'imaginaire n'est-il pas l'illusoire et donne-t-il matière à l'idée. Mais ce qui permit à Freud d'y faire la descente au trésor dont ses suivants furent enrichis, c'est la détermination symbolique où la fonction imaginaire se subordonne, et qui chez Freud est toujours rappelée puissamment, qu'il s'agisse du mécanisme de l'oubli verbal ou de la structure du fétichisme." *Ecrits*, p. 464.

We have already discussed the forgetting of proper names, and we will come to the phenomenon of fetishism shortly. For the moment, however, we are concerned only with specifying the role of the imaginary within the structure of the symbolic. As we have seen, this structure is also that of the unconscious primary process; its metonymic movement produces unending transference and displacements, concatenations but also fragmentation. Nevertheless, just as the allegedly "primary" process of the unconscious requires a no less "primary" censorship, or more precisely, repression, in order to constitute itself as a process, the symbolic needs the imaginary-metaphorical moment of fixation, in order to assure the minimum of determination necessary for any articulated structure.

Here we touch on the problem of what Freud described as *Urverdrängung*, "primal repression." Without recourse to some such irreducible, initiating but also internally incoherent notion, it is difficult to conceive of the possibility of a drive's "attaching" itself to – that is defining itself in terms of – an ideational-representative; and since "attachment" – also known as *cathexis* – is an essential aspect of the drive as such, the theoretical fiction of a "primal repression" must be regarded not as an external "vicissitude" of drives, but as a necessary part of their *destination*. Considered in a purely subjective register, this reciprocal dependency can only appear to be paradoxical and circular: on the one hand, the unconscious presupposes (primal) repression as its enabling other (be it in the form of the ego or of the super-ego); on the other, primal repression likewise presupposes the differentiation of the psyche into unconscious – preconscious-consciousness, in order to have a space within which it can occur in the first place.

Such paradoxes, however, lose something of their logical absurdity when it is recognized that they are structural effects of differential articulation. The apparently vicious circle describes the necessary form of signification. Meaning – the signified – is an effect of the signifying chain; yet without some such "meaning-effect," the chain itself would be unthinkable.

Thus, viewed from the structural perspective of differential signification, the imaginary and the symbolic must be considered primarily as forms of articulation. The subject of the imaginary, as described in the mirror-stage, is *le moi*, the reflexive ego of self-consciousness. Yet while this subject may appear to be present and identical, the very process of identification disrupts and divides it. Insofar as its identity is determined as self-consciousness, any and all divisions must be comprehended within the unity of a self; by contrast, the conception of a subject as a configuration of signifying chains is a notion that is not compatible with the conception of the autonomous ego as self-consciousness, however dialectically conceived. For the symbolic network of signification can never be totalized, even by dialectical negation. This essential incompatibility should be kept in mind when encountering Lacan's use of dialectical terminology: as is the case whenever he "borrows" a particular philosophical vocabulary, his use of it is always commanded by strategic imperatives: that of revealing an element of irreducible heterogeneity and difference there, where identity had previously been assumed.[13]

Independently of its volition or designs the narcissistic ego of the imaginary signified – of the *énoncé*, the statement – is thus reinscribed in the symbolic as the eccentric subject that signs itself over to the signifier with a slip of the pen. It thereby subjects itself not merely *to* the utterance, but *in* the process of *uttering* (*l'énonciation*), in the sense of the shifter discussed earlier. This subject of the utterance is not simply diametrically or symmetrically opposed to the subject of the statement, the *moi*. Rather, and in sharp contrast to the purported unity and identity of this *moi*, the subject of the uttterance is necessarily split and suspended between the statement as meaningful utterance, and the excessive overdeterminations of the signify-

---

[13] Mikkel Borch-Jacobsen has argued, in *Lacan, le maître absolu*, Flammarion: Paris 1990, that Lacan's theoretical armature is decisively determined by Alexandre Kojève, whose lectures on Hegel (1933–1939) were enormously influential in France. Although such influence should obviously not be underestimated, it cannot, I believe, sufficiently account for the Heideggerian elements in Lacan's elaboration of the heterological nature of language. In Lacanian/Sassurian terms, the Hegelian dialectic ultimately subordinates the signifier to the signified, difference to identity. This explains why Kojève himself refuses to acknowledge that the Heideggerian notion of history constitutes a viable alternative to Hegel. Cf. A. Kojève, *Introduction à la lecture de Hegel*, Gallimard: Paris, 1947, p. 575, note: "Heidegger has taken up the Hegelian themes of death; but he completely neglects those of Struggle and Work; moreover, his philosophy does not succeed in accounting for History."

ing chain. Left to its "own" devices – that is, to the metonymic movement of the signifier – the subject would become a hopeless *drifter*; it is as *moi* that the drift is stopped, but only through imaginary (dis-)simulation. As shifter, the subject remains suspiciously shifty.

The subject of the utterance thus emerges not only as a drifter, always on the run, on the "rails," at home nowhere, but moreover – to cite the English word used by Lacan – as a "fader".[14] Lacan illustrates this "fading" by referring to certain so-called "expletives," like the French *ne*, used primarily in subjunctive phrases to stress the counterfactual moment of desire or of affect. An approximate equivalent, in American English, would be the word, "really?!", meaning everything and nothing, and confirming, by antiphrasis, the tenuous "reality" of the communicative process. A counterpart in conversational German would be the expression "*genau!*," "exactly". Such "expletives" *fill out* the *fall out* of the signifier.[15]

But as its name indicates, such filling is even shiftier than the shifter. For the "I" as shifter still would seem to occupy one place at a time, and thus to be entirely compatible with the subject of the signified, one whose identity and presence – as author of a message and as creator of meaning – is never radically called into question. By contrast, a "filler," such as *ne*, is closer to what Freud, in his discussion of dreams, refers to as "determinatives": markers that have no semantic meaning of their own, but which function purely syntactically. In this particular case, *ne* also alludes to a process of denial or distancing, which is particularly appropriate for the "fading" of the subject of the unconscious:

The unconscious, beginning with Freud, is a chain of signifiers which repeat themselves insistently somewhere (on another stage, he writes), thereby intervening in the fissures offered it by actual discourse and by the thinking that it informs.[16]

---

[14] Since the subject constitutes itself through the movement of the signifier, "it disappears as subject in the signifiers, for it only becomes" and "is" in and through the "fading that constitutes its identification." *Ecrits*, p. 835.

[15] Such "expletives" can also play a decisive role in jokes, as I have sought to demonstrate; cf. Samuel Weber, "Laughing in the meanwhile," MLN (Fall, 1987), Johns Hopkins University Press, Baltimore 1988, pp. 704–705.

[16] "Subversion du sujet", *Ecrits*, p. 799; Sheridan, p. 297.

The "fissures" mentioned by Lacan are, as it were, the materialization of difference in "actual discourse." Difference materializes as a gap, a fissure, a hole or shadow that interferes with the semantic progress of discourse, puncturing and punctuating it. Such interruptions, as Freud emphasized in his discussion of dreams, constitute the favored markers of the unconscious. Despite its name, then, an "expletive" like *ne* does not so much fill up a hole as mark its borders.[17] As with the (in)famous Watergate tapes, expletives are always deleted from official declarations, since they are obscene, not only in what they say, but in their interruption of all meaningful statement. If what is obscene belongs off-stage – a dubious etymology but nevertheless a suggestive one – expletives are obscenity itself: self-effacing, they are often barely heard, interrupting the flow of speech, while at the same time engendering the illusion of a flow by covering up its incoherence. In spoken, communicative discourse, they are the perfect cover-up, Watergate *avant la lettre*. Which is why they are virtually inaudible in ordinary, spoken language, whose semblance of continuity they assure; it is only in the merciless rendition of transcription that the full force of the expletive is revealed (if it is not censored out before publication).

Perhaps the most prevalent "expletive" of this sort, in spoken American English, is hardly a word or part of discourse at all, in the grammatical sense, at least. It is the ubiquitous "uh . . ." that scans the speech of most Americans, in varying degrees. In so doing, it functions as an exemplary trace of what constitutes the subject. The notion of the unconscious is Freud's attempt to describe this lack. In American spoken English, its most characteristic expression, perhaps, is the *uh . . .*

The structure of the symbolic, the symbolic as structure, thus stands out in sharp contrast to the imaginary. Symbolic is the play of differences that manifests itself in and as the concatenation of signifiers. While the imaginary reduces differential

---

[17] In German, what most closely corresponds to the French, *ne*, is, perhaps surprisingly, the word, *ja*, as, for instance, in the phrase, "Das habe ich ja nicht bestellt." The "ja" functions merely to intensify the statement ("I didn't order that!"), it says "yes" to the statement, which is often a denial, and in so doing, says "no" to the real or suspected "no" of the other. See: "Laughing in the Meanwhile," pp. 691–706.

articulation to the ostensibly dualistic relationship of representative and "represented," in which the latter term is presumed to guarantee preconstituted identity and presence, the symbolic is representation primarily in the sense of a *Darstellung*, of a performance destined for *another stage*, or more precisely, for a *theater* in which the representation simultaneously produces and dislocates the represented. What is thereby "represented," however, is not, as one might expect, the signified, but what Lacan insists upon calling: the subject. In one of his most famous formulations, he describes the place of this subject by demarcating the sign from the signifier. If, as in the celebrated definition of Peirce, quoted by Lacan, the sign can be said to represent "something to someone," the "signifying order," by contrast,

constitutes itself through the fact that a signifier represents a subject for another signifier. This is the structure of all the formations of the unconscious, be it the dream, the lapsus, or the joke. It is also the structure that explains the originary division of the subject.[18]

The representation of the subject by the signifier is thus no simple reproduction of something that – virtually or actually – was already present. Rather, it is a movement of division that constitutes the subject. Represented by this movement of signifier to signifier, the subject cannot be suitably articulated in the present indicative or in any of its modalities, such as the present perfect. By contrast, the present participal, through which the subject is determined through its participation in an on-going (verbal) process, marks the subject's subjection to a movement of signification. Another aspect of this subjection is articulated, as already discussed, by the future past. And yet, there is another tense in French – if indeed it is really a tense at all – capable of indicating the elusive status of the subject of signification: the *imperfect*. In French, the imperfect designates not merely a "before," which once *was*, but which no longer is; by virtue of its incompleteness and imperfection, it can also articulate a "not yet." In this sense, it functions as what grammarians call a "past future" (*futur du passé*); like the future

---

[18] "Le registre du signifiant s'institue de ce qu'un signifiant représente un sujet pour un autre signifiant. C'est la structure, rêve, lapsus et mot d'esprit, de toutes les formations de l'inconscient. Et c'est aussi celle qui explique la division originaire du sujet." *Ecrits*, p. 840.

past of the "will have been," this "past future" also implies a conjectured "reality." Take, for example, the French sentence: *"Un pas de plus, il était dans la rue,"* which in English can be rendered idiomatically only with the far less ambiguous conditional phrase: "One step more and he *would have been* in the street," but which literally says: "One step more and he *was* in the street." What is decisive here is precisely the undecidability of this temporal–conjectural distinction, and the fact that it results from the differential structure of the signifier. As part of a process of signification, the signifier always anticipates a signified. At the same time, however, it also refers back; and inasmuch as it is always more or less determinate, each signifier derives from, or has its point of departure in, a previously determined signified.

Unlike the sign in Peirce's definition, then, Lacan's signifier is based on a distinctive function; rather than being construed in relation to a central presence or present tense (as is the case of the sign), the before and after of the signifier are "centered" around a difference. As a distinctive element, the signifier always differs from itself and "is" only in this difference: not merely to other, similarly differential terms, but to itself. To be identifiable, each signifying mark must be repeated, must be *iterable*, as Derrida argues.[19] Its identity is thus *imperfect* in the most "literal" sense: it can never fully take place because its place is a function of divergent metonymic chains. Which is why, as Lacan often writes, the signifier takes place "in [the] place of the other," (*"au lieu de l'Autre"*): both "in the place of the Other," and "instead of another." As signifier, language is "intrinsically" substitutive, and hence, figurative. But since each figure always *gestures* toward another figure, the process of configuration is addressed at a destination it can never attain.

The subject of both the signifier and the symbolic is necessarily incomplete, and it is there, in the force-field of such imperfectability, that the ostensible identity of the imaginary ego *will have been* inscribed, albeit in invisible, self-effacing characters. The "I" takes place, takes its place in the shadow of an "uh . . ." To retrace the genealogy of this shadow, it may be

[19] J. Derrida, *Limited Inc.*, trans. S. Weber, Northwestern University Press: Evanston, 1989.

useful to return, once again – assuming, that is, that we ever left it – to the mirror stage.

The mirror stage appears to be clearly pre- and extra-linguistic when considered from a genetic perspective, as a developmental "stage." The process of narcissistic identification sets in before the child has learned to speak, and it appears to occur independently of language, in the ostensible silence of infancy. It seems to involve a purely dualistic relationship of the child to its reflection. Furthermore, the relation Lacan establishes between the precocity of birth and the belated development of motor and sensory powers in humans, as compared with other mammals, would seem itself to betray what Lacan might call an imaginary mode of argumentation, structured upon the opposition of the organic and the perceptual. Moreover, the consequences of the mirror stage appear to be conceived in terms of a dualistic structure: the ego competes with itself as with an alter-ego. However, the text of the "mirror stage," upon which this reading is based, turns out itself to be incomplete and imperfect; what is lacking, or rather, effaced, is precisely that aspect of the *figure* which distinguishes it, as signifier, from a *Gestalt*: its *gesture*. It is this that will become – or rather, will have been – its most decisive moment: the gesture of desire. This aspect appears in print only in 1958, in an article already mentioned, Lacan's "Remarks on the paper by Daniel Lagache." Moreover, it is introduced in such a matter of fact manner, that its omission from the published paper is almost instantaneously forgotten. The context is defined by the question of the Other (capital O): that is, by the function of alterity or heterogeneity in discourse. In contrast to Lagache's "personalistic" interpretation of Freudian doctrine, Lacan stresses the impersonal structure "of this Other, where discourse is situated"; such alterity, he continues, reaches to "the purest moment of the mirror relation." What is this "purest moment"? Lacan locates it

in the gesture by which the child at the mirror, *turning around* to the person carrying it appeals with a look to the witness who decants, by verifying it, the recognition of the image from the jubilant assumption, in which, to be sure, *it* [such recognition] *already was*.[20]

---

[20] "Car l'Autre où le discours se place, toujours latent à la triangulation qui consacre cette distance, ne l'est pas tant qu'il ne s'étale jusque dans la relation

The present participle indicates an ongoing movement: that of the child, *turning around*, seeking to "decant": to purify, separate, decontaminate "the recognition of the image" from its "jubilant assumption," in which such recognition *already was*: was already at work. What is not said here, but what is implicit, is that in that recognition something *else* was at work as well, something capable of adulterating it, and which thereby requires a confirmation that Lacan compares here with "decanting." A liquid is decanted for at least two reasons: to separate it from its sediment or precipitate, and, correlatively, to preserve its homogeneity, or purity. We recall that one of Lacan's favorite figures for describing the manner in which the signifier falls out into the signified is precisely that of a certain "precipitation." The signifier precipitates out as a sediment that attaches to every signified. This is why the "recognition of the image" that "already was" at work in its "jubilant assumption," must necessarily be as *imperfect* as the tense through which it is articulated: such recognition "already was" in the "jubilant assumption," and yet it never was fully *there*, since it is precisely the jubilant assumption that makes "verification" necessary.

It is this imperfection of the child's jubilant recognition – its contamination by something *else*, something unsettling, that impels the child to *turn around*, for such verification can only come from somewhere else, from another place. It does not take place in the ostensibly perceptual relationship of the child to the mirror, of subject to object, or even, despite appearances, of subject to subject. It takes place in the encounter of look and look. The look is no longer determined by the object it seems to perceive: the mirror image, but rather by its encounter with another look. This turning, from object or image, to look, marks not merely the movement of the child, but the *Kehre* of Lacan as well. In it, the ethological perspective that initially marks the mirror stage, turns away from the descriptive discourse of Gestalt psychology and moves toward the *theater* of the symbolic. What is now added to the mirror image is the *glance of the other* and the *gesture* of turning around that *returns* the child to the signifier.

spéculaire en son plus pur moment: dans le geste par quoi l'enfant au miroir, se retournant vers celui qui le porte, en appelle du regard au témoin qui décante, de la vérifier, la reconnaissance de l'image, de l'assomption jubilante, où certes *elle était déjà.*" *Ecrits*, p. 678.

With the appearance of this *gesture*, a problem noted in our previous discussion of this text begins to be clarified, if not decanted. In the original version of the text of the mirror stage, the effect of the reflection upon the child seemed to result from its recognition of the image as its own likeness. Yet what remained unclear was just how this recognition could produce such jubilation. In the later essay, recognition as such is no longer enough; instead, in its stead, there appears the anxiety which causes the child to twist back, turning around, and in this gesture, to seek the confirming look of another. Recognition of the "same," in the guise of a mirror image, is no longer described simply as a means by which the child seeks to compensate for physiological helplessness. Instead, the jubilant reaction does not relieve the child from having to seek something like an acknowledgment of the other. In this sense, recognition is no longer a process organized around two poles: child and mirror image, subject and object. Instead, it emerges as a triadic relation in which acknowledgment emanates not from the self-identical ego, but from the "person who carries it," that is, from the place of the Other.

At the same time, the twisting and turning of the child marks a decisive articulation in Lacan's thinking itself. The linear temporality of a before and after is no longer adequate to measure the *gesture* at stake here. The acknowledgment "was" – and Lacan stresses the imperfect here – "already" at work in the jubilant reaction (including, perhaps, Lacan's own jubilation at *his* discovery of the signification of the mirror stage . . .). That the tense of this turn should, as I have indicated, be the imperfect, suggests that the discovery involves more than simply meets the eye:

But this "already" should not deceive us about the structure of that tertiary presence: it owes nothing to the anecdotal figure that incarnates it.[21]

In the later text, "Of our antecedents," dealing with the same problem, Lacan stresses the fact that the personal identity of the other is a matter of indifference; what is important in the

[21] "Mais ce déjà ne doit pas nous tromper sur la structure de la présence qui est ici évoquée en tiers: elle ne doit rien à l'anecdote du personnage qui l'incarne." Ibid.

production of this reaction is the sheer fact of "being there."[22] The other, whose role as witness is, in Western societies, at least, generally (but not always) assigned to the mother, can in essence be determined neither as an individual, nor as a social function, nor as a subject in general. Indeed, it is nothing more or less than the differentiality upon which discourse depends, but which itself is not so much discursive as *gestural*. Like the "uh...", this other takes the place of the signifier, whose imperfection appears as a fading in and out, or as an interruption. The realm of the signifier is not confined to the verbal discourse it makes possible, but includes the *appeal* and the exchange of looks, "that most evanescent of objects, for it appears only on the margins." Such gestures and appeals may antedate verbal discourse, but their structure is homologous to its condition, that of the signifier.

The "clarification" of the essay on the mirror stage thus sets the stage of a very different theater, albeit one that was already "on the scene." The mirror stage is not negated or invalidated, far from it; it is given a new twist by a *gesture* that turns away from the image in a silent *appeal* to the *look* as such. The place of the subject is thus no longer framed by the mirror, but relegated to the enabling margins of the visible. On this margin, the manifestation of a certain "prematuration" is replaced by another lack, a "much more critical one, the concealment of which is the secret of the subject's jubilation."[23] The new twist, the look that is lacking, sets the stage for a very different kind of drama: that of desire conceived as the desire of the other.

---

[22] "Ce qui se manipule dans le triomphe de l'assomption de l'image du corps au miroir, c'est cet objet le plus évanouissant à n'y apparaître qu'en marge: l'échange des regards, manifeste à ce que l'enfant se retourne vers celui qui de quelque façon l'assiste, fût-ce seulement de ce qu'il assiste à son jeu." ("What is manipulated in the triumph of the reception of the bodily image in the mirror is that most evanescent object, which only appears on the fringe: the exchange of glances, manifest in the turning-around of the child toward the person who aids it, be it merely through the fact that the person is there witnessing the game.") *Ecrits*, p. 70. In this mention of the "most evanescent" of objects that appears "only on the margin," Lacan alludes to that most elusive theory of the "*objet petit a*" – the object small a – which thereby makes a fleeting appearance here, in the margins of this book. See also below, Appendix A, where the relation of the *object a* to anxiety is explored.

[23] "Cette fonction est d'un manque plus critique, à ce que sa couverture soit le secret de la jubilation du sujet." Ibid.

❖❖❖

8

"When someone speaks, it gets light": demand

❖❖❖

Nowhere is the peculiarity of Lacan's "return to Freud" more apparent than in his insistence upon a term Freud rarely employs, and certainly never as a central theoretical concept: *desire*. The German word generally held to correspond to the French, *désir*, *Begehren*, is not to be found in the voluminous Index to the German edition of Freud's collected works; instead one finds the term *Begierde*, without any page reference, but with cross-references to *Gier*, and in parentheses to *Erregung*, *Gelüste*, *Wunsch*.[1] One may thus infer that the problem is at best of peripheral importance in Freud's writings; and insofar as one takes these texts *at their word*, this conclusion is difficult to refute. Indeed, it is difficult to situate *desire* in respect to the words that take its place in Freud, words such as wish, excitation, drive, libido, eros, etc. In thus ignoring the word, Freud would appear to continue a tradition of thought which has increasingly excluded "desire" from rigorous scientific discourse and relegated it to the languages of poetry, theology or at best, morals.[2] One should thus recognize the degree of provocation involved in Lacan's breaking with this tradition by determining desire to be the "the manifestly constitutive vector

[1] S. Freud, *Gesammelte Werke*, vol. XVIII, S. Fischer Verlag: Frankfurt am Main, 1968.
[2] An exception, perhaps, is still to be found in the philosophy of Hegel, and in particular in *The Phenomenology of Spirit*, where the term *Begierde* signifies a relation of sensibility that must be overcome in the development of self-consciousness. If Hegel, possibly through Kojève (see below, p. 128), alerted Lacan to the significance of this notion, the Lacanian "dialectic of desire" is ultimately incompatible with the Hegelian notion of their negation and transcendence, their *Aufhebung*, in and through self-consciousness. The "dialectics of desire" will turn out to be precisely what excludes all such *Aufhebung*, the transparency of self-consciousness and the reflexive totalization of the subject through conceptual discourse.

of the Freudian field of experience [or experiment: *expérience*]," and by defining the subject as a "subject of desire."[3] If Lacan's provocative emphasis upon desire should not be overlooked, to accept it as self-evident would also be to blunt its force. If the interpretation of a text seeks to be more than mere paraphrase, the introduction of terms absent or even alien to the text is hardly to be avoided. However, in order to impose themselves, such terms must call attention to an absence that structures the text. Let us attempt to trace the contours of this absence in Freud's work by investigating the concept which most closely approaches that of desire, without however completely coinciding with it: that of the *wish*.

The theory of the wish is developed by Freud primarily in *The Interpretation of Dreams*. In the section on wish-fulfillment, he reconstructs the genesis of the wish as follows: 1. The psychic apparatus strives to keep itself as free as possible from stimuli, a process described by Freud as that of a reflex apparatus; 2. The "exigencies of life", however, interfere with this striving and force the apparatus to move in a different direction. These exigencies confront the psyche first in the form of major somatic needs: "The excitations produced by internal needs seek discharge in movement . . . but the situation remains unaltered, for the excitation arising from an internal need is due not to a force producing a momentary impact, but to one which is in continuous operation." Freud adds:

A change can only come about if in some way or other (in the case of the baby, through outside help) an "experience of satisfaction" can be achieved which puts an end to the internal stimulus. An essential component of this experience of satisfaction is a particular perception (that of nourishment, in our example) the mnemic image of which remains associated henceforward with the memory trace of the excitation produced by the need. As a result of the link that has thus been established, the next time this need arises, a psychical impulse

---

[3] The entire sentence reads: "Pour nous, le sujet a à surgir de la donnée des signifiants qui le recouvrent dans un Autre qui est leur lieu transcendental: par quoi il se constitue dans une existence où est possible le vecteur manifestement constituant du champ freudien de l'expérience: à savoir ce qui s'appelle le désir." ("For us, the subject must emerge from the given of the signifiers that cover it over in an Other that is their transcendental site: whereby it constitutes itself in an existence that makes possible the vector that is manifestly constitutive of the Freudian field of experience: which is to say, desire.") *Ecrits*, pp. 655–656.

will at once emerge which will seek to re-cathect the mnemic image of the perception and to re-evoke the perception itself, that is to say, to re-establish the situation of the original satisfaction. An impulse of this kind is what we call a wish; the re-appearance of the perception is the fulfillment of the wish; and the shortest path to the fulfillment of the wish is a path leading directly from the excitation produced by the need to a complete cathexis of the perception. Nothing prevents us from assuming that there was a primitive state of the psychical apparatus in which this path was actually traversed, that is, in which wishing ended in hallucinating. Thus, the aim of this first psychical activity was to produce a "perceptual identity" – a repetition of the perception which was linked with the satisfaction of the need.[4]

Let us interrupt Freud's account here, which goes on to describe the genesis of reality-testing as a necessary "detour on the way to wish-fulfillment," in order to underscore the essential moments of his wish theory. We should begin by examining the relationship and the difference between need and wish. A condition of the wish is the so-called "experience of satisfaction," i.e. the satisfaction of a somatic need. The satisfaction of this need involves three moments: first the need can be filled only by particular objects determined by the need; hunger, for example, can, insofar as it is a physical need, be relieved only by some kind of nourishment and not by water. Secondly, the elimination of tension brought on by need [*Bedürfnisspannung*] is linked to a *perceptual image*; here we should again stress the fact that this image depends not upon the perceived *object* of satisfaction, but rather upon its spatio-temporal coincidence with the experience of satisfaction. Thus, from the very beginning, the image [*Bild*] functions less as a copy [*Abbild*] than as a signal. Yet it is also clear that such signals cannot be completely arbitrary. Certain objects, persons, and scenes, including perspectives, such as those studied by Spitz, from which the nursing child sees the mother's face, are necessarily linked to experiences of satisfaction and to the perceptions associated with them. The fact that the mother plays an important role in this initial experience of satisfaction, sets the stage for her later psychical function.

Thus, according to this scenario, wish differs from need. Yet, at the same time, it appears as a kind of second-order

---

[4] S. Freud, *Interpretation of Dreams*, SE, v, pp. 565-566.

satisfaction of a need. It is described in terms of a tendency to reproduce the initial perceptual image – which meanwhile has become a "memory-image" – as something that is independent of external reality, namely as an hallucination. Hallucination, accordingly, would constitute the essence of wish-fulfillment. Nevertheless, even in this schematic presentation, it should already be clear that the fulfillment of a wish is not entirely analogous to the satisfaction of a need. If hallucination is the essence of wish-fulfillment, its way of "fulfilling" a wish is certainly different from the manner in which a real object satisfies a need. In contrast to the satisfaction of needs, wish-fulfillment is characterized by a certain negativity: its scene is not that of physical objects, but the psychic realm of repetition and representation. What constitutes this realm is precisely the absence of that which is represented and wished. For something like a wish to arise in the first place, objects of need must be lacking. But this lack is not that by which an object, for instance, can be said to be absent from or negated by an image of it. What counts here is not the constitutive absence of the original in the copy, but a more general absence of object as such. It is this condition that makes it possible for perceptual images, or more precisely: for memory traces to function more or less arbitrarily as signals or signs. Finally, insofar as wishing relies primarily on outside help, the "helper" helps to constitute the wish, by means of a certain *power*. This power helps to bring about an experience of satisfaction, but at the same time transcends it.

In light of the ensuing description of the psyche, this initial model of the wish, which treats it still primarily as the epiphenomenon of unsatisfied need, may seem inadequate. For as they develop, wishes acquire a relative autonomy; they can no longer be derived from unsatisfied need, and operate according to their own laws: those of the primary process. Yet insofar as the unconscious can "do nothing but wish," as Freud remarks in *The Interpretation of Dreams*, its laws must themselves be grounded in the structure of the wish. First sketched out in that book, this structure is more fully elaborated in later texts, in which Freud foregrounds the peculiar negativity already mentioned. Principal revisions to his initial account of the wish stem from the related discoveries of infantile sexuality and the Oedipus complex. Concerning the latter, we shall limit the discussion, at this point, to those aspects of it that are of particular relevance to the structure of the wish.

Of primary importance is the prohibition of the original love object, the mother, and the consequences it has for *desire*. If this word now supplants the term "wish," it is because the Oedipus complex involves a degree of structuration difficult to reconcile with the concept of the wish. With respect to the prohibition of incest, Freud describes, in *Totem and Taboo*, the movement of what he calls *Trieblust*, translated by Strachey as "instinctual desire":

The prohibition owes its strength and its obsessive character precisely to its unconscious counterpart, the concealed and undiminished desire – that is to say, to an internal necessity inaccessible to conscious inspection. The ease with which the prohibition can be transferred and extended, reflects a process that falls in with the unconscious desire and is greatly facilitated by the psychological conditions that prevail in the unconscious. The instinctual desire is constantly shifting in order to escape from the barrier *[Absperrung] against which it finds itself*, and endeavors to find substitutes – substitute objects and substitute acts – in place of the prohibited ones. In consequence of this, the prohibition itself shifts about as well, and extends to any new aims which the forbidden impulse may adopt. [My italics][5]

Both here and in the case of infantile sexuality, prohibition seems to be the result of some initial event, and to apply to an object that at first really was there. Yet, we cannot read the above lines too literally: the *drive* "finds itself" only through the resistance of the *barrier*, which is nothing but the *bar* of the *signifier*. Such a reading seems to say more than Freud wants to say. And yet, it is perhaps the only account consistent with his notion of a wish, which, as we have seen, emerges from the absence of the object as such; a wish can come about only if its object (as the object of a need) is missing. Thus, what occurs diachronically in the experience of the individual subject, must already be structurally prescribed by the way in which the absence is articulated. The absence of the object, condition of possibility of the wish, develops into the incest prohibition forbidding that the mother (or father) be taken as the primary

[5] S. Freud, *Totem and Taboo*, SE, XIII, p. 30.

love object. This very prohibition, however, opens the possibility of displacement and condensation, the two moments constitutive of the primary process. We may thus conclude that although, as a matter of *empirical* fact, the prohibition applies to the parents, the latter function as personifications of a structural category: the signified. The prohibition of incest thus articulates the movement of articulation as such, insofar as it depends upon the *barring* of the signifier, which splits it and causes it to fall out as a signified. It is this movement that Freud retraces when describing the trajectory of *Trieblust*, which "is constantly shifting in order to escape from the barrier [*Absperrung*] against which it finds itself, and endeavors to discover substitutes – substitute objects and substitute acts – for those that are forbidden. In consequence of this, the prohibition itself shifts about as well, and extends to any new aims which the forbidden impulse may adopt."

It might be objected that Freud is concerned here only with an abnormal form of desire – namely the ambivalent desire of obsessional neurosis – which he then links to the rites and ceremonies involved in taboos. This is doubtless correct, and yet, if neuroses are singularly illuminating objects of study, it is because their very *singularity* brings *general* tendencies and structures of psychic life to light. While the specificity of the different kinds of neuroses should not be overlooked, Freud never permits any doubt concerning the ubiquity of ambivalence – above all in respect to the intimate and constitutive *complicity between wishes and prohibitions*. In "The most prevalent form of degradation in erotic life," (1912) Freud writes:

However strange it may sound, I think the possibility must be considered that something in the nature of the sexual drive itself is unfavorable to the achievement of absolute gratification. When we think of the long and difficult evolution the drive goes through, two factors to which this difficulty might be ascribed at once emerge. First, in consequence of the double inception [*des zweimaligen Ansatz*] of object-choice, with the incest barrier arriving in between, the ultimate object of the sexual drive is never again the original one, but only a surrogate for it. Psychoanalysis has shown us, however, that when the original object of a wishful excitation becomes lost in consequence of repression, it is often replaced by an endless series of substitute objects, none of which ever give full satisfaction. This may explain the lack of stability in object-choice, the "craving for excitement," which is so often a feature of the erotic life of adults.[6]

The second "inception," involving the reduction of polymorphous sexuality to genitality, is inscribed in the structure of the first. Sexuality is afflicted and undermined by the substitution that constitutes it, and which in turn is the effect of prohibitions and repression. These define the *unconscious* character of sexuality, for whether we are concerned with wishes, drives or desires, we are always dealing with unconscious structures. Thus, while the goal of sexuality may be understood as wish-fulfillment, it begins to emerge that the latter is very different from an "experience of satisfaction": there is "something in the nature of the sexual drive that is unfavorable to the achievement of total satisfaction." The wish, we recall, was described by Freud as the reproduction not of experienced satisfaction, but of a representation or perception associated with such an experience. We now begin to see just how *tenuous* such an *association* can be: both precarious, and yet by virtue of its very precariousness, all the more tenacious.

In *Beyond the Pleasure Principle*, Freud describes this structure of desire in terms of the dynamics of the drives. What we previously have referred to as "negativity" now emerges as "difference":

The repressed drive never ceases to strive for complete satisfaction, which consists in the repetition of a primary experience of satisfaction. No substitutive or reactive formations and no sublimations will suffice to remove the repressed drive's persisting tension; and it is the *difference in amount* between the pleasure of satisfaction which is demanded and that which is actually achieved that provides the driving factor which will permit of no halting at any position attained. [My italics][7]

Given the resistance of such a movement to closure, we can see why the process described here cannot be covered by the concept of "wish" – no matter how closely related to it it may be. The wish that is "fulfilled" in dreams has the form of a *predication* constructed from latent dream-thoughts. These, however, are "thought" according to the laws, and above all,

[6] SE, xi, pp. 188–189.
[7] S. Freud, *Beyond the Pleasure Principle*, SE, xviii, p. 42. See the discussion of this passage by Serge Leclaire, in: *Psychoanalyser*, Paris, 1968.

according to the *subject-object grammar of* the secondary process, of the system preconscious-consciousness, while the movement of displacement, involving what Freud also calls "facilitations" or "paths," operates according to the laws, and above all, according to the differential *graphics* of the unconscious, the primary process, which "writes" in the wake of the signifier. In his later writings, Freud increasingly uses the term "drive" [*Trieb*]; yet even this notion is too narrow to describe adequately the particular way in which psychic energy is structured by "representatives"; and we should be mindful of the considerable ambiguity of this term in Freud; it can refer either to the *energy psychically represented* by ideas and affects, or to the representative itself. Indeed, it seems as though a third concept is needed to account for the movement of desire. Let us attempt to retrace its structure as described by Lacan.

Desire for Lacan – and undoubtedly for Freud as well – is essentially unconscious in structure. The latter is therefore determined by the unconscious, which in turn, as we have seen, is an effect of the signifying structure of language. As Lacan writes:

> The unconscious exists, not because there is unconscious desire, in the sense of something impenetrable, heavy, a Caliban or even animal-like, which emerges from the depths in all of its primitiveness, in order then to raise itself to the higher level of consciousness. Quite to the contrary, if there is desire, it is only because there is the unconscious, i.e. a language, whose structure and effects escape the subject: because at the level of language, there is always something that is beyond consciousness, which allows the function of desire to be situated.[8]

Desire is thus structured differentially and as a metonymic movement; it is oriented less by objects than by signifiers. In "The instance of the letter," Lacan writes that desire is always a desire for something else: *"le désir d'autre chose – de la métonymie."*[9]

[8] Jacques Lacan, "Psychanalyse et médicine," *Lettres de l'École freudienne*, no. 1. (1967), p. 45; cited in: M. Safouan, "De la structure en psychanalyse," *Qu'est-ce que le structuralisme?*, Paris: Editions du Seuil, 1968, pp. 252–253.
[9] Sheridan, p. 167; *Ecrits*, p. 518. In "Subversion of the subject" Lacan comments upon his formula for desire: "Human desire is the desire of the Other" – in the sense of a subjective genitive: i.e. man desires not the other, but *as another*, "en tant que l'Autre." Desire of the Other means accordingly, desire instead of the other, in a place, however, that is continually displacing

Yet insofar as desire is directed towards something else which "itself" can never simply be a self-identical object, it is not only desirous *of another*, but is "itself" another's desire. It is "the desire for the other's desire," the desire *of* a signifier, defined as the signifier of another desire. Let us elaborate upon this formula, which comprises the core of Lacan's theory of desire. This is perhaps the point in Lacan's thought where he is most indebted to Kojève's reading of Hegel. Lacan never concealed this debt, acknowledging Kojève as his "master," even if he went on to place increasing emphasis upon the distance that separated his thinking from the philosophy of Hegel.[10] Kojève's reading of *The Phenomenology of Spirit*, which places considerable emphasis on the master-slave dialectic and on the liberating process of work, traces how the struggle for recognition necessarily develops out of Hegel's problematic of desire [*Begierde*]. So long as the desired end entails the consumption of natural objects, the subject is defined as a natural being caught up in the struggle for self-preservation. Only a desire seeking not a natural object, but rather acknowledgment through another desire raises the subject above its natural and material existence to the level of pure self-consciousness. What ensues from this account is the struggle for mastery. In this interpretation, desire seeks recognition from another desire. Recognition, however, is a moment in the autonomous constitution of self-consciousness. The master-slave dialectic thus represents only a stage in the development of consciousness, played out between two of its forms. As a reader of Freud, however, Lacan maintains that this dialectical moment of self-consciousness cannot set the stage for the *scene of desire*, since the latter is essentially unconscious. Yet how can Lacan at the same time adopt the notion of desire – as desire for the other's desire, and as desire for recognition through the other – without situating this process in a dialectic of self-

---

itself. The subjective genitive of desire is contrasted by Lacan with the unconscious as the "discourse of the Other"; in the latter case the genitive is objective, in the sense of *de Alio in oratione*, as Lacan remarks. Cf. *Écrits*, p. 814ff; Sheridan, p. 312.

[10] Cf. above all "Subversion of the subject . . .", where Lacan discusses in some detail his relation to Hegel and declares it to be "entirely didactic." *Écrits*, p. 794. Sheridan, p. 293. Needless to say, such declarations hardly can be taken at their word.

consciousness? To do so, he must develop a radically non-dialectical notion of the Other.

In a paper on "The direction of treatment and the principles of its power," Lacan writes:

> If desire functions in the subject by virtue of the conditions imposed upon him by the existence of discourse, namely, that his need must go by way of the processions [*défilés*] of the signifier; – if, on the other hand [. . .] the concept of the Other is to be determined as the locus of the deployment of speech (as that "other scene," of which Freud speaks); – then it must be supposed . . . that human desire is the desire of the Other.[11]

As Lacan remarks, we are not dealing with a process of identification here – for, as we will see, the metonymic movement of desire excludes any kind of identification – but with "the condition that obliges the subject to find the constitutive structure of its desire in the very rift [*béance*] opened by the effect of the signifiers in those who come to represent the Other for it, insofar as its demand is subjected to them."[12]

We encounter here the three terms that will play a determining role in Lacan's theory of desire: need, demand, and desire. Need is the least difficult to grasp; it refers to the dependency of the human organism which requires empirically determined objects to satisfy certain natural wants. Although Freud makes no strict terminological distinction between need and desire, our examination of the Freudian notions of "wish" and "drive" has suggested how different the two are from each other. The difficulty begins with Lacan's notion of demand. Let us start by citing a passage from "The signification of the phallus," in which demand is distinguished from need:

---

[11] "Si le désir est en effet dans le sujet de cette condition qui lui est imposée par l'existence du discours de faire passer son besoin par les défilés du signifiant; – si d'autre part, comme nous l'avons donné à entendre plus haut, en ouvrant la dialectique du transfert, il faut fonder la notion de l'Autre avec un grand A, comme étant le lieu de déploiement de la parole (l'autre scène, *ein anderer Schauplatz*, dont parle Freud dans la *Traumdeutung*); – il faut poser que, fait d'un animal en proie au langage, le désir de l'homme est le désir de l'Autre." *Ecrits*, p. 628. Sheridan, p. 264.

[12] "Cette condition que le sujet a à trouver la structure constituante de son désir dans la même béance ouverte par l'effet des signifiants chez ceux qui viennent pour lui à représenter l'Autre, en tant que sa demande leur est assujettie." *Ecrits*, p. 628, Sheridan, p. 264.

Demand in itself bears on something other than the satisfactions it calls for. It is demand of a presence or absence. Which is what is manifest in the primordial relation to the mother, pregnant as it is with that Other to be situated *this side* of the needs it can satisfy. Demand constitutes the Other as already possessing the "privilege" of satisfying needs, that is to say, the power of depriving them of that alone by which they are satisfied. This privilege of the Other thus outlines the radical form of the gift of that which the Other does not have, namely, that which is called its love. In this way, demand annuls (*aufhebt*) the particularity of everything that can be granted by transforming it into a proof of love, and the very satisfactions that it obtains for need are degraded [*sich erniedrigt*] to the level of being no more than the demolishing of the demand for love (. . .)[13]

Thus demand, which as Lacan writes elsewhere, is always a demand for love, does not seek concrete objects of satisfaction. Instead, it is demand for presence or absence, for power. And while this power may indeed make possible the satisfaction of needs, as that "outside help" mentioned by Freud in his description of the child's dependency, as such it transcends any of its concrete actions. The "privilege" of this power is expressed first, in the *withholding or deprivation* of objects of satisfaction, and second, in its peculiar way of giving, for it bestows what it does not have: love. Thus, the demand for love not only *differs* from the satisfactions it obtains, it also tends to "depreciate and degrade" them, in order to defend its trans-cendence against obliteration through the particularity of such satisfaction.

How then are we to understand this notion of demand? At first sight, it seems linked to the child's condition of depend-ence, of *Bedürftigkeit*, as Freud called it. To satisfy its needs, the child is of necessity dependent upon outside help. Yet, at the same time, demand stands in sharp contrast to the real sphere of

---

[13] "La demande en soi porte sur autre chose que sur les satisfactions qu'elle appelle. Elle est demande d'une présence ou d'une absence. Ce que la relation primordiale à la mère manifeste, d'être grosse de cet Autre à situer *en deçà* des besoins qu'il peut combler. Elle le constitue déjà comme ayant le 'privilège' de satisfaire les besoins, c'est-à-dire le pouvoir de les priver de cela seul par quoi ils sont satisfaits. Ce privilège de l'Autre dessine ainsi la forme radicale du don de ce qu'il n'a pas, soit ce qu'on appelle son amour. C'est par là que la demande annule (*aufhebt*) la particularité de tout ce qui peut être accordé en la transmuant en preuve d'amour, et les satisfactions même qu'elle obtient pour le besoin se ravalent (*sich erniedrigen*) à n'être plus que l'écrasement de la demande d'amour [. . .]" *Ecrits*, pp. 690–691. Sheridan, p. 286.

need. As the transcendental condition of possibility of satisfaction, demand cannot coincide with any concrete need. Lacan's pairing of the words "privilege" and "deprivation" suggests that demand might be defined as a kind of general negation of dependency, which could lead one to infer that the subjective basis of demand is not need, but *anxiety*. Although this line of thought is not explicitly pursued by Lacan,[14] a footnote in *Three Essays on the Theory of Sexuality* gestures in this direction:

For this explanation of the origin of infantile sexuality I have to thank a three year old boy, whom I once heard calling out of a dark room: "Auntie, speak to me! I'm frightened because it's so dark." His aunt called back to him: "What good would that do? You can't see me." "That doesn't matter," replied the child, "when someone speaks, it gets light." Thus, what he was afraid of was not the dark, but the absence of *a loved one*, and he could promise to calm down once he had obtained proof of that person's presence.[15]

Anxiety is thus relieved by "proof" of the "presence" of "a loved one," and it is in this manner that "demand" is answered. This answer in turn involves a linguistic operation: it is voiced and elicits a promise (the child "promised to calm down once he had obtained evidence of the beloved person's presence"). It marks a new stage in the assumption by the subject of its relation to language; instead of merely crying, the child increasingly uses articulated speech to draw attention to its needs. As Lacan remarks, "with demand we find ourselves in the domain of what is actually articulated."[16] It is demand, not need, that "opens the way to unconscious desire"[17]; it is "an approach" to desire and not desire itself. Why?

A scene from *Beyond the Pleasure Principle* provides elements of a response. The passage has received widespread attention ever since Lacan interpreted it as exemplifying the relation of demand to desire. Freud describes a "game invented and played by" his grandson, "a little boy of one and a half":

The child was not at all precocious in its intellectual development. At the age of one and a half he could say only a few comprehensible

---

[14] See below, chapter 10, "The witch's letter."
[15] S. Freud, *Three Essays on the Theory of Sexuality*, SE, VII, p. 224, note.
[16] J. Lacan, "Les formations de l'inconscient," *Bulletin de Psychologie* XI, p. 251.
[17] Ibid.

words; he could also make use of a number of sounds which expressed a meaning intelligible to those around it. He was, however, on good terms with his parents and their one servant-girl, and tributes were paid to his being a "good boy." He did not "disturb" his parents at night, he conscientiously obeyed orders not to touch certain things or go into certain rooms, and above all he never cried when his mother left him for a few hours. At the same time, he was greatly attached to his mother, who had not only fed him herself, but had also looked after him without any outside help. This good little boy, however, had an occasional disturbing habit of taking any small objects he could get hold of and throwing them away from him into a corner, under the bed, and so on, so that hunting for his toys and picking them up was often quite a business. As he did this he gave vent to a loud, long-drawn-out "o-o-o-o," accompanied by an expression of interest and satisfaction. His mother and the writer of the present account were agreed in thinking that this was not a mere interjection but represented the German word *fort* ["gone"]. I eventually realized that it was a game and that the only use he made of any of his toys was to play "gone" with them. One day I made an observation which confirmed my view. The child had a wooden reel with a piece of string tied round it. It never occurred to him to pull it along the floor behind him, for instance, and play at its being a carriage. What he did was to hold the reel by the string and very skillfully throw it over the edge of his curtained cot, so that it disappeared into it, at the same time uttering his expressive "o-o-o-o." He then pulled the reel out of the cot again by the string and hailed its reappearance with a joyful "*da*" [there]. This, then, was the complete game – disappearance and return. As a rule one only witnessed its first act, which was repeated untiringly as a game in itself, though there is no doubt that the greater pleasure was attached to the second act.[18]

Freud interprets the game in two ways and, as we shall see, the two need not be mutually exclusive. First, the child "compensates himself" for his "great cultural achievement – the renunciation of instinctual satisfaction – which he had made in allowing his mother to go away without protesting." The way he compensates for this is "by himself staging the same disappearance and return with objects within his reach," thereby repeating and symbolizing the mother's departure and return with the wooden reel – that is, with a language of things. Second, Freud suspects that behind this game is some act of vengeance; for the child not only passively accepts or symboli-

[18] S. Freud, *Beyond the Pleasure Principle*, SE, XVIII, pp. 14–15.

cally recuperates the mother's absence, but instead acts it out again in its game. It is as if the child were "defiantly saying, 'All right then, go away! I don't need you. I'm sending you away myself.'" Freud's interpretation was later confirmed – this time in relation to the father who had been called away to the front.

In this example we see how the presence and absence of the mother is at first repeated and symbolized by means of a thing-language. Yet beyond this, we observe the beginnings of a linguistic form – that of the signifier, in Lacan's terms. The presence-absence alternative is signified by the difference between the two sounds, "o-o-o-o" and "a-a-a-a," functioning at first as phonemes. What interests Lacan are not so much the objects used to symbolize the mother's departure and return, as this phonematic opposition, which forms a bridge between sign-language and the language of the signifier. What role then do presence and absence play in the game?

First of all, they signify the possibility of narcissistic identification as in the mirror stage. This is evidenced in a footnote Freud adds to his description:

A subsequent observation fully confirmed this interpretation [i.e. that the game symbolized the mother's disappearance and return]. One day the child's mother had been away for several hours and on her return was met with the words "Baby o-o-o-o!", which were at first incomprehensible. It soon turned out, however, that during this long period of solitude the child had found a method of making himself disappear. He had discovered his reflection in a full-length mirror which did not quite reach to the ground, so that by crouching down he could make his mirror-image "gone."[19]

The presence-absence of the mother forms the matrix of narcissistic identification; according to Lacan, it is out of this that the ego first emerges as the figure of irremediable alienation. Yet, as we have already heard, the demand for presence or absence must itself be situated in the realm of actual articulation. Unlocalizable in the imaginary register alone, demand opens the way to unconscious desire, i.e. to the symbolic. As Lacan remarks in reference to the story of Freud's grandson, "demand is first linked to the premises of language." Yet, what are these "premises"?[20] There are at least two: first, that

---

[19] SE, XVIII, p. 15, note.
[20] "Les formations de l'inconscient," p. 251.

language presupposes the absence of what it speaks about – its referents. This is similarly the presupposition of language conceived as a signifying system; the referent is not only presumed to be absent; it *is* the absent other. And this is precisely the first aspect of the child's game: in throwing away and retrieving objects, it can at will set in motion and control the *Fort-Da* (gone-there) alternation. In so doing, the child is an active subject mastering both the game and its symbolism. The child acknowledges the mother's absence, yet only insofar as it can make use of it – that is, only insofar as absence can be used (and appropriated) to further its own identification and ego constitution. Representation and articulation operate only in a limited sense here – only insofar as they can be enlisted and put to use in the making-present of an identity. It is in this sense that we understand Lacan's assertion that "demand is linked to an identifying and idealizing function."[21] So long as language qua representation is viewed essentially as absence, it virtually effaces itself in the voice of a speaker, to whose presence it seems dialectically to bear witness.

Yet a second presupposition of language arises when it is no longer considered merely as a *signifying* system, but instead as a *distinctive* one. Here language is seen as a movement of difference in which the moment of absence is given priority; this absence is always related to the negation of a presence and of a signified. This presupposition is implicit in the doubling of the object-language by the phonemes O – A: in this apparently superfluous doubling of symbolization, the sign is replaced by the signifier and the ego is supplanted by the subject of the unconscious. With the entry of the subject into the language of the signifier – into verbal language in this case[22] – it enters into a

---

[21] Ibid.

[22] As the previous discussion of Saussure has suggested, it would be a mistake to equate "verbal" discourse with "language" qua signifying function. To be sure, "verbal" is not simply a descriptive category: to speak of "words" presupposes an interpretation of what constitutes a word. If the word is "intuitively" defined by its morphemic content: i.e. as having a minimal meaning, in linguistic practice words are ambiguous, and such ambiguity, far from simply adding to the minimum semantic condition, tends to foreground the dependence of its signification, like all signification, upon "contextual" and syntactic factors. In the particular case under discussion, two remarks are in order: first, that it is differential signification, presented in the form of the phonemic (or semantic) opposition, which defines the couple, o-o-o/a-a-a.

structure of articulation in which direct identification no longer functions; the subject can never again hope to find itself in the signifier, because the latter only receives its identity by virtue of its place in the signifying chain. Signifiers "are," only by virtue of their difference. The subject is thereby split between the "said" and the "saying," between the enunciated and the enunciation; it is inscribed in a structure of representation that cannot be traced back to an original presence, but is instead constituted by an irreducible movement of repetition.

This, however, also modifies the status of the Other: as the addressee of the demand, the Other offers a guarantee of its *claims*. In a linguistic perspective, this Other is the reservoir and resource of meaning, "the treasure trove of signifiers," as Lacan puts it (*"trésor des signifiants"*).[23] Moreover, it is a treasure in the sense of a code; the signifier here functions primarily as a sign, as the representative of a signified and as the sender of a message whose content is the presence of the sender himself. And it is certainly no accident that in the case described by Freud, what assures the child of the presence of the person it loves is not seeing her, but hearing her voice. "When someone speaks, it gets light," says the child, thereby rediscovering what Jacques Derrida describes as the metaphysics of presence, that is, phonocentrism.[24]

In this sense, the Other of demand guarantees the meaning and presence of articulation. Lacan can thus write that demand is "at home in what is *actually* articulated," since only demand – and the Other it calls upon – can *claim* any such "actuality" of articulation. But demand, as articulation, is not merely imaginary, though it constitutes the basis and medium of the Imaginary. In demand, need goes the way of the signifier, that is of symbolic articulation, even if demand itself seeks an imaginary realm, "beyond articulation": an absolute presence or absence.

The opposition of presence and absence of the Other in demand, however, initiates a movement which cannot be

---

And second, that it is this relationship of binary opposition, presence or absence, either/or, that prevails in the constitution of the ego.
[23] *Ecrits*, p. 806; Sheridan, p. 304.
[24] *Of Grammatology*, passim.

restricted to these two poles. Lacan indicates the trajectory of this movement in "The signification of the phallus":

It is necessary then that the particularity thus abolished [*aufgehoben*] by demand reappear *beyond* demand. It does in fact reappear there, preserving, however, the structure contained in the demand-for-love's unconditionality. By a reversal that is not simply a negation of the negation, the power of pure loss emerges out of the residue of an obliteration. In place of the unconditionality of demand, desire substitutes the "absolute" condition: this condition unties the knot of that which in the proof of love rebels against satisfaction. Thus desire is neither the appetite of satisfaction, nor the demand for love, but the difference that results from the subtraction of the first from the second, indeed, the very phenomenon of their splitting (*Spaltung*).[25]

Desire thus entails not only the difference between the satisfaction of particular needs, and an unconditional demand for love, but difference itself, i.e. "the phenomenon of their splitting." Desire is the absolute condition insofar as it designates a movement of differential articulation based on the other – on difference. Yet at the same time it preserves the structure "contained" in the demand-for-love's "unconditionality," for desire's own movement is interminable; as such, desire must also function "unconditionally." The "object" of desire, signifier of another desire and of the Other's desire, always points to *another* signifier. In so doing, it refers not only to its own condition but beyond it as well – to *other* conditions. Just as hallucinatory wish-fulfillment presupposes the absence of the original object of satisfaction; just as the displacement of desire is occasioned by the loss of the original object (the mother) and the assumption of the incest prohibition, so desire presupposes the denial of need while privileging demand. Desire thus emerges on the fringes of denial.

[25] "Il y a donc une nécessité à ce que la particularité ainsi abolie reparaisse *au-delà* de la demande. Elle y reparaît en effet, mais conservant la structure que recèle l'inconditionné de la demande d'amour. Par un renversement qui n'est pas simple négation de la négation, la puissance de la pure perte surgit du résidu d'une oblitération. A l'inconditionné de la demande, le désir substitue la condition 'absolue': cette condition dénoue en effet ce que la preuve d'amour a de rebelle à la satisfaction d'un besoin. C'est ainsi que le désir n'est ni l'appétit de la satisfaction, ni la demande d'amour, mais la différence qui résulte de la soustraction du premier à la seconde, le phénomène même de leur refente (*Spaltung*)." *Ecrits*, p. 691; Sheridan, pp. 286–287.

Demand

This Other of desire can thus no longer be located in some kind of code, since a code implies a collection of signs based on a particular *system of signifieds*. This Other of desire is instead the *locus of the discourse of the unconscious*; it can only be placed as the difference between the "said" and the "saying," between signified and signifying, or more exactly as the movement of signifiers which itself always takes place upon "another stage." This Other locale thus traces the contours of that dislocation, that "transcendental" locus, where any possible combination or configuration of signifiers must in turn always be another signifier referring to something beyond itself. This Other, like the other of demand, befalls the subject in a variety of ways: for example, in the form of the third "person." As Freud stresses in his book on jokes, the third person is an essential element of the joke (though not of humor), for a joke only is one insofar as the listener laughs at it. Yet just as the exemplary embodiment of the Other of demand is the mother, so the Other of desire is personified in the father, for it is he who introduces the law of desire through the incest prohibition and the threat of castration. If we consider the Other as the dislocation of the signifier, it cannot be incarnated in the living identity of a person; here as well, the locale remains closed, *barred*. What is important is not the person of the father, but his role as guardian of the law.[26] Lacan often stresses the fact that this Other "does not exist",[27] it is barred, always elsewhere, inaccessible. Lacan names the mode of this inaccessibility the *name-of-the-father (le nom du père)*.

---

[26] The "father" is guardian of the Law, but not Legislator. The law is not given by anyone, "there is the Law," and the "there" marks the place of the Other. This place can be represented by the father, whom Lacan describes as "représentant originel" [original representative] of the Law. But if the father can exercise this function, it is less as a person than through his name, which in turn, as signifier, presupposes the radical absence of the signified. This is why it is above all in the place of the *dead* father that this name assumes its structuring power. This is the sense of the parricide, allegorically recounted in *Totem and Taboo*. It is only in inter-dicting himself, that the "father," qua "function," can become the effective site of the Name of the Father. It is therefore of more than anecdotal interest that in November, 1963, Lacan interrupted the seminar he had planned to devote to the "Names-of-the-Father," after its first session, as a response to the exclusion of his name from the list of training analysts. The text of that session has now been translated into English by Jeffrey Mehlman, and published in the *Dossier on the Institutional Debate*, October 40, pp. 81–95.

[27] *Ecrits*, pp. 820, 826; Sheridan, pp. 317, 323.

Yet while the name-of-the-father is the signifier of that place from which desire receives its law via prohibition, this law is enforced only by virtue of another signifier, which structures desire and which perhaps can only be named *improperly*, as the "phallus."

9

The signification of the phallus

Let us begin with a scene from a film: a little girl stands naked before a mirror and observes herself. Suddenly, she places her hand on her body, covering her sex. End of scene. Or perhaps the beginning of another? (To be re-viewed in "Of our antecedents."[1])

What the mirror image represents for a subject that cannot yet control its body is an image of totality. The unity of the ego will follow from an identification with this reflection of the body as a full *Gestalt*. What counts here is a sense of wholeness. Yet what happens when the image is no longer whole? And what if it is lacking in a way that can never be remedied? This is precisely what the little cinematic scene displays: observing herself in the mirror, the girl suddenly notices that something is missing; she responds to this "perception" by trying to conceal (or in some way, make up for) the absence. The mirror image is no longer whole. Would it have been different if, instead of a little girl, there had been a little boy?

Let us hear what Lacan has to say:

Certainly there is in all this what we call a hitch . . . a margin that all thought has avoided, skipped over, circumvented, or blocked whenever it apparently succeeds in sustaining itself through a circle, be it dialectical or mathematical.[2]

What then is this *margin* that ever since Freud appears as the shadow of the circularity with which thought seeks to sustain itself, haunting it with the ghost of the squaring of the circle?

---

[1] *Ecrits*, p. 70.

[2] "Assurément il y a là ce qu'on appelle un os. [. . .] Cette marge que toute pensée a évitée, sautée, contournée ou bouchée chaque fois qu'elle réussit apparemment à se soutenir d'un cercle: qu'elle soit dialectique ou mathématique." *Ecrits*, p. 820; Sheridan, p. 318.

This stumbling block, or as Freud calls it, this *"gewachsener Fels,"*[3] has a name: castration. The question, what that name names – whether a fear, a threat or a "complex" – can for the moment be left unanswered. Only two things seem certain: first, whatever castration may be, it's not good. Second, it is nothing less than the hinge upon which Freudian psychoanalysis turns. How so and why, are the questions to which the Lacanian theory of the phallus seeks to respond.

To answer these questions we must attempt to retrace the path that led Freud to the theory of castration. Freud's thinking on the subject crystallizes slowly. The matter first comes up in the context of his "Analysis of the phobia of a five-year-old boy,"[4] "little Hans," and it is discussed at length in his essay "On the sexual theories of children"[5] published in 1908. Yet, it is not until 1923 that Freud will elaborate fully the significance of his discovery in his essay on "The infantile genital organization of the libido,"[6] where he sets forth the theory of the phallic phase. Let us first summarize the main features of this theory as itself a theory of meaning and of signification before attempting to describe its significance for psychoanalysis.

The essay, "On the sexual theories of children," describes the castration complex as one of those "false theories of sexuality" that nevertheless contain "a grain of truth." (215) "The first of these theories, which builds upon a neglect of sexual difference," according to Freud, "consists in attributing to everybody, including women, a penis just like the one the boy knows of from his own body." (215)

As Freud clearly states, the reasons for this attribution are essentially narcissistic:

The penis is already in childhood the key erogenous zone and the most important auto-erotic sexual object, and the child's appreciation of its value is logically reflected in his *inability to imagine a person similar to himself* without this essential part. [215–216, my emphasis]

---

[3] S. Freud, "Analysis Terminable and Interminable," SE, x, p. 252; GW xvi, p. 99.

[4] SE, x.

[5] S. Freud, "On infantile sexual theories," SE, ix. Page references to this work will be given in parentheses in the body of the text.

[6] SE, xix, pp. 141–145. References to this essay will be given in parentheses in the body of the text.

Freud continues:

> If a little boy obtains a sight of his little sister's genitals, what he says shows that his prejudice is already strong enough to warp the perception; he does not remark on the lack of the penis but invariably says, as if to console and reconcile: the . . . is still small, but when she gets bigger, it, too, will grow. (216)

The narcissistic moment is already apparent in this first formulation, which actually has more to do with the point of departure of the castration complex than with the complex itself. The ego – the boy's in this case – persistently endeavors to find itself, its mirror image, in others. Hence, the boy's "inability to imagine a person similar to himself without this essential part," viz. the penis. Hence, too, his disavowal of the perception that does not confirm this expectation; the boy does not remark on the lack of the penis, but only that it is still small. Castration is discussed here only as one of many infantile theories of sexuality. Nevertheless, Freud already claims that it applies to young girls as well as to small boys; he does not, however, elaborate on this. As already stated, it is in 1923 in "The infantile genital organization of the libido," that Freud first grounds the universality of castration in a theory of the primacy of the phallus, or the so-called "phallic phase." He begins by correcting his earlier thesis that "the primacy of the genitals is not completed in the early period of childhood, or only very imperfectly."[7] He now claims instead that "the approximation of childhood sexuality to that of adults goes much farther" than he had at first believed; yet at the same time, Freud points out a significant difference between the "infantile genital organisation" and "the final genital organisation of the adult." The difference lies in the fact that

for both sexes in childhood only one kind of genital organ comes into account – the male organ. The primacy reached is, therefore, not a primacy of the genitals, but of the phallus.[8]

Thus begins one of the liveliest and most significant debates in the history of psychoanalytic theory; although Freud admits he does not have enough observational material to support fully

[7] SE, XIX, p. 142.
[8] SE, XIX, p. 142.

his presumption of the primacy of the phallus in both sexes, he nevertheless insists that it is invested with the same psychic significance for girls as well as for boys. And despite increasing skepticism and criticism from within the psychoanalytic movement itself – on the part of Ernest Jones, Melanie Klein, and Karen Horney, among others – Freud sticks to his thesis, even if the empirical evidence in support of his conviction that "the real female genitals never seem to be discovered" by the young girl (145), appears ever more dubious. It is difficult, therefore, to avoid suspecting that Freud's position in this decisive debate is determined by "phallocentrism," as Jones calls it. Is one to conclude, then, that Freud, and certain central psychoanalytical tenets, are as badly tainted by "male chauvinism" as has often been charged?[9] Why privilege the phallus in such an obviously one-sided manner?

To even address this question adequately, much less respond to it, the precise significance of this *privilege* must be discussed, which means, first of all, to determine the place it occupies within the general context of Freudian theory. The first, obvious, but nevertheless hardly trivial aspect that should be noted about that place is its proximity to what Freud refers to as castration. At first glance, it would seem as if Freud construes that proximity in terms of a genetic derivation:

> It seems to me [. . .] that the significance of the castration complex can be rightly appreciated only when its origin in the phase of phallic primacy is also taken into account. (144)

Although Freud concedes that there are experiences of separation in childhood development that prepare the child for the experience of castration – e.g., the loss of the nipple after nursing and the daily production of its feces – "the castration complex," he insists, "should be a term reserved for the occasion when the idea of such deprivations comes to be

---

[9] For a counter-argument, cf. Juliet Mitchell, *Psychoanalysis and Feminism*, London, 1974, p. XIII: "The greater part of the feminist movement has identified Freud as the enemy. It is held that psychoanalysis claims women are inferior and that they can achieve true femininity only as wives and mothers. [. . .] I would agree that popularized Freudianism must answer to this description; but the argument of this book is that a rejection of psychoanalysis and of Freud's works is fatal for feminism." Mitchell's understanding of Freud is strongly influenced by her reading of Lacan.

associated with the loss of the male organ." (144, note) Is the priority Freud here attributes to the phallus sheer evidence of the naturalistic bent of his thought, the fetishization of an anatomical condition, rather than a theory that is itself supposed to explain fetishism? Or is it an adequate description of a state of affairs which has its basis not in anatomy, but in a specific cultural and social tradition, which, however vast, is still far from being universal? Can the theory of the phallic phase and the universality of castration be applied to women as well as to men? Why should the feminine psyche be conditioned by the *loss* of something which *in reality* cannot have been lost, since it was never possessed?

As Lacan comments, "it might be a good idea to re-examine the question by asking what could have imposed upon Freud the evident paradox of his position."[10] His response is that Freud's phallocentrism is the result of "the intrusion of the signifier into the human psyche, which is strictly impossible to deduce from any pre-established harmony of this psyche with the nature it expresses."[11] Accordingly, the phallus must be understood as that which *marks the passage from the imaginary to the symbolic, from demand to desire,* as a discontinuous and conflictual one. The favored name for this discontinuity and conflict is "castration." Having established just what the Lacanian hypothesis is, let us try to determine the degree to which it is inscribed or prefigured in the writings of Freud.

We have already pointed out that castration presupposes the conviction that all human beings have a penis. This belief has its origins in a narcissism said to be common to both sexes. Freud maintains this position by asserting that what counts, for the psyche, is the perception not of one's own body, but of others'. The belief in the ubiquity of the penis is always held in relation to the other. The totality of one's body-image, the narcissistic condition for the development of the ego, is, however, called in question by the perception of the absence of the penis. Called into question, but not simply shattered. The invisibility of the penis can in fact help to confirm its existence; according to some early childhood phantasies interpreted by Melanie Klein, the

---

[10] J. Lacan, "La signification du phallus," *Ecrits*, p. 688; Sheridan, p. 284.
[11] *Ecrits*, p. 555; Sheridan, p. 198.

(father's) penis is contained inside the mother's body. Here we have a concrete example of the theory of perceptual identities discussed earlier at work, for a child's perception is certainly not disinterested or objective. It is motivated and conditioned by a curiosity which itself serves the interests of the narcissism expressed in the demand for love.

Nevertheless, self-expression here is at the same time self-alienation, since the demand is dependent upon the hetero-geneity of the other in the movement of signification. Since the other addressed by the infant is (in modern Western middle-class culture) generally the mother, it is here that the drama of castration unfolds. Demand, however, is articulated in the medium of the imaginary and this in turn has particular implications for castration. First, the *perception of the female genitals* is misconstrued as the perception of an absence, of a "lack" or "loss"; that is, as castration in a narrow or even literal sense. The alternative logic that structures both demand and its medium, the imaginary, thus remains in force, since the subject is presented with the choice: absence or presence. The Other – in this case, the mother – is the seat of a code formed as a system of signs; its message thus presents itself as one consisting of signs that refer to an (absent) referent. The exemplary organ of this is therefore the *voice*, insofar as it can claim to assure the presence of the (beloved) speaker: "When someone speaks, it gets light." In its pretension to presence, however, the voice sets itself apart from articulation understood as a movement of signifiers or as a play of difference. On the contrary, it tends to reduce difference by determining it as the interval between itself and the being of the speaker – between sign and referent. Hence, we see how the imaginary structure of demand – with the mother in the position of the utterly Other – is actually supported by the invisibility of the maternal phallus. The mother *does not have* a penis, and yet precisely by virtue of this not-having, she can present herself as *being* the phallus. For what is decisive, Lacan insists, to all understanding in this question, is the awareness that the phallus functions psychically not as an organ, but as a particular kind of representation, a *simulacrum*:

In Freudian doctrine the phallus is not a phantasy, if by that we mean an imaginary effect. Nor is it as such an object (partial, internal, good, bad, etc.), in the sense that this term tends to accentuate the reality obtaining in a relation. It is even less the organ, penis or clitoris, that it symbolizes. And it is not without reason that Freud used the reference to the simulacrum that it represented for the Ancients. For the phallus is a signifier, a signifier whose function in the intrasubjective economy of analysis is perhaps to raise the veil of the function it had in the mysteries. For it is the signifier destined to designate the effects of the signified in their entirety, i.e. insofar as these effects are conditioned by the presence of the signifier.[12]

The phallus is thus situatéd, decisively and incisively, on the border that separates the imaginary from the symbolic. It emerges out of the gaps of a perception that apprehends only presence or absence. Within the phantasmatic economy of human desire the phallus is, therefore, a *simulacrum*: it presents similarity instead of the dissimilar, symmetry in place of the dissymmetrical. It is a perception that strives to be identical, but it is not a perceptual identity (except in the Freudian sense of that term). What it represents is not the absence of a presence, but a difference impossible to apprehend in terms of presence or absence. What it represents, but only by effacing it, is the differential relation of the sexes. The trace of this effaced difference it then names: "castration." This name also designates the "falling out" of the signifier with – and *as* – the signified. This is what Lacan is driving at when he writes that the phallus is the signifier that designates "the effects of the signified in their entirety, insofar as they are conditioned by the presence of the signifier." What, however, are these effects of the signified and how does the "presence of the signifier" condition them?

These effects belong to the imaginary mode of articulation, whose structural basis, the transcendental signified, is always

---

[12] "Le phallus dans la doctrine freudienne n'est pas un fantasme, s'il faut entendre par là un effet imaginaire. Il n'est pas non plus un objet (partiel, interne, bon, mauvais etc...) pour autant que ce terme tend à apprécier la réalité intéressée dans une relation. Il est encore bien moins l'organe, pénis ou clitoris, qu'il symbolise. Et ce n'est pas sans raison que Freud en a pris la référence au simulacre qu'il était pour les Anciens. Car le phallus est un signifiant, un signifiant dont la fonction, dans l'économie intrasubjective de l'analyse, soulève peut-être le voile de celle qu'il tenait dans les mystères. Car c'est le signifiant destiné à désigner dans leur ensemble les effets de signifié, en tant que le signifiant les conditionne par sa présence de signifiant." *Ecrits*, p. 690; Sheridan, p. 285.

already conditioned by the signifier. In this respect, it must be remembered that, whatever else it may be, the phallus is first of all the idea of something that in reality has never existed: the maternal penis. Once the child establishes that this idea has no positive or objective referent, the significance of the phallus is split for it: on the one hand, the phallus becomes a kind of negative idea of a particular non-being; it signifies the total presence of the mother – a presence that can claim to be non-objective and transcendental, since it withdraws itself, or is withdrawn, precisely in the granting of the satisfaction of need. It *is* as the negation of the particular satisfactions and objects of satisfaction it grants; it *is* precisely *as* their degradation and belittlement. The phallus thus operates as the pure representation of absence, a representation that is pure because it represents nothing, and hence, coincides, qua representation, with what it represents, without leaving the slightest trace or residue. In this sense, the phallus is the perfect simulacrum: one that can claim to be utterly self-identical in the pure ideality of representation. The phallus then would be pure sign, were it not for the fact that it does not completely disappear or dissolve into diaphany; instead, it reappears inscribed as the distinctive trait of the male body, and above all, of the paternal body. Or more precisely: it is not the phallus that reappears, but instead that which it initially seems to represent, before it reveals itself in the claim to *be* the non-being of the maternal penis, before, that is, it takes off upon the path of pure representation.

The phallus now appears in a second phase Lacan calls "privation." Rather than appearing as the mark of the transcendental being of the mother, it now appears as that which she neither *is* nor *has*: as the exclusive property of the father and simultaneously as that which the mother, in her negativity, can neither be nor have, but only desire. In the first phase, coinciding with the mirror stage, the child tries to be the phallus in order to satisfy the desire of the mother: to confirm her completeness, on the one hand, and to partake in it, on the other. Now, however, the child sees itself excluded by the father from identifying narcissistically with the phallus as absolute being and with the mother as presence. Moreover, the child only feels the force of this exclusion when it learns that even the father cannot possess the phallus, but only speak in its name.

Thus, while the father may be the locus of a prohibition, this prohibition also applies to the "law-giver" himself, turning him into a *symbolic father* or into what Lacan calls the name-of-the-father, and which might also be rendered as the *naming* of the father (subjective and objective, genitive and genitor). Only with the naming of this name, does the phallus become for the subject the signifier of its desire, that is, of its relationship to the symbolic, and the symptom of its split articulation in and through the signifier.

Thus, the phallus, in the course of its movement, otherwise known as castration, describes the operation that transforms the signified demanded (and the signified of demand) into the signifier of desire; that is, it transforms it into what it always *will have been*, insofar as the subject is structured in and through the signifier. In the problematic of the phallus and of castration, we see how the structure of language conditioning the subject converges with the destination of the individual. As Lacan remarks, "the phallus is the privileged signifier of the mark in which the role of the Logos and the arrival of desire converge."[13] Two moments thus come together in the phallus: first, the structure of the signifier as the differential element of articulation. The phallus is the mark of this structure insofar as it functions as a *negative representation*, which however does not negate (and surpass) itself in the process; that is, it does not function according to the totalizing teleology of dialectical sublation. The signification of the phallus is constituted through castration, even and especially if "nothing" is castrated. In this sense the phallus is the signifier of signification in general, the signifier of difference. To put it more precisely, the phallus marks the *bar* and the *barrier*, which itself is meaningless, but which renders signification possible. Lacan alludes to this relationship and function in his description of the moment in the famous painting of the Pompei villa when the phallus, which otherwise is always depicted as veiled, is revealed.

It then becomes the bar which, at the hands of this demon (shame) strikes the signified, marking it as the bastard offspring of this signifying concatenation.[14]

---

[13] "La formation de l'inconscient."
[14] *Ecrits*, p. 692; Sheridan, p. 288.

It is through castration that the phallus is constituted as a signifier. Castration is thus nothing other than an effect upon the subject caused by the falling out or *striking down* of the signifier. This function of the phallus thus derives from the structure of language conceived as a movement of signifiers, a movement to which the subject is sub-jected. This subjection not only splits the subject, but also supports and suspends it in the incessant reiteration of an irremediable division: not between subject and object, but between enunciated and enunciation, signified and signifier. It is in this sense that the individual subject is dependent upon the symbolic, or as Freud writes in a letter to Fliess, upon that "prehistoric, unforgettable other, who is never equaled by anyone later."[15] This Other, however, is not a person or even a subject, but instead that "somewhere else," that localized difference which emerges from and moves towards the signifying chain. This negative place, this "dislocation" comes to be occupied by various instances: first by the mother as that utterly Other in the sense of the demand for love; then by the father as the forbidding, castrating instance which also introduces the law; and finally by the phallus "itself," as the selfless, self-effacing mark that bars the place and splits the subject. While the phallus thus marks the *decisive* moment of bifurcation in the trajectory of the subject, it at the same time remarks the structural condition of the latter's subjection – to language as medium of articulation and of difference. After this mark, there is no going back; and yet before it, there is no going forward. As the phallic object of the mother's desire, a child is marked by castration even before it is born.[16]

In this respect, it may be said that structure, in a synchronic sense, enjoys a certain priority over the diachrony of individual development. But it is a structure of dislocation, not of deter-

---

[15] S. Freud, Letter of December 6, 1896, in: *The Complete Letters of Sigmund Freud to Wilhelm Fliess, 1887–1904*, translated and edited by Jeffrey Moussaieff Masson, Cambridge & London: The Belknap Press of Harvard University Press, 1985, p. 213.

[16] In support of the priority of the symbolic over the empirical, genetic development of the individual, Lacan often cites the passage from Freud's discussion of "little Hans," in which Freud tells the boy that "long before he was in the world . . . I had known that a little Hans would come, who would be so fond of his mother that he would be bound to feel afraid of his father . . ." SE, x, p. 42.

mination, much less of predetermination. This is a priority that is implicitly at work in the writings of Freud, for instance, in his metapsychological reflections on "primal repression," a primacy that cannot be construed coherently in chronological terms. This form of repression is supposed to differentiate the psychic apparatus and yet, as it is also a purely intrapsychic instance, it must presuppose this differentiation. Yet as soon as one ceases to consider primal repression as an intrasubjective product and begins to see it as an effect of the signifier in the structuring of the subject, the paradox becomes intelligible. It can be understood as an allegory of the difference that *renders* discursive logic and its linearity possible while simultaneously restricting and displacing them. It is in this sense that Lacan can claim that language is the condition of the unconscious, for the unconscious "is" only (before) the bar that strikes and sub-jects the subject to the signifier.[17]

On the one hand, then, the phallus performs the function of the signifier in general, as it falls out with the signified; on the other hand, however – and we now come to its second moment – it is a *specific*, determinate signifier, not a transcendental one. It is from this perspective that one can begin to understand the particular importance Freud attributed to castration *vis-à-vis* other experiences of separation, such as the loss of the nipple or the production of feces. What sets the phallus apart is a particular fixation on a signified, which, to be sure, is the case for every particular or determinate signifier. This means that the imaginary function of the phallus – or of anything else, for that matter – can never be wholly surpassed by its symbolic function. For the imaginary bars the way, not just in the sense of blocking the way, but also in that of staking it out, demarcating it and fixing its trajectory. Without such an imaginary bar, the phallus would be nothing but a "pure signifier," and we would be unable to speak of it or name it in any other way. It would thereby dissolve into a diaphany so pure that the symbolic function itself would disappear. For the symbolic to function, the signifier can never be pure or self-identical, but instead must

---

[17] "Le langage est la condition de l'inconscient," Lacan asserts in *Radiophonie* (*Scilicet* 2/3, Paris, 1970, p. 58) – and not the reverse. If one can speak of an ontology, therefore, in respect to Lacan, it is not one of the Unconscious, but of language qua signifying function.

always be slightly out of sync, slightly deranged, slightly: imaginary. This is the imaginary moment of the phallus: its localization and materialization as the representative of the male member; and since it is imaginary, it can never entirely fulfill its symbolic function. Some other imaginary determination is always possible, indeed, inevitable. That is, the possibility of a substitution is inevitable. It is this necessary possibility that marks the symbolic moment of the imaginary, contaminating it no less than it, in turn, contaminates the symbolic that it nevertheless *renders* possible.

Which is why, as the (in part imaginary) signifier of the signifier, the phallus displays the limits of formalization, and at the same time the necessity of naming; for it must be determined as a particular mark, linked to a particular content and context, in short: to a signified. The peculiarity of this signified, however, resides in the fact that, within the economy and development of the subject, it indicates that the signified can appear only as an effect of the signifier. As the particular signifier (of a specific signified), the phallus can thus take its place in numerous "symbolic equations": it may be equated with the child, as "the little one"[18]; with excrement, "as something that can be detached from the body" (i.e. the phallus menaced by the threat of castration); with the body of the mother, as that which is lacking, and with money, as that which circulates. Its representation by the Ancients as an erect penis points just as much to the movement and tension of desire, as it does, negatively and implicitly, to a detumescence marking the frailty and evanescence of pleasure. And even if it might be difficult to verify the etymological assumption that "phallos" derives from "phanein," this association reminds us of its indubitably intimate and ambivalent relationship to the imaginary realm of *phenomenality*, as well as to that of phantasy and phantasm. In this respect, the phallus is the phenomenon that is conspicuously absent: it *is* the conspicuousness of absence.

Perhaps, then, instead of trying of find out "what the phallus *is*", we would do better to ask, "What *about* the phallus?" "How do things stand with it?" To this the response will be,

---

[18] S. Freud, "On transformations of instincts as exemplified in anal eroticism," SE, XVII, p. 128.

about the phallus stand circum-stances, which cause it to fall due constantly. Because its stance depends upon circumstance, it stands to reason that it must fall due. For it marks an outstanding debt, a debt out of all proportion that can only be settled – i.e. deferred – according to the laws of the symbolic. Thus the phallus "is" the "Fall" itself, fortunate or unfortunate: the case of the signifier falling out with(in) the signified. The aura of the phallus is this fallout.

In the light of this aura, we see why Lacan's response to the charges directed against the theory of the phallus is unequivocal: the phallocentrism of Freud aims at deconstructing all "centrism," insofar as the phallus stages the drama of the signifier. As the phallus, the signifier is struck down as the signified. The signified *is* the signifier *struck down*. This act of determination is violent and illicit, and yet as such, it is the origin of all law. The striking down of the signifier is performed in the name of the father, but the "father" here names the name of a name that has no present or presentable reference. What it names is the interminable circulation that it terminates, precisely through being struck down. This is why the phallus does not debut as the product of a particular culture. Rather, it is part of the theater of language, the condition of "culture" as well as of "nature," as of everything that bears a name. Yet no one knows better than Lacan, perhaps, that the phallus nevertheless remains a particular signifier, tied to the margin of a text. Of *a* text, and not of *the* text. Which is why no formalization can ever entirely replace reading. And why reading never takes place in general.

Reading in this sense – and it is the sense of the Return to Freud announced by Lacan – means relearning how to be *struck* by the signifier. And by its stage. In the theater of the unconscious, one never gets over being stage-struck.

Appendix A

❖❖❖❖❖❖❖❖❖❖❖❖❖❖❖❖❖❖❖❖❖❖❖❖❖❖❖❖❖❖❖❖❖❖❖❖❖❖❖

Beyond anxiety: the witch's letter

❖❖❖❖❖❖❖❖❖❖❖❖❖❖❖❖❖❖❖❖❖❖❖❖❖❖❖❖❖❖❖❖❖❖❖❖❖❖❖

The incompleteness in the story of the Fall, the fact that anybody could have the idea of telling Adam something he could not possibly understand, disappears once we consider that the speaker is language, and that therefore it is Adam himself who speaks. That leaves the serpent. [. . .] And here I must confess that I am incapable of attaching any definite thought whatsoever to it.

That the man of science ought to forget himself is entirely true; nevertheless it is therefore also very fortunate that sin is no scientific problem, and thus no man of science has an obligation [. . .] to forget how sin came into the world. If this is what he wants to do, if he magnanimously wants to forget himself in the zeal to explain all of humanity, he will become as comical as [the Copenhagen bookseller] Soldin, who, in a fit of self-oblivious enthusiasm, and carried away by his chatter, has to ask his wife: "Rebecca, am I the one who is speaking?"

S. Kierkegaard, *The Concept of Anxiety*[1]

I

In the "Descriptive index of major concepts" that Jacques-Alain Miller assembled to guide readers of the *Ecrits*, a term is missing which, indeed, occurs infrequently in the volume. The term is *angoisse*, anxiety, and its infrequency in the 1966 collection of texts deserves more consideration that it has received. For it is anything but self-evident. Three years previously, in 1962–63, Lacan had lectured for an entire year on the subject. And to judge from his opening remarks – as they are recorded in the unauthorized, but nevertheless widely circulated text to which I shall refer, while awaiting its publication as volume X of *Le Séminaire* – the importance of anxiety as a problem was no more self-evident at the time than it has proved to be since. The choice of it as the subject of the year's lectures having apparently come as a surprise to many of his listeners, Lacan begins by emphasizing its necessity within the context of his thought:

You shall see, I believe, that anxiety is precisely the point of rendez-vous where all of my previous discourse awaits you, including a certain number of terms which up to now may have seemed to you to be insufficiently related. You will see how anxiety is the terrain where these terms tie in with each other and thereby assume more clearly their place.[1]

If anxiety was thus to supply the "terrain" upon which the Lacanian discourse was to demonstrate its coherence, it is not entirely suprising if the "setting" has been eclipsed by the scenario. It is as if the destiny of the problem reflected the particular theoretical role it was called upon to play: that of serving as an introduction to another problem, one more specifically and (in the meanwhile) more recognizably Lacanian, that of the *lack*:

In other words, anxiety introduces us, with the greatest possible accent of communicability, to the function of the lack or fault (*la fonction du manque*), inasmuch as it is radical for our field.

The topic of anxiety, then, which allows the hitherto somewhat disparate membra disjecta of Lacan's terminology to come together and take their proper places, at the same time and in the same process has its own place clearly defined: that not merely of a "terrain," but of a *passage-way*. This passage must be negotiated, but it also must in a certain sense be left behind. For the work to be done, and in particular the work of the analyst, takes place elsewhere, as Lacan recalls at the very end of these lectures:

I have often asked you what the analyst's desire must be so that work might be possible there, where we are trying to bring things, *beyond the limit of anxiety*. (7.3.63)

The lectures on anxiety thus have the task of establishing this "limit," and thereby of preparing its *overcoming*: "Anxiety can

---

[1] "Vous le verrez, je pense, l'angoisse est très précisément le point de rendez-vous où vous attend tout ce qu'il était de mon discours antérieur et où s'attendent entre eux un certain nombre de termes qui ont pu jusqu'à présent ne pas vous apparaître suffisamment conjoints. Vous verrez sur ce terrain de l'angoisse, comment, à se nouer plus étroitement, chacun prendra encore mieux sa place." (11.14.62)

only be surmounted when the Other (capital O) has named itself." This self-naming of the Other, Lacan announced, would comprise the topic of his lectures of the following year, which were to deal with the Names of the Father. But as is well known, this project had to be deferred for a decade, following the interruption of his teaching at Sainte Anne. When finally the time had arrived for the Other to name itself, *les noms du père* had now been doubled by "les non-dupes errent." And anxiety, presumably, had long since been left behind.

2

Lacan was not the first who had sought to put anxiety in its (proper) place, to be sure. Freud himself had already made a similar attempt. With dubious success. For Freud, too, anxiety presented itself as an unavoidable station along the way to the new discourse he sought to establish. In one of his earliest essays, he endeavored to demarcate "anxiety neurosis" from the then more familiar and more general category of "neurasthenia." Libido that could not be discharged through sexual activity, he argued, was transformed into anxiety. Subsequently, Freud modified this thesis in the context of his later theory, asserting that anxiety was the reaction of the ego to danger, and above all, to that of an object-loss (of which "castration" was considered to be the exemplary instance). In the later perspective, anxiety is described less as a disturbance of the psyche, than as its attempt to protect itself from such disturbances.

Freud's discussion of anxiety thus turns upon a question that it will never entirely resolve: Is anxiety a constitutive process by which the psyche maintains its coherence and identity, or does it ultimately entail their dissolution? To be sure, as Freud pursues the notion of "danger," to which anxiety is said to be a reaction, the opposition – between identity and nonidentity, internal and external – that such a question presupposes, has to be refined. *A danger*, by definition, entails a certain exteriority with respect to that which it endangers, an aspect that Freud retains in his notion of "real" or objective danger. The more realistically danger is considered, however, the less it can be used to define anxiety, which, as Freud laconically remarks, is rarely the most realistic, in the sense of effective, response to an objective menace. The danger to which anxiety may be considered a response, therefore, cannot be defined purely from its realistic, external side; it must in some way be related to that which it endangers, the functioning of the I. If the latter consists above all in the production and maintenance of stable cathexes, in particular of a visual nature, this explains why Freud defines the danger faced by anxiety in terms not merely of the "loss of objects," – which would still suggest a relation to objective reality – but rather, more rigorously, as a loss of perception, a *Wahrnehmungsverlust*, since it is in such a loss that a true danger to the ego is articulated.

The notion of "perceptual loss" can be used to describe the peculiar indeterminacy that, according to Freud – who here follows a venerable tradition – distinguishes anxiety from fear. The danger of a loss of perception is determinate, inasmuch as it is necessarily attached to familiar images, situations and representations. The threat of "losing" these, by contrast, entails much more than the possibility of their simple disappearance. The danger of perceptual loss cannot be understood strictly in terms of the negation or absence of a particular perception, although this can often be the triggering factor. The danger itself, however, is not perceptual; rather, it involves what Freud calls "trauma": a shock that prevents the I from retaining and maintaining fixed cathexes (that is, energy more or less stably invested in representations).

In this context, it should not be forgotten that such a "trauma" is only the reverse side of the process by which not only "perceptions," but also "desires" themselves are constituted. If the essence of danger, qua "perceptual loss", can be described by Freud as that of the trauma, it is because the formation of what *The Interpretation of Dreams* calls "perceptual identities" (*Wahrnehmungsidentitäten*), and hence of "wishes" (if not of desire itself), entails the very relationship out of which the trauma emerges: *the radical divergence of representation and signification.* A perceptual identity, it will be remembered, arises when a memory trace or image is reproduced in a quasi-hallucinatory manner, in order to repeat the experience of satisfaction with which it has remained associated. The radical discrepancy between the representation, and that which it signifies, but cannot represent – for the simple reason that a shift in tension is not as such representable – is the structural essence both of the heterogeneity that separates all desire from its "object," and of the "trauma" discerned by Freud as constituting the ultimate danger to which anxiety responds.

Considered from this perspective, it is precisely Freud's inability to resolve the problem in terms of the alternative already described – Is anxiety functional or dysfunctional? Is the danger to which it responds essentially external or internal? – that constitutes the interest of his discussion. The reality of anxiety and of the danger to which it reacts, emerges as neither simply external nor internal, neither straightforwardly functional, nor dysfunctional; the functioning of the psyche is, intrinsically, as it were, bound up with an irreducible exteriority, with an alterity that it simultaneously denies and affirms. It denies it by giving it the form of an object that can be represented, and it affirms it by treating that representation as the mere material of a "cathexis," of a libidinal "investment," the signification of which must be sought elsewhere.

But, the reader will doubtless want to protest, just who or what is this "it" being referred to? Does not such an account confuse, or at least conflate, Freud's theoretical discourse with its object, the psyche? To this charge, I would reply as does Freud at the beginning of Chapter 7 of the *Interpretation of Dreams*, concerning the criticism that all accounts of dreams only falsify the latter. Freud affirms the statement as a description (yes, the recounting of the dream does disfigure it), but denies it any critical value (no, such disfiguration does not disqualify itself as an access to the dream). This is the distinctive involvement of what I have elsewhere called "psychoanalytical thinking."[2] The "it" of the discourse of psychoanalytical theory, like the Id that theory seeks to describe, entails a region of indeterminacy in which object and subject, signifier and signified, far from being clearly distinct, tend to redouble one another in a play of mirrors and shadows that one should not too hastily disqualify as "imaginary." It is this area of indeterminacy that Freud's discourse highlights, precisely by

[2] See Samuel Weber, *The Legend of Freud*, University of Minneapolis Press: Minneapolis, 1982.

demonstrating, more implicitly than explicitly, how and why the oppositionally structured alternative of "real" and "neurotic," of "external and internal," of functional and dysfunctional, is incapable of articulating the dynamics of anxiety. At the same time, the synthetic aim of comprehension makes it inevitable that the same discourse seeks to define and delimit that unruly "area" and thus to reinstate precisely the distinctions that it also tends to neutralize. The result is a text like *Inhibition, Symptom, Anxiety*, in which the argument follows a seesaw movement of self-revocation not unlike that described by Derrida in his reading of *Beyond the Pleasure Principle* in *The Post Card*.[3] The Freudian theory of anxiety is perhaps most revealing in the manner in which it comes to resemble what it is ostensibly intent on describing: the tension between the traumatic tendency of object-cathexes to dissolve, and the counter-effort of the Ego to arrest and channel that tendency. If, despite such resemblance, Freud's discourse *on* anxiety avoids becoming a discourse *of* anxiety, it is precisely because it allows its own movement to go on in function of that tension, rather than seeking to protect it from it.

3

This unresolved ambiguity and tension in the Freudian theory of anxiety reflects the manner in which the latter remains bound to the I: bound up, that is, with the effort of the subject to bind itself to and with representations. Or, to put it in more traditional terms: for Freud, anxiety is inseparable from the effort of the psyche to organize itself and to maintain its identity, however problematic, divided, and conflictual such identity will necessarily have to be. In Lacan's lectures, by contrast, the accent rests upon the need to go beyond the notion of the I – not necessarily in the sense that term has in the writings of Freud, but rather in those of the Ego-Psychology that dominated the International Psychoanalytical Association in the early sixties. To read Freud properly for Lacan is to uncover the necessity of

---

[3] Jacques Derrida, *The Post Card: From Socrates to Freud and Beyond*, trans. Alan Bass, University of Chicago Press: Chicago, 1987.

looking beyond the Ego in order to understand the origins and structure of anxiety:

> How does it happen that the movement of reflection [. . .] brought [. . .] first Rank and then Freud, who follows him on this point, to situate the origin of anxiety at a pre-specular, pre-autoerotic level, at that level of birth where no one, in the entire analytical chorus, would ever dream of speaking of the constitution of an *Ego*. There is something here which proves that even if it is possible, once the *Ego* is constituted, to define anxiety as a signal [. . .] in the *Ego*, this can hardly be exhaustive.[4] (1.23.63)

Lacan returns to this point in a later lecture:

> The *Ego* is the site of the signal. But it is not for the *Ego* that the signal is given. [. . .] It is so that the subject – it cannot be called otherwise – may be alerted to [soit averti] something. (2.27.63)

That "something," to be sure, is not merely an "original lack or fault," but rather the object *o*, the "cause" of desire and also the elusive embodiment of the Other. The latter can only embody itself – that is, its heterogeneous unself – by falling out with itself, and this leaves behind an "object" that is other than the object as we usually construe it: that is, as an object that can be represented, or at least symbolized. The object *o* is, by contrast, precisely not accessible to symbolization, it is what falls out of the signifying chain, or what it leaves behind. Nor can this strange object be reflected in a mirror, since, like the Moebius strip with which Lacan at times compares it, it has no definable, fixed border; indeed, its structure seems to *be* that of such a twisted border. More precisely, it seems to be situated at the intersection of the Imaginary and the Symbolic, and to serve the function of guaranteeing "the alterity of the Other":

> With respect to this *Other*, dependent upon this *Other*, the subject inscribes itself as a quotient; it is marked by the unique trait (*le trait unaire*) of the signifier in the field of the *Other*. Well, it is not for nothing if I can put it this way: that it slices up the *Other (met l'Autre en rondelles)*. This is a remainder, in the sense of a division, a residue. This remainder, this ultimate other, this irrational [number], this proof and sole guarantee, finally, of the alterity of the *Other*, is the *o*. (11.21.62)

---

[4] Lacan finds support for this assertion in "the phenomena of depersonalization" known to accompany severe anxiety, phenomena that are "the most contrary to the structure of the Ego as such."

The witch's letter

[It is just this *residue*, produced by the precipitation of the signifier, that the child encounters when it averts its gaze from the mirror and turns around in search of a verification that might "decant" the moment of recognition from the jubilation that accompanies it; what it finds is the look of the other, which in turn, as Lacan emphasizes, is one of the paradigmatic manifestations of the object *o*. [See above, p. 116ff]

Since this *o*, object of desire par excellence, safeguards the alterity of the Other by localizing the lack/fault (le manque) in its place, the Freudian notion of object-*loss* is, for Lacan, misleading. The object *o* is constituted rather by its very ability to *be lost*, or more precisely, to be "ceded." Anxiety, therefore, arises not from the loss of an object, but rather from the loss of this loss, or, as Lacan puts it, "when the lack comes to be lacking" (*quand le manque vient à manquer*). At the same time, such a process is necessarily associated with the *o*, since it has the paradoxical function of embodying what precisely cannot have a body without being distorted and defaced.[5] The "loss" that triggers anxiety, then, is not that of an object that once was possessed, but rather the effacement, through objectification, of what Lacan refers to as the "lack."

Anxiety results, then, from the process by which the Other

---

[5] Lacan describes this self-effacement of the *manque* in terms obviously indebted to Heidegger's description of the "disclosure" of Being, which conceals itself all the more thoroughly in and through revealing itself. The "lack of a lack" similarly echoes Heidegger's account of the (self-)effacement of the ontological difference between Being and beings. It should be added that Lacan's relation to Heidegger itself appears to follow a similar pattern. Heidegger is mentioned at the beginning of the lectures on anxiety, but only in order to remark that the latter's questioning of the Being of beings, and in particular, his thematization of Being-toward-Death, "does not really take the way of anxiety," but is oriented rather toward the question of care (*Sorge, souci*). (11.14.62) That Lacan should approach the problem of anxiety in terms of *lack* and of *fault*; that the *o* is determined as a mode of *falling*; that the *uncanny* is described by him as the "key" to anxiety, which in turn is related essentially to the effect of *isolation*: all this will be quite familiar to readers of *Being and Time*, § 40. But Lacan's posture toward Heidegger here merely repeats that of Heidegger toward his own forerunners, in particular toward Kierkegaard. Whether or not such an effort to blur the traces of a debt is itself not part and parcel of the theory (and practice) of anxiety – as the anxiety of theory itself, beyond any particular set of "influences" – is a question that deserves more attention than can be given it here. I have discussed this question in a different context in the essay "The debts of deconstruction" in: Samuel Weber, *Interpretation and Institution*, University of Minnesota Press: Minneapolis, 1986.

paradox of this is that only such effacement and defacing can guarantee the place of the Other. For without the intervention of the *o*, a situation would arise that Lacan describes as being *manic*:

> In mania what is involved is the non-functioning of the *o*, and not merely its misrecognition. It is through this that the subject is no longer weighed down (*lesté*) by any *o*, and sometimes, without any possibility of freedom, is delivered over to the infinite metonymy and pure play of the signifying chain. (7.3.63)

The difficulties involved in the notion of the *o* are thus the measure of its importance. It holds the line, as it were, between the symbolic gone wild and the imaginary gone wrong, between the infinite metonymizing of signifiers and the unending mirroring of narcissistic identification. And it is in anxiety that the subject encounters this peculiar "object," not as something that is "over against," but rather implied by its own position in respect to the desire of the Other. It is from this perspective that Lacan approaches the significance of "danger" in regard to anxiety. In contrast to Freud, for whom the notion is inseparably bound up with the traumatic "helplessness" of the I in the face of excessive quantities of excitation, Lacan construes danger as related to the desire of the Other insofar as it addresses the subject as its "cause," thereby placing it radically into question:

> [The subject] is alerted (by the anxiety-signal) to something that is a desire [. . .] which concerns nothing other than my being itself, that is to say, which puts me in question [. . .] which does not address itself to me as to someone present but rather as to someone who has been awaited (*attendu*), or even more, as to someone who has been lost, and whose loss is also urged (*qui sollicite ma perte*), so that the Other may rediscover itself there – that is anxiety. The desire of the *Other* does not recognize me, as Hegel believed [. . .] It challenges me (*me met en cause*), questioning me at the very root of my own desire as *o*, as cause of this desire and not as object. And it is because this entails a relation of antecedence, a temporal relation, that I can do nothing to break this hold other than enter into it. It is this temporal dimension that is anxiety and that is also the dimension of analysis. (2.27.63)

One begins to envisage here just why Lacan should attribute such central significance to anxiety and also why this significance should require a perspective that looks "beyond the limits of anxiety." Anxiety assumes a decisive position in Lacan's "enseignement" – his teaching, but also his doctrine – because it confronts the subject with "the truth of the lack/fault," in the form of the object *o* as "cause" of desire. This desire, in turn, emanates from an other, whose alterity admits of no further derivation. The encounter of the subject with this irreducible heterogeneity, through the intermediary of the *o*, must bear the mark of a certain non-knowledge. The latter is certain, insofar as anxiety, as Lacan puts it, is what "does not deceive" (*ce qui ne trompe pas*). But that *about* which anxiety does not deceive is the fact that one can know nothing of the particular, determinate *o* that the subject represents for the desire of the Other. This is summarized by Lacan at the end of his lectures on anxiety:

anxiety manifests itself clearly from the very beginning as relating – in a complex manner – to the desire of the *Other*. From the very first I have indicated that the anxiety-producing function of the desire of the *Other* was tied to the fact that I do not know what object *o* I am for this desire. (7.3.63)

The certain non-knowledge, the fact that I cannot know just what I am for the desire of the other, indicates clearly that the object of anxiety cannot be a cognitive object. In this sense, Lacan can describe anxiety as that which puts cognition into question (or, more literally, "into cause": *la mise en cause de la connaissance*) (5.8.63). For cognition, at least as traditionally construed, requires objects constructed according to the model of narcissistic identification with the mirror-image, with the "*i(o)*" (the imaginary object). By contrast, the *o*, which the subject encounters in and as anxiety, is precisely that which cannot be contained in the mirror-image and which Lacan compares on the one hand to the frame of a window, citing the drama of the Wolfman, and on the other, to the curtain of a theater. The *o*, far from being an object accessible to cognition, is that which allows a certain place to demarcate itself. At the same time, the process of demarcation, insofar as it is bound to the *o*, is itself in a certain sense incomprehensible.

Where, then, does this leave the discourse "on" or "about" anxiety? The discourse that seeks to make out the proper place of its subject, to fix its borders, map out its terrain? How hospitable a terrain can it offer to disparate terms seeking to bind themselves together into a more coherent whole? Is such a scenario even thinkable other than as the acting-out of anxiety itself? And if it is such, what will its consequences be? Already in the initial lecture of the series, Lacan indicates that he is in no way unaware of this problem:

If you know therefore how to come to terms with anxiety (*vous arranger avec l'angoisse*), it may help us to move forwards if we try to see how that works; as for me, I wouldn't know how to introduce it without determining it in some way or other – and therein lies perhaps a snag. One should not come to terms too quickly with anxiety. (*Il ne faut pas que je l'arrange trop vite*). (11.14.62)

That this remark should be followed immediately by a reference to Kierkegaard and to "existentialist" philosophy, from which Lacan seeks to distinguish his own approach, does not alter the fact that the name of the Danish writer recurs throughout these lectures whenever the theoretical status of anxiety is at issue. Yet it is only in the final session that this problem is fully addressed:

I do not know if one has been sufficiently aware of Kierkegaard's audacity in speaking of the *concept* of anxiety. What can this possibly mean if not the affirmation that, *either* the concept functions in a Hegelian manner, entailing symbolically a veritable grasp of the real; *or*, the sole grasp (*prise*) that we can have – and it is here that one must choose – is that afforded us by anxiety, the sole and thus ultimate apprehension of all reality (*seule appréhension et comme telle de toute réalité*). (7.3.63)

If an adequate discussion of the choice embodied in Lacan's lectures on anxiety must await their publication, one can still, in a preliminary way, question the manner in which he envisages this *choice*: can one enclose anxiety in an alternative of this kind? If there is a "concept" of anxiety, must its "hold" or "grasp" – the *Griff* of the *Begriff* – be defined either in terms of anxiety or of its Hegelian *Aufhebung* in thought? The word used by Lacan instead of the German *Griff* is *prise*, which, as the participle of *prendre*, to take, suggests not merely "getting a handle on", but also a *pinch*, as of salt or sugar. Thus, the word itself is suspended in the alternative set out by Lacan: either anxiety can be considered a concept through which we get a true hold upon the real, or we are beholden to it, we feel its pinch. Another possible approach can be retraced in Freud's essay, *Inhibition, Symptom, Anxiety*, beginning with its remarkable title that establishes a sequence but not a conceptual or totalizing synthesis. The serialization of the problem also leads Freud to question the usefulness of the oppositional logic generally used in the elaboration of concepts:

It is time to reflect. We are apparently searching for an insight that will reveal to us the essence of anxiety; we are looking for an either-or that will distinguish truth from error. But that is hard to come by, anxiety is not easy to grasp. So far we have reached nothing but contradictions, between which it was not possible to choose. I now propose that we proceed differently: we will try to collect, impartially, everything that we can say about anxiety, and in so doing renounce the expectation of a new synthesis.[6]

Since I have discussed this text at length elsewhere,[7] I will limit myself here to noting that Freud's discussion of the "indeterminacy" of anxiety does not hesitate to inscribe that indeterminacy in the text in ways that conjure up the risk of compromising the value of its theoretical argumentation, considered, that is, from the standpoint of traditional scientific standards. If the core of anxiety relates to what I have described as the "traumatic" discrepancy between representation and signification, the same divergence is assumed by Freud as a principle of his metapsychological discourse: not as the small o, but as that large "X," which we take over into each new formula without really knowing just what it represents.[8]

Yet another approach, however, is suggested by the following remark of Kierkegaard:

Anxiety is a determination of the dreaming spirit. [...]Awake, the difference between myself and my other is posited; sleeping, it is suspended, dreaming it is a signified nothing. The actuality of the spirit constantly shows itself as a figure that tries out its possibility but which disappears as soon as the spirit seeks to take hold of it: a nothing, that can only bring anxiety.[9]

[6] S. Freud, *Inhibition, Symptom, Anxiety*, W. W. Norton: New York, 1959, p. 58.
[7] *The Legend of Freud*, pp. 57ff.
[8] S. Freud, *Beyond the Pleasure Principle*, Bantam Books: New York, 1972, p. 58.
[9] S. Kierkegaard, *The Concept of Anxiety*, Princeton University Press: Princeton, 1980, pp. 41–42, translation modified.

The discourse of Lacan, in contrast to that of both Kierkegaard and Freud, is one which seeks and offers "guarantees." The quasi-concept of the *o*, "guarantee of the otherness of the Other," also opens the perspective of that move "beyond the limits of anxiety," so that another sort of "work can be possible," that of analysis itself:

> To be sure, this requires that the analyst be one who has been able, in whatever small measure, by whatever way, by whatever edge, to cause his desire to return to that irreducible *o* and thereby provide the question of the concept of anxiety with a real guarantee. (7.3.63)

"Anxiety," Lacan assured his listeners, "is only overcome where the Other names itself." (7.3.63) In the discourse that follows the lectures on anxiety, this naming will make ever less mention of anxiety. The term drops out of Lacan's discourse, in large measure. Is this a sign that the problem it entails has indeed been overcome? Or could it be that by thus dropping out, anxiety assumes the role of the *o* in Lacanian discourse itself? In any case, it would not have been the first time that such an event had occurred. In the lectures on anxiety, Lacan calls attention to the way in which Freud, by missing the point in his analysis of Dora, by misconstruing the character of feminine desire, reveals something that a more insightful procedure might well have obscured: "*La chose freudienne,*" – the Freudian thing – "is what Freud let fall, what he overlooked, the matter he dropped, but it is precisely this that, in the guise of all of us, still leads the hunt after his death." (1.23.63)

From this, however, to infer that anxiety might be a name for *la chose lacanienne,* would be to offer a conjecture that little if any explicit evidence would seem to support, much less authorize. Except, perhaps, if one recalls the manner in which Lacan himself construed authorization:

> Let us proceed from the conception of the Other as the site of the signifier. In the context of this site, no authoritative statement can have any guarantee other than its very enunciation, since it is futile for it to look for any such in another signifier, which under no circumstances can appear outside of this site. That is what we formulate in saying that there is no metalanguage that might be spoken, or, more aphoristically, that there is no Other of the Other. The legislator, who claims to make up for this by erecting the Law, does so as an impostor.

But not so the Law itself, nor whoever acts on its authority.[10]

The question raised by Lacan's conclusion is: how can one act on the authority of a Law that derives, as it were, from a site from which one is barred? How, unless it is through the bars themselves, which demarcate an area in which we, as subjects, first person plural or singular, never quite succeed in taking (our) place. Let us therefore in conclusion, in lieu of a conclusion, take a look through, and at, these bars, albeit in an area that seems quite remote from that we have been discussing.

Peter Greenaway's film, *The Draughtman's Contract*, tells the enigmatic story of a cocky, successful young draughtsman, Neville, who accepts an offer to make twelve sketches of the estate of Lord Herbert, in exchange not just for money, but for services to be rendered him by Lady Herbert. As his work progresses, a number of strange, unaccountable objects crop up in his, and our, field of vision, a field that is determined by an apparatus that he carries around with him, and that he uses to frame and construct his drawings. Wholly absorbed by his work, and by his relation to Lady Herbert, Neville is taken entirely by surprise when the daughter of Lady Herbert, Miss Sarah Talman, suggests to him that the objects mentioned may not be as inconsequential, nor his situation as simple, as he seems to believe. On the contrary, she continues, these curious objects could well be indications of a conspiracy to do away with Lord Herbert, in which Neville might now be involved, however unwittingly.

What is of particular interest in the context of our discussion, however, is the "theory" – Miss Talman's word – with which she seeks to explain to her increasingly disconcerted listener,

---

[10] "Partons de la conception de l'Autre comme du lieu du signifiant. Tout énoncé d'autorité n'y a d'autre garantie que son énonciation même, car il est vain qu'il le cherche dans un autre signifiant, lequel d'aucune façon ne saurait apparaître hors de ce lieu. Ce que nous formulons à dire qu'il n'y a pas de métalangage qui puisse être parlé, plus aphoristiquement: qu'il n'y a pas d'Autre de l'Autre. C'est en imposteur que se présente pour y suppléer, le Législateur (celui qui prétend ériger la Loi). Mais non pas la Loi elle-même, non plus que celui qui s'en autorise." *Ecrits*, p. 813. Sheridan, pp. 310–311. The designation of the Legislator as an "impostor" goes back at least to Rousseau's *Social Contract*. For a discussion of this text, see Paul de Man, "Promises," in *Allegories of Reading*, Yale University Press: New Haven, 1979, and Samuel Weber, "In the name of the law," *Cardozo Law Review*, vol. 11, nos. 5–6, July–August, 1990, esp. 1533–38.

just why and how he might make an easy prey for possible conspirators:

Mr. Neville, I have come to the conclusion that a really intelligent man would make a mediocre painter. For painting requires a certain blindness, the partial refusal to take all the possibilities into account. An intelligent man will know more about what he draws than what he sees with his eyes, and in the space between knowing and seeing, he feels himself more and more . . . confined, incapable of following out an idea with any consequence, fearing that the judicious will not take pleasure in his work, if, in addition to what *he* knows, he does not put into it what *they* know. You, Mr. Neville, if you are an intelligent and therefore a mediocre draughtsman, would have to welcome the fact that a theory such as I have proposed could indeed be constructed based upon the clues contained in your paintings. If, however, you are, as I have heard people say, a talented draughtsman, then I could imagine that you might assume that the objects which I have brought to your attention testify to no plan, indicate no deviousness and do not amount to any sort of accusation.

Sarah Talman's theory, taken by itself, would hardly amount to more than a clever reworking of Socrates' mockery of the rhapsode, Ion, who sings about things without knowing what in the world they really are. But the shot itself accentuates a dimension that is not simply that of the Platonic mimesis: the dimension of space itself, or rather, the interval between space and place, which is not necessarily equivalent to "the space between knowing and seeing." The shot shows Neville in profile, silhouetted in the lower left foreground, while Lady Talman stands above and behind him, addressing not so much Neville as the spectators, camera, or both. But what is most striking in this frame is precisely its framing: almost, but not quite convergent with the actual frame of the shot is Neville's frame, which forms a second, heavy black border within which the artist's head is located, whereas Lady Talman's is outside. And yet, not entirely either, for the plumed column of her hat rises first above Neville's frame, and then right out of the picture as such. The clever and 'talented' artist, Neville, takes the frame that he carries around with him for granted, as an instrument. He knows no anxiety, except perhaps when the force of Lady Talman's words begins to take hold. For the spectator, to be sure, it is precisely the presence of those curious objects that don't "fit in," that raise the issue of the frame by pointing elsewhere, to another place, to the "space between knowing and seeing" within which the "intelligent man" feels increasingly "confined."

Anxiety, it may be recalled – Nietzsche, among others, made the point – is related etymologically to the idea of "confinement" (*Angst*, from *Enge*: narrow): to "lack," if you will, but above all, to a lack of *breath*. Anxiety is perhaps what one feels when the world reveals itself to be caught up in the space between two frames: a doubled frame, or one that is split, who can tell? Frames in which we are no less framed than is poor Neville.

A final remark. Toward the conclusion of his thesis on *The Concept of Anxiety*, Kierkegaard comes up with a striking figure to describe anxiety, "the pivot upon which everything turns:"[11]

Anxiety discovers destiny, but just when the individual wants to put his trust in destiny, anxiety turns around and takes destiny away, because destiny is like anxiety, and anxiety, like possibility, is a "magic" picture.[12]

The Danish word that is here rendered as "magic picture" is: *Heksebrev*, literally: witch's letter. A "witch's letter" is a "set of picture segments of people and animals that recombine when unfolded and turned."[13] If we ever get "beyond the limits of anxiety," beyond transference, or to any of the other "beyonds" one might conceive, we might well find a witch's letter waiting there to greet us.

[11] *The Concept of Anxiety*, p. 43.
[12] Ibid., p. 159.
[13] *The Concept of Anxiety*, translator's note, p. 254.

Appendix B

❖❖❖

Transferring the heritage: psychoanalysis and criticism

❖❖❖

Shortly before Christmas, 1985, a brief article appeared on the last page of the Parisian daily, *Le Monde*, under the headline:

JACQUES LACAN

"BELONGS" TO HIS SON-IN-LAW

The text of the story reads as follows:

On the 11th day of December, 1985, the First Chamber of the Paris Civil Court recognized the rights of Jacques-Alain Miller, as the testamentary executor and trustee, [. . .] over the work of Jacques Lacan. J.-A. Miller, Lacan's son-in-law, and the Editions du Seuil, had brought several charges against the association, *APRES*, for publishing a transcribed version of the seminar of Jacques Lacan, on "Transference," in its internal bulletin, *Stécriture*. [. . .]

The Association, *APRES*, is found guilty of copyright violation; the court orders distribution of the bulletin to be stopped, existing copies to be destroyed, and damages to be paid.

It should be noted, however, that the individual members of the association are exonerated of any further responsibility. Moreover, the only part of the sentence to be executed, for the time being, concerns the ban upon distribution: the court leaves it up to the parties involved to decide whether or not to publicize the verdict (*signifier . . . le jugement*). This decision, therefore, may perhaps not be the epilogue of this "murky affair" (*cette ténébreuse affaire*).

The Balzacian allusion with which the article concludes was hardly lost upon the readers of *Le Monde*: the "case" of the purloined papers of Jacques Lacan raised the very issues around which the writings of Balzac – but also those of contemporary literary theory more generally – incessantly swirl: the question of the rights of an author and, correlatively, that of the status of a "work," literary or other.[1] It is the enduring power of this

[1] I have discussed the relation of author to work in Balzac's writings in

question that makes the Paris case more than merely a "fait divers," more, that is, than a French version of what in English is called a "human interest story." Which is why this curious affair merits consideration.

First, however, some necessary background information. The association *APRES*, an acronym signifying "Association for the Research and Establishment of the Seminars," was constituted in 1983, two years after the death of Lacan, by researchers and analysts including many former members of the Ecole Freudienne de Paris, the institution founded by Lacan and then dissolved by him, amid general confusion and much protest. The group described its purpose as that of "elaborating a theory of the transition from the spoken to the written word of Lacan." The results of its efforts are published in a bulletin which takes its name from a word play of Lacan: "Stécriture." The groups sees the "originality" of its "method" reflected in the production of a "critical apparatus" and of a text, which, unlike the authorized edition of Miller, does not efface the multiplicity of sources that is at its origin. This multiple origin includes: the stenographic record of Lacan's lectures, the notes of his listeners, the many tape recordings that were made by them, and, last but not least, the various interpretive interventions of the editorial collective itself.

By thus retaining a certain textual plurality, or, if one prefers, a certain intertextuality, in which not merely the speaker, Lacan, is inscribed, but also his listeners and even certain of his readers, Stécriture endeavors to produce "a collective version" of the Seminar that is "as close as possible to Lacan."

The question, to be sure, is: just how close is close? Or rather, given the nature of this particular case, just how close is *just*, or at least, legal? How close can one get to Lacan without violating French copyright law – this is the question that the editors, and lawyer, of Stécriture seek to elaborate, if not to resolve. "Stécriture does not pretend (*prétend*: claim) "to publish" Lacan and thus to compete with the Editions du Seuil."[2] But if

---

Unwrapping Balzac: A Study of "La Peau de Chagrin," University of Toronto Press: Toronto/Buffalo/London, 1979.
[2] The Editions du Seuil have published a number of Lacan's seminars and are under contract to do yet others. The publishing house was also a co-plaintiff with Miller in this case.

Appendix B

Stécriture is not publishing "Lacan," what is it publishing under the title, "Transference in its Subjective Disparity, its Putative Situation, its Technical Excursions"? How, in short, can one publish a text that comes as "close as possible to Lacan" without infringing upon the "droits d'auteur," firmly in the hands of the literary executor, Jacques-Alain Miller? There is only one possibility: by contesting that there is any author at all, at least in this particular case. This is precisely the way taken by Stécriture.

The text from which I have been quoting, entitled "Who is the author of 'Lacan's' Seminar?", begins by raising precisely this question: "The spoken work constituted by the 'Seminar' of Jacques Lacan poses, in a very particular manner, the question of the 'right of the author'." Lacan, Stécriture argues, like Foucault, never thought of himself as an "author", once even going so far as to assert that, "contrary to my friend, Lévi-Strauss, I will not leave behind a work." Where there is no work, however, there can be no author, the latter always being defined as the originator or creator of the former. And if there is one issue upon which both Miller and Stécriture agree, it is that "the spoken work constituted by" Lacan's Seminar is not really a work at all, or at least, not the work of an author. Stécriture supports this assertion by referring to the peculiar nature of Lacan's *enseignement*, his "teaching," which, it argues, did nothing less than "put into practice the theory he developed."

One of the more conspicuous tenets of this theory is that the subject receives its message in a more or less distorted – Lacan says "inverted" – form, on the rebound, as it were, from the Other that is in part constituted by its interlocutors. Given the constitutive importance of such interaction, the oral teaching of Lacan cannot be considered to be the sole or exclusive product or property of an author. (In view of this argument it is hardly surprising that the seminar chosen to serve as a test-case of this approach would be that dealing with "transference." We will have occasion to return to this matter shortly.

Stécriture might have strengthened this argument, theoretically if not legally, had it cited a passage from the essay entitled "Subversion of the subject and dialectic of desire," which indicates just how complex the issue of authorial rights can become in a Lacanian perspective. In his essay, Lacan has been elaborating the significance of what he calls "the paternal function," in the light – or rather, in the chiaroscuro – of his "conception of the Other as the site of the signifier." He then goes on to describe the kind of legality that derives from this place:

Let us proceed from the conception of the Other as the site of the signifier. In the context of this site, no authoritative statement can have any guarantee other than its very enunciation, since it is futile for it to look for any such in another signifier, which under no circumstances can appear outside of this site. That is what we formulate in saying that there is no metalanguage that might be spoken, or, more aphoristically, that there is no Other of the Other. The legislator, who claims to make up for this by erecting the law, does so as an impostor.[3]

How is it possible, however, to "act on" the "authority" of a Law that is not so much *made*, as *received*, or, as Sheridan translates it, "assumed"? How can one conceive of "authority" without an author? How are we to be sure that such a law is itself legitimate? What if it were only *powerful*, based on more or less opaque force? Would it still be legally binding?[4]

The French expression used by Lacan, *s'en autoriser*, is reflexive, but the turn back upon itself that it articulates turns the subject inside-out, as it were, making it dependent upon a place that is beyond the compass of subjectivity. It is the turn itself that appears to constitute the authoritative move, and it turns out to be a linguistic turn. For the only guarantee of any statement of authority is, as we have read, "its very enunciation." Yet, how is this enunciation to be determined, if its only law is that of difference, or, in Lacanian terminology, that of the Other? In short, what is the relationship between a determinate statement, an *énoncé*, and an *énonciation*, the process of utterance? How do the rules of the State, or of a certain stasis, relate to the dynamic play of signification?

The decision of the Paris Court in favor of the plaintiffs and against Stécriture, offers one response to this question. First of all: the law of March II, 1957, as well as Article 509 of the French

---

[3] *Ecrits*, p. 813. Sheridan, pp. 310–311 (translation modified).
[4] These are questions that Jacques Derrida has addressed in a recent article dealing primarily with Walter Benjamin's *Critique of Force*, but which also discusses Montaigne, from whom Derrida takes the title of the essay: "Force of Law: The 'mystical Foundations of Authority,'" *Cardozo Law Review*, pp. 919–1046.

New Code of Civil Procedure, explicitly include oral lectures as one of the "works," the reproduction of which is subject to copyright regulation. Lacan's declaration that, unlike his friend, Lévi-Strauss, he will not leave behind a work, has in this perspective no legal value whatsoever, however significant in other ways it might turn out to be. Secondly, there are other speech acts of Lacan, which, although they may be of lesser theoretical interest, and indeed, may even seem to contradict that theory, *are* legally binding. One such is the duly signed and notarized will, in which Lacan "names as my testamentary executor, insofar as the totality of my published and non-published work (oeuvre) is concerned, M. Jacques-Alain Miller. He will exercise all the prerogatives attached to the moral right according to the law of March 11, 1957." Between two *énoncés*, then, the one stating that Lacan will leave behind no work, the other, that his entire work, published as well as unpublished, shall be administered by Miller as prescribed by French copyright law – how is one to choose? If the "authority" of a statement derives only from its utterance, how is it to be acted upon?

In Lacanian terms: If the subject is constituted by its "submission to the signifier,"[5] i.e. to an alterity that can never be reduced or retraced to the same, how is one to conceive the process of such an authorization? What is the relation of the Law or laws of language to the laws of the State? Of its statements and the process of stating, of enunciating? How in general does authority as such *take place*, if this place, as site of the signifier, is not one that can ever be simply, or definitively, *taken*?

These are just some of the questions that the dispute over the Lacan legacy stirs up and calls us to reconsider. But this case becomes even richer in its *enseignement* when we consider the other side, which, in this instance is not that of the Other, not at least to begin with, but that of the Author: the "co-author" and "testamentary executor," Jacques-Alain Miller. A year before he actually brought charges against Stécriture, Miller published an interview that he had given in which he discusses his work as the editor of Lacan. In this text, entitled *Conversation on the*

---

[5] Sheridan translates Lacan's *soumission* as "subjection." Cf: *Ecrits*, p. 806; *Selection*, p. 304.

Seminar,[6] Miller addresses the criticism later to be formulated by
Stécriture, above all, that of not having satisfactorily fulfilled the
"function of editor and guardian of the work, conferred upon
me by Lacan in the most legal of forms." It has not been easy, he
acknowledges, to do this while "continuing and animating the
truth of his teachings." (66) Coming as it does shortly before the
end of the interview, such an admission suggests that there is
no easy response to the critiques addressed to him. Nevertheless, elements of a response are furnished by Miller's editorial
practices, such as his decision not to publish Lacan's texts with a
critical apparatus, as did Stécriture:

> the lectures of Lacan could have justified an entire critical apparatus:
> references, citations, clarifications of difficulties. However, by common
> consent [between Miller and Lacan, presumably] the Seminar is
> presented without any critical apparatus . . . (49)

Miller gives no particular reasons for this decision, beyond
alluding to the need for keeping the teachings of Lacan "alive"
(*vivant*). He also refers to a similar decision taken by the editors
of the *Collected Works* of Heidegger. Yet the interview as a
whole makes it quite clear just why there is no place in his
edition of Lacan for what he calls "la glose universitaire":
academic notes and commentary. What is to be avoided,
ultimately, is what has happened to psychoanalysis in the
Unites States, or for that matter anywhere where the teaching of
Lacan has not (yet?) taken hold. In France, as in "all other
romance-language countries," the interest in psychoanalysis is
intense, Miller notes. On the contrary, in areas

> where this teaching has not been received, for example in the United
> States, the fashionable vogue enjoyed by psychoanalysis in the
> post-war years has disappeared. If interpretation is predetermined by
> norms, which (in turn) always borrow their definition from social
> ideals, it loses its distinctive force (*vertu*), and the subject supposed to
> know (*le sujet supposé savoir*), which is essential to the functioning of the
> experience (or the experiment), crumbles (*se délite*). This has happened
> wherever Lacan's teaching has not taken hold. (59)

Miller's allusion to Lacan's notion of the "subject supposed
to know," indicates that in his eyes, the establishment of an

[6] J.-A. Miller, *Conversation sur le Séminaire*, Navarin, Diffusion Seuil: Paris, 1985.

authoritative text, without distracting notes and references, is inseparable from a desired reinforcement of "transference" on the part of the reader:

> According to Lacan's definition, knowledge is the structural pivot of transference. One can, therefore, certainly have a "transference to Lacan" [. . .], on the basis of the knowledge laid down and articulated as a work. Moreover, the form of the work is such that this knowledge conserves a dimension of supposition.

Having thus established the importance, in reading Lacan, of the supposition of an all-knowing subject, Miller goes on to point out that this subject should not be confused with an author:

> Lacan undoes the position of the author as someone who knows what he is saying, such that the dimension of supposition persists, and that in place of truth – to refer to his discourse – there is precisely this supposed knowledge, not the author identical to himself. (64–65)

Although the accent here is placed upon the supposition of knowledge rather than upon knowledge itself, it is clear that such a supposition cannot impose itself in a void. If knowledge is to be supposed, and if this supposition is to *impose* itself upon readers, it will have to respect the forms of cognition, even if its contents will prove to be elusive. Miller seeks to describe this by emphasizing the *systematic* character of Lacan's thought. The subject supposed to know articultates itself in Lacan's work not through a refusal or an absence of systematization, but through the tireless transformation of each successive system by what follows in a thought-process that constantly calls itself into question. (44) "I believe that Lacan continually thought against Lacan," Miller remarks, while also acknowledging that such questioning is obscured by the often apodictic, formulaic character of Lacan's affirmations: "The cutting edge of his formulas does not alter the fact that their exact theoretical value is related to the moment of their enunciation." (45–46)

Once again, we find ourselves back at the problem of "enunciation," the enigma of which is hardly resolved by introducing, as Miller does, the Hegelian notion of "moment." For the movement of the Signifier, unlike that of the Concept, is not circular, its "chain" is no daisy-chain, nor does it spiral toward totality. How "exactly" therefore "theoretical value" can be determined, insofar as it depends upon a movement of signification that is not just ongoing, but is dislocated in each of its moves, is a question that Miller, in this interview at least, does not address.

In the meanwhile, to be sure, one reply has been furnished, provisionally at least, by the First Chamber of the Paris *Tribunal de Grande Instance*. It should be noted that the name of this court is not easy to render in English, which has a Small Claims Court, but no Large Claims Court. More interesting, to be sure, is the fact that the French title condenses several of the problems we have been discussing. The term, *Instance*, recalls both Freud's use of its German version, *Instanz*, to designate the different systems of the psyche, and Lacan's designation of the *letter* in psychoanalysis as an *instance*. The English translation of this word as *agency* obscures the conflictual *urgency* that marks the word both in Lacan's and Freud's writings, where it designates not merely the executor or executive, but the precariousness of all stable institutions given the pull of divergent forces that prevails. This sense of the term both points to the need for a judge and judgment in respect to conflicting parties, and also suggests how fragile such sentences, and indeed, the authority in whose name they are spoken, inevitably must be. The etymology of the term, *in-stare*, designates not just the fact of being present, but rather the necessity of such presence being continually renewed and reaffirmed. Hence, the relationship, often noted by Lacan, between "instance" and "insistence," or even "persistence." It is this insistent drive that is arrested in the Instance that the German translators of Lacan sought to preserve when they translated the word into German as "Drängen": the "Urging" or "Urgency of the Letter." An urgency is not entirely the same as an agency.

What gets lost is the notion that the very "instance" that is called upon to adjudicate, and indeed, to pronounce judgment, is itself part and parcel of the conflicts it seeks to resolve. In short, the Court has power, but does it have authority over the Signifier? And if it does, from where does that authority derive its legitimacy? In democratic societies, one is prone to point to the people as the source of all authority; but it remains to be seen in what sense the people, as a collective subject, can

claim to dictate the law to language, if all subjectivity only comes
to be in and through the movement of signifiers.

The *Tribunal de Grand Instance* delivers its verdict, recognizes
rights and prohibits all reproduction, distribution, exchange and
circulation by Stécriture of its version of the Seminar on
"Transference." It also "stays" the execution of its verdict,
except for the ban on distribution, pending appeal. "Transference" is thus stopped, provisionally, until an authorized version
can be produced. The "law" of language, however, as elaborated by Lacan and before him by Freud, "knows" no such stop-
page, just as the Unconscious is said to "know" no contradiction. The overdetermination of unconscious inscription, as
in dreams, both requires interpretation and at the same time
can never be exhausted or rendered fully by any interpretation.

Interpretation thus is construed and practiced less as a faithful
rendition than as a struggle for power, or rather – in the
Nietzschean sense of the phrase, as a *Wille zur Macht*, a will
toward power. Such power is not something that can be reached,
attained, in a place that one might hope to occupy (in German:
besetzen, "cathect"), once and for all. Rather, it entails a constant
struggle that Freud in the *Interpretation of Dreams* describes as one
of "Selbstüberwindung," which is to say, *overcoming of Self*, and
not, as the Standard Edition would have it, "self-discipline."[7]

Certainly, inasmuch as all interpretive practice necessarily
attempts to establish its authority, the distinction between self-
discipline and self-overcoming inevitably becomes blurred;
nevertheless, the fact remains that today, psychoanalysis,
where it is informed not only by Lacan, but by the more general
movement of thought of which Lacan is an outstanding
"instance" and yet by no means the only such: that is by what
we call today "poststructuralism" – that psychoanalysis has
become one of the areas in which the a-licit Law of language
struggles to impose the problematic rights of the author.
Another such area is, of course, the study of literature.

This has, of course, been the case ever since the beginnings of
Western thought. It is a case that has been made against

---

[7] S. Freud, *The Interpretation of Dreams*, chapter 7: "The forgetting of dreams,"
Avon Books, p. 563.

literature ever since Socrates – or was it Plato? – excluded the poets from the just state. They were banished for "forgetting themselves," for allowing themselves to be carried away by their mimetic impulses. In so doing, Plato argued – mimetically, through the mouth of "Socrates" – that the poets forgot or abdicated their diegetical responsibilities, and thereby forfeited their place in the *polis*:

> Do you know the first lines of the *Iliad*, in which the poet says that Chryses implores Agamemnon to release his daughter, and that the king was angry and that Chryses, failing of his request, heaped curses on the Acheans in his prayers to the god? You know then that [. . .] the poet himself is the speaker [there] and does not even attempt to suggest to us that anyone but himself is speaking. But in what follows he delivers his speech as if he himself were Chryses and tries as far as may be to make us feel that not Homer is the speaker, but the priest, an old man. And in this manner he has carried on nearly all the rest of his narration about affairs in Ilium, all that happened in Ithaca, and the entire *Odyssey*. (393a–b)[8]

As the possibility of such "mimetic" narration, poetry poses a danger to the statesmen, the "guardians" who if they must imitate, "should from childhood on imitate what is appropriate to them." (395c) By "likening himself to another," by speaking with the voice of another, the poet undermines the authority of his discourse. The verdict is ironic, but without appeal:

> If a man [. . .] who was capable by his cunning of assuming every kind of shape and imitating all things should arrive in our city, bringing with himself the poems which he wished to exhibit, we should fall down and worship him as a holy and wondrous and delightful creature, but should say to him that there is no man of that kind among us in our city, nor is it lawful for such a man to arise among us, and we should send him away to another city, after pouring myrrh down over his head and crowning him with fillets of wool . . . (398a–398b)

Reading this passage today, we are liable to react with a certain condescension, as though the irresponsibility of language was no longer a problem for us, schooled as we are on Bakhtin and Barthes, and protected by International Copyright Conventions. Were we to react in this manner, however, we

---

[8] Plato, *The Collected Dialogues*, ed. E. Hamilton and H. Carins, Pantheon Books: New York, 1961, pp. 637–638.

would be pulling the wool over our eyes: the issues that preoccupied Socrates and Plato are still very much with us. To confirm this, we need only reflect for a moment on the importance, in our own writing, on the one hand of quotation marks, and on the other, of proper names, in particular those of authors and titles. Without the latter, how could we identify "works"; without the former, their meaning? Imagine what would become of our jobs, and of our practice as teachers and students, scholars and critics, were we no longer able to rely upon quotation marks to distinguish direct from indirect discourse, or to demarcate the writing of others from what we claim as our own?

For almost a century, reflection upon literature has been occupied, and indeed increasingly so, with the problem of authoritative discourse: from Henry James and Percy Bullock's thematization of point of view to Wimsatt and Beardsley's critique of the intentional fallacy; from Bakhtin's polyphonic-dialogic theory of the novel, to Barthes' obituary of the author and to the more cautious, more historical investigation of Foucault, literary practice and critical theory have grown increasingly suspicious of authorial positions and discourse. Until fairly recently, however, criticism almost always stopped short of reflecting upon the implications of such suspicions for its own 'position' and project, and with good reason. For if the "omniscient narrator" is at best unreliable and at worst an illusion, what of the Critic? To what kind of authority can the discourse of criticism legitimately lay claim?

The response most recently in vogue, in the US at least, of certain neo-pragmatist critics such as Stanley Fish, is that it is the "community of interpreters" alone that authorizes interpretation. But such an answer merely begs the question it pretends or claims to address. Constructing a collective subject to serve as the authoritative instance accomplishes little, if that subject is construed to have the same, self-identical, undivided structure as the individual critic it is meant to supplant. For the divisions with which we are confronted, today no less than in the past, affect communities no less than individuals. The question therefore to be addressed is not just: how does a community constitute itself, but also: what does the notion of community entail? Indeed, if we feel impelled to recur to this notion today, it is because our interpretive practice calls into question the establishment of precisely such communality. What is involved in interpretation is not so much the analysis of works, perhaps, as the imposition of meanings always more or less at the expense of other, competing schemes. Interpretation would therefore address neither the meaning of works, nor even the condition under which such meanings take place, but the very process of "taking place" itself; that is, of *taking place away* from other place-holders. The real object of interpretation would be the place itself, as site of division and conflict, and this would determine its practice as negotiation and as strategy.

It is in allowing us to explore the nature of such divisions and conflicts, in their structural and structuring effects, that psychoanalysis has an important and probably indispensable contribution to make to current theoretical discussions. Let us return then to one of the areas opened by psychoanalysis, and which seems particularly promising in this regard: that of *transference*. The history of its use by Freud provides a useful way of approaching the problem. In *The Interpretation of Dreams*, the German word *Übertragung* is employed to designate the distortions of the dreamwork, which shifts from one represen-tation to another in order to accomplish its goal: that of producing a distorted, self-dissimulating fulfillment of a con-flictual wish. *Übertragung*, the German word that literally corresponds to the Greek *metaphorein*, thus describes both the particular dream-device of *displacement* (*Verschiebung*), and the more general instability of psychic energy that is characteristic of the primary process and of the unconscious in general. Freud describes this primary process in terms of the volatility and mobility of its cathexes, that is, of the manner in which energy is attached to representations. This he contrasts with the secon-dary process, to which he attributes a greater stability. In it, energy is bound in a more enduring way to representations, to "intellectual identities" as he calls them (*Denkidentitäten*), in contrast to perceptual identities, which are epitomized not in the perception of stable, self-identical objects, but in the equivocal imagery of the manifest dream content.

What is striking, however, is that this opposition of primary and secondary process, of volatile and stable cathexes, does not suffice to account for the phenomenon of transference, which exhibits traits of both processes: as distorted representation, *Übertragung* presupposes the volatile movement, the "carrying-over" from one place or thought or image to another; but at the same time, like "metaphor" itself, it also entails an element of fixity, indeed of fixation. What is perhaps most significant of all, however, is that these two elements, movement and fixation, do not simply oppose one another, as one might expect, but rather converge and overlap: the movement of representation is fixed, arrested but the fixation/arrestation turns out to constitute another kind of movement. The movement is fixed and arrested, inasmuch as the process of symbolization has come to rest in the manifest dream-content; but it is also in movement, insofar as the apparently stable content leads us inevitably in multiple directions: forward, into the future, through the fact that the dream depends upon its belated narration in order to function and indeed, to be; it only comes to be the morning after, as it were, in its distorted reproduction; and backward, toward the infantile complexes that are always more or less at the origin of the dream. In this sense, then, the dream does not merely make use of *Übertragung*: it has the structure of an *Übertragung*.

This curious conflict of fixation and mobility, which also entails a form of repetition, is what emerges with increasing emphasis in Freud's later use of the term to designate the pivotal mechanism in the analytic situation itself. The analysand, instead of remembering – that is, instead of representing the past as past, and hence, as representable – repeats the past as though it were the present. The past, instead of being remembered, is re-enacted. Again, we are confronted with a movement of repetition that is simultaneously submitted to the constraints of a certain fixation. The differences of the present are ignored and thereby reduced to sameness.

What, however, gives this latter usage of the term "transference" its specific quality is that its fixation is bound up with the figure of the analyst, who becomes the object of love, hate, or both at once. Freud stresses that transference becomes increasingly intense as the analysis progresses, that is, as the analysand begins to approach, to articulate and to assume the conflicts of desire involved in neurosis. The projective mechanism of transference is a way of both acknowledging and resisting that development: the split in the subject is bridged, as it were, by an amorous (or antagonistic) relation to the Other, whose role in the analysis is played by the analyst. By being treated as the object of erotic passion, this Other is thus made into an object of love, the reality of which is no longer to be questioned. The Other is no longer analyst, but beloved, no longer agent of the signifier, but quintessential signified. The conflict is no longer within the subject, but between subjects construed as self-identical egos.

Such transference, Freud emphasizes, poses the greatest dangers to the analytic process, but at the same time it is its only chance of success. For only by means of such transferential projection can analyst and analysand hope to "work through" the resistant and conflictual reality of the signifieds of desire in order to reach its signifying passion.

There is every reason to believe that something very similar is at work in our dealings with texts in general, and with literary texts in particular. If, at least, by "literary" we mean something akin to what Kant had in mind when, in the Preface to the *Critique of Judgement*, he noted that it is "primarily in those forms of evaluation which are called aesthetic" that we find that "embarrassment concerning principles" in which judgment has no universals to fall back on in its confrontation with particular cases, in which it therefore has no choice but to fall forward, as it were. Faced with the inexhaustible multiplicity of experience, with an alterity which cannot be subsumed under existing knowledge, what the judging subject does is something not so very different from the analysand, or for that matter, from the literary critic. In order to judge, the subject considers the particular thing that confronts it *as though* it were the product of an "understanding" like our own, and yet sufficiently different from ours to comprehend what we cannot. Faced with the singular unknown, what the subject does is to suppose a subject that knows, that comprehends what we do not, because it has produced it according to its knowledge. Through such an assumption, the judging subject seeks to assure itself that the unknown is, at least potentially, knowable.

This, for Kant, constitutes the a priori, transcendental principle of what he calls "reflective judgment": it is "reflective" because properly understood, it tells us nothing about the object, nothing about the other to be judged, but only about a "law" – if it can be called that – the judging subject gives to itself in the process of judging the unknown (that for which no general law or concept can be found). And it is this that Kant finds at work in that most exemplary case of reflective judgment: aesthetic judgements of taste. Thus, the entire Kantian conception of beauty as "form," as purposiveness without purpose, depends upon this initial, initiating assumption: that of an Author, having produced a – his – work. However, the fact that this judgment is defined by Kant as being "reflexive" also renders that assumption of authority fictional: it applies not to the object but to the judging subject; it is an "as if." And yet, the status of this as-if, of this assumption, proves difficult to determine in any univocal way. For what does it entail to assume such an Author, while at the same time "knowing" that it is "only" an analogy, a projection of the knowledge we desire? Can such an assumption, which does not or should not constitute a statement about reality, be "really" assumed, as a pure fiction? Were it recognized to be a pure product of the subjective imagination, would it still operate to enable investigation, and thus to prepare us to discover the missing universal law, rule or concept?

What the psychoanalytic theory of transference suggests, is that such assumptions, or projects, can never be made innocently or as mere heuristic devices, for the simple, or rather complex, reason that the subject only comes to be through such a process. If this is so, there is good reason to suspect that it will take more than exposure of the various Intentional Fallacies to rid us of its literary correlative, the Authorial assumption. Perhaps what we should try to think about are ways not so much of escaping from it, as of putting it into play; in this case, however, it might just be criticism itself that turns out to have a leading part.

Index

Index